IN FORBIDDEN CHINA

THE D'OLLONE MISSION
1906-1909
CHINA-TIBET-MONGOLIA

Frontispiece

IN FORBIDDEN CHINA

THE D'OLLONE MISSION
1906-1909

CHINA-TIBET-MONGOLIA

VICOMTE D'OLLONE

BERNARD MIALL

SECOND EDITION

WITH 126 ILLUSTRATIONS
A MAP AND A PORTRAIT

GYAN

Published by

Gyan Publishing House
5, Ansari Road
Daryaganj, New Delhi-110002
Phone: 011-47034999, 9811692060
E-mail: books@gyanbooks.com

Distribution Network
gyanbooks.com
India, USA, Canada, UK, Australia, France

ISBN : 978-81-212-3573-0 (PB)
First Published, London, 1912

2nd Impression 2020

Printed at: Gyan Press, Delhi.

In Forbidden China
Author: Vicomte D'ollone

IN FORBIDDEN CHINA

THE D'OLLONE MISSION

1906–1909

CHINA—TIBET—MONGOLIA

BY

VICOMTE D'OLLONE

MAJOR IN THE FRENCH ARMY

TRANSLATED FROM THE FRENCH OF THE SECOND EDITION

BY

BERNARD MIALL

WITH 126 ILLUSTRATIONS, A MAP, AND A PORTRAIT

T. FISHER UNWIN

LONDON: 1 ADELPHI TERRACE

LEIPSIC: 9 INSELSTRASSE

1912

CONTENTS

LIST OF ILLUSTRATIONS

INTRODUCTION

THE OBJECT OF THE MISSION

A LIMITLESS plain, broken by lotus-covered lakes, whose waters are ploughed by junks of monstrous form ; a land of innumerable isles and hills, all bearing flags, turrets, and pagodas ; a land resembling an enormous artificial park, the apotheosis of the factitious, the conventional ; a land whose inhabitants are all alike : men with slanting eyes, long robes, gentle and calculated movements, incapable of a virile gesture or a frank word ; a country at once uniform, artificial, peaceful, and traditional ; the same to-day as it has been since history began ; a country incapable of transformation—let those who prefer to retain so convenient an opinion of China close this book at the commencement ! Here they will read only of formidable mountains, enormous snowfields, torrential rivers rolling through abysmal gulfs ; of warlike, war-worn, and violent races, as different from the conventional Chinese as are we ourselves.

All the western provinces of the Middle Empire are merely territories won by conquest from non-Chinese populations. Yet the word "won" is deceptive. The Chinese are content to occupy the fertile valleys, where the superiority of their arms, their organisation, and their numbers assures them of the advantage ; and there they have built strong fortresses, connected by roads across the more accessible passes. They have thus cast over the country a kind of network, of which the meshes isolate and imprison each range of mountains. Driven from the fruitful soils, relegated to the high table-lands and the rugged slopes, isolated in groups by the valleys, which are held by their conquerors, the majority of the natives have been forced to recognise the domination of the Chinese, or at least their supremacy ; but they have retained their own language and their own customs. Yet three groups of these peoples have resisted conquest by an invincible opposition, so that they retain to-day, in the heart of China, their perfect independence ; they are the Miao-tze in Kwei-Chu, the Lolos in Sze-Chuan, and the Si-Fan in the north of Tibet ; and their countries, forbidden to the foreigner, are the only portions of the globe which are to-day unexplored.

Here we encounter a surprising fact : all observers are at one in agreeing that one at least of these races —the Lolos—presents a type, a character, and customs entirely different from most of the rest of the yellow races. The first to meet them, Dr. Thorel, the companion of Francis Garnier, did not hesitate to declare that they formed a "black branch of the Caucasian race," and all succeeding travellers, far from questioning this opinion, have emphasised the probable kinship of the Lolos with the Indo-European race. At the same time it was discovered that these supposed savages possessed a system of writing quite peculiar to themselves, as well as numerous books, which no one could decipher. Were they a primitive people, still imperfectly developed, or were they still in possession of something more than the vestiges of a civilisation destroyed by the Chinese?

Hence a problem of some interest. Are there, in the heart of China, populations which do not belong to the yellow race? If so, did they come from elsewhere? In that case, we must discover by what road they arrived;

search for the traces of their passage, and the colonies which they would probably have left along their route; determine what was their starting-point, and to what original family we should refer them. Are they autochthonous, or did they come upon the ground at so remote a period as to have been established there before the beginnings of history? In that case the Far East must no longer be regarded as the cradle of the yellow race; on the contrary, the latter must have come from elsewhere, dispossessing the ancient masters of the soil; and if so it must have absorbed many of the latter, so that its boasted homogeneity is only a fiction.

All these questions, arising one by one, had begun to interest many eminent thinkers in all countries. To solve them the first step was to obtain precise data concerning the non-Chinese races; to travel thither and observe them on the spot. But the countries which they occupy are so vast that no one man's lifetime would suffice for the task. After a first reconnaissance in China, in 1904, the following plan occurred to me:—

First of all, the three independent territories must be explored. There would only there be a possibility of finding completely unmixed populations which would reveal the appropriate characteristics of their race; next we should look for these characteristics among the half-subjected tribes, and finally among the populations of Chinese aspect which dwell in the surrounding territories.

A voyage of exploration thus conceived would embrace an immense domain. How many sciences would claim their part therein! Geography would demand the maps of the three unknown regions, and the revision of the maps of all the countries, as yet imperfectly explored, which divide and surround them; History, the tale of the vicissitudes which, after two thousand years of warfare, have resulted only in the partial establishment of the Chinese supremacy over half the Empire. Archæology and Epigraphy would demand the discovery and reconstruction of all the monuments and inscriptions which record the phases of those struggles. Ethnography and Anthropology would expect the collection of traditions, customs, principles of social and political organisation, and somatic types and characteristics ; while Philology would ask for the vocabularies of these teeming populations, and the explanation of their methods of writing. Or, to be precise, the traveller must seek to assemble the first elements of a positive knowledge of these important matters, leaving to those that follow him the task of correcting errors and filling up gaps.

The reader need not be alarmed by such an enumeration. All the scientific booty of the expedition has been apportioned among seven volumes, intended for the specialists, the publication thereof being assured by vote of Parliament. Here will be found only the description of picturesque lands and races, and the narrative of an exploration which had its moments of excitement, for we were penetrating countries regarded as impenetrable.

*
* *

The explorers of old were fortunate. What a field was open to their enterprise! The fabulous kingdoms of Mexico and Peru, the marvels of India, the vast prairies of America, the Siberian steppes, and the great lakes of Central Africa. Moreover, the discoveries which made their names immortal, and multiplied tenfold the inheritance of humanity, demanded only the resolve to undertake them ; nowhere were the discoveries of continents ill-received. To-day all that could be has been explored ; all that is left to the discoverer is the waste remnants of the earth ; a part of the Antarctic, and a few corners of Tibet ; savage populations in precipitous mountains ; all that has been regarded as too difficult of access or not worth the trouble of discovery.

Yet no period has exhibited such a fever for exploration. The remotest corners of the earth are attained; the mountains are scaled, the natives conciliated, questioned, and measured. The more inaccessible a country, the greater the desire to learn of it. What is the meaning of this ardour? What Golden Fleece do our modern Argonauts hope to win? What profit can science and humanity expect of so many efforts? Has not exploration become a superior form of sport for the adventurous; for those who are wary of the banality of our civilisation, and hope to gain a sensational fame by triumphing over obstacles reputed as insurmountable?

Certainly the idea of an active, violent, physical existence, reflecting one's own will, involving the daily risk of a life preserved only by strength or cunning, is one that holds a powerful attraction for men of strong will and adventurous mettle. But a discoverer must think of other things than the mere expenditure of energy; he must follow a higher and more useful object.

The object of exploration is not what it was. Formerly men sought to know the face of the globe; as for the distant peoples whom the lack of means of communication isolated from our daily life, they were merely the subject of curiosity or the source of profit. Now, thanks to invention, distance exists no longer; the races live in mutual contact; and we wonder with some anxiety what the appearance of these new-comers upon the stage of the world may mean to us. Who are they? Whence come they? What have they done hitherto?

When, as in the case of the yellow races, there is a question of a mass of five hundred millions of human beings, the solution of such problems becomes of absorbing interest. Among those that seek the solution it excites a profound emotion, such as the discovery of one more island, one more inhabited range, is powerless to afford. The child of the age of steam and electricity must plunge into the midst of civilisations that have suffered no change ; he finds the past, which he believed was dead ; he explores not only space, but also time. Successively, as he penetrates farther and farther into these remote and isolated lands, he ascends the river of the ages, and all the forms of human society, from that of the period of Louis XIV. to those of the Middle Ages, pass in procession before him ; and when at length he stands upon the boundless steppes or the bristling ranges, he finds himself among the Barbarians of antiquity.

Those who conquered Cyrus, checked Alexander, ravaged the Roman Empire, conquered Asia and the half of Europe, are still there and have not changed. Scythians, Huns, Turks, Mongols, Tibetans, or Lolos, the Barbarians are neither extinct nor powerless. Among them we can understand and revive the past ; the conflict which still persists between the children of nature and of civilisation explains the stages of human history.

Will these Barbarians again have their hour, as they have had it so often in the past? For two hundred years they have surrendered or retired, vanquished by the musket and the rifle; but firearms, having given the advantage to the enemy, are to-day passing into their own hands. Will they succumb in the embrace of science, or shall we see them, armed with improved rifles and cannon of the latest type, utilise the railroads built by ourselves in order to recommence their terrible incursions?

Dreams—idle phantoms ! It is true they are only a handful ; but who has numbered their brothers by race, apparently subjected, apparently Chinese, yet always ready for adventure : Long-hairs, Taipings, and Boxers? Do not let us forget that the Barbarians already installed in the Roman Empire ensured the success of the invaders.

Let us not despise these hordes, powerless though

they appear. We should see them by the sombre light of many terrible memories. Let us learn what they are worth, and what possibly unlimited assistance the surrounding multitudes might offer them. Even if the future escapes them, even if they are condemned without appeal, let us not lose this occasion, which is about to disappear for ever, of learning somewhat of those who once made the world tremble. They cannot much longer resist the onset of progress : as victors or vanquished they must at least suffer change.

We shall have known the last Barbarians.

THE D'OLLONE MISSION.

Sub-Lieut. de Boyve. Commandant D'Ollone. Captain Lepage. Captain de Fleurelle.

To face page 19.

IN FORBIDDEN CHINA

CHAPTER I

FROM HANOI TO SZE-CHUAN

On the 6th of August, 1906, the projected expedition of exploration which I had elaborated, and which had obtained the suffrages of the Society of Geography, was approved by M. Etienne, the Minister of War, and the Mission was constituted. With its leader were appointed, successively, Lieutenant de Fleurelle—since Captain—of the Artillery, entrusted more especially with the work of geographical and topographical research; Lieutenant Lepage—since Captain—of the Colonial Artillery, a diploma'd scholar of the School of Oriental Languages, and familiarised, by a five years' residence in China, with the use of the language, who would act as the chief interpreter of the Mission ; and Sergeant-Major de Boyve—now Sub-Lieutenant—of the Cavalry, who was entrusted with the details of transport. The secondary staff was to be composed of Annamites and Chinese.

The Minister of Public Instruction, the Minister of the Colonies, the general Government of Indo-China, the Academy of Inscriptions and Belles-Lettres, and the French Asiatic Committee, while granting us financial assistance, lent us a moral support which was even more precious. In order to emphasise the scientific character of an expedition which was exclusively military in the composition of its superior staff, and therefore might disturb the touchy Chauvinism of the Young Chinese press, our Mission was placed under the official patronage of the Society of Geography; and I take this opportunity of expressing our gratitude for the effectual and indefatigable assistance which we received from that body during a period of more than three years.

In December, 1906, we sailed for Indo-China. Two months were spent in various ethnographical expeditions across Cambodia, Cochin-China, and Tonkin, and along the Chinese frontier of Kwang-Tong; for several of the races which we purposed to study are represented in Indo-China, and we had at the outset to verify these elements of comparison.

At Hanoi I was badly disappointed in a matter concerning the constitution of my subordinate staff. I wanted to have by us a few reliable men—men who would not desert under any circumstances, and who would be capable of rendering effectual assistance in case of attack. I had asked, and while yet in Paris had obtained, the promise that ten Annamite sharpshooters should be attached to our party as orderlies; they would wear civil costume, and nothing would distinguish them from ordinary servants—except their fidelity. However, the Governor-General was of opinion that the presence of these ten soldiers, even without arms or uniform, would be liable to alarm the Chinese. We were therefore obliged to content ourselves with civil servants. This was by no means the same thing; nothing could force them to follow us into regions reputed to be dangerous; unaccustomed to handle arms, they would be useless to us in an emergency; we could not even ask them to mount guard at night, but should be forced to rely upon ourselves.

Nevertheless, Annamites, even though civilians, were, as servants, infinitely preferable to the Chinese. If we could take them as far as Tonkin they could not possibly return alone, so that their interest would be ours. I engaged four; at once cooks and "boys," who had already been to Yunnan in the service of consuls, officers, and engineers, and who spoke French and Chinese passably well; their wages were to be paid only when the Mission was completed, which was a fair guarantee of fidelity

Extremely methodical, prompt and well-behaved, as is usual with the Annamites, they rendered us every service we could expect from them. But how many difficulties would have been evaded by the presence of ten resolute men, ready to obey to the death, and what security they would have afforded!

From the frontier of Tonkin to Yunnan-sen is sixteen days' ride on horseback. To relate the incidents of this journey would be an almost comical archaism, since to-day a railway—opened on the 1st of April, 1910—enables one to complete it—by a slightly different route, it is true—within two days. We will therefore leave some future traveller the pleasure of discovering Mong-Tze, which is certainly, of all the cities of China, the richest in monuments of sculptured stone; the beautiful Grottoes of the Swallows, Sin-Ngan-fu; Tong-Hai, with its lake and mountain, Tzu-Shan, sprinkled with graceful pagodas hidden by a wood of pine-trees, a wood full of the flashing of waterfalls, assuredly one of the fairest scenes to be found in China; and the lake of Cheng-Kiang, with its picturesque, temple-covered island. At one step we will proceed to Yunnan-sen, the capital of Yunnan, which was really the starting-point of our journey of exploration.

The previous conceptions which I had formed of the means of entering the country of the Lolos, whether from the writings of travellers, or thanks to the advice proffered with such friendly generosity by two of the explorers who had approached the independent population most closely—Captains de Vaulserre and de

Marsay—had told me that the obstacles to be overcome were of three kinds.

Firstly, the formal opposition of the Chinese authorities. They are suspicious of all intercourse between foreigners and the rebels. Again, if disaster were to overtake the explorer, his Government would infallibly seek reparation from China, and China does not like to admit that this territory has evaded her supremacy. If, on the contrary, he were to succeed, what a proof of the pusillanimity and incapacity of the mandarins, who cannot even enter the country!

The second difficulty would be to find servants to accompany us. It would not do to count upon our Annamite boys: they would never dare to follow us; as for the Chinese, any Chinaman who sets foot upon Lolo territory is killed or reduced to slavery.

The third difficulty arose from the organisation of the Lolos themselves; they are divided into a multiplicity of clans, all of which are jealous of and at war with one another. Colborne Baber, the celebrated English traveller, whose observations are so valuable, explains why he was forced to content himself with travelling around the country of the Lolos. "We would willingly receive you among us," said the Lolos, "but we could not pass you over to our enemies."

None of these obstacles appeared to me as invincible. The last was the very difficulty against which I had had to contend, in company with the administrator Hostains, among the cannibal tribes of the Ivory Coast. Would the Lolos prove to be more difficult?

As for the other two difficulties, I knew of some one who would assist us to cope with them—Father de Guébriant, the Pro-Vicar Apostolic of Kien-Chang, a region bordering on the west of the Lolo country. All travellers that way spoke of his services and his

ENTERING YUNNAN-SEN BY CANAL FROM THE SOUTH.

To face page 22.

eminent qualities. Indefatigable and intrepid, he had travelled, almost as much for the love of science as for the sake of evangelisation, the whole of the vast region confided to him—a region which was in great part unknown. Only the country of the Lolos had remained closed to him; twice the formal prohibition of the Chinese authorities had checked him at the moment when he was preparing to enter it; and one can imagine the impatience which gnawed at the heart of this apostle and explorer at the sight of the mountain ranges, the home of the Lolos, which overlooked his dwelling at Ning-Yuan-fu, and at the foot of which he had been checked for a period of twelve years.

Even before we left France I had written to him asking him secretly to select and engage the indispensable staff of servants and interpreters, for his reputation and the confidence which he inspired might perhaps determine some bolder spirits to follow us, especially among his Christians; and he, with numerous and devoted agents at his service, would surely be able to obtain for us the help of some Lolo frontier chieftain. If all these arrangements could be made in absolute secrecy, before the fact of our existence was even known, on our arrival we should only have to hasten into Lolo territory, and the mandarins, taken by surprise, would not have time to oppose our plans.

If Father de Guébriant would consent to help us, he would afford us the most invaluable assistance.

His reply awaited me at Yunnan-sen. He entirely approved of my proposals, and he generously offered to accompany me, and to find among his Christians the necessary assistants, on the condition that I should come alone or with only one companion, for a larger number would alarm the suspicious Lolos. But he warned me that before the end of April he expected to leave his residence in order to visit his bishop, if I did not before then advise him of my arrival.

It was then the 15th of April, and it was reckoned

a hard fortnight's march to Ning-Yuan-fu. Moreover, it was essential to buy good horses, to obtain passports for Sze-Chuan, and to hire pack-horses or mules—in short, to make preparations which usually consume a considerable period of time. Would not the Father have left before the arrival of even a rapid courier?

Happily the obligation of losing not a moment if I wished to succeed suppressed all hesitation. I set out immediately, with Sergeant-Major Boyve, making forced marches. Lieutenants de Fleurelle and Lepage, on their part, would make a study of the conquered Lolos of the eastern Yunnan, and explore the country of the independent Miao-Tze.

It was a time of feverish activity. The French consul, M. Arnould, witnessed our departure for the Lolo country with misgivings; but, being unable to oppose the instructions I had brought from Paris, he did his utmost, as did the vice-consul, M. Soulié, to obtain from the Chinese authorities the necessary documents and the transport animals, which all over China are subject to the control of the mandarins.

In two days all was ready. Moreover, our baggage was reduced to the simplest expression—a bed and a canteen apiece.

We took with us only two Annamites and a Chinese interpreter; but the prudent Chinese administration, being responsible for our persons, supplied us with an escort of ten soldiers, who were sent by five different authorities: the Viceroy, the Tao-Tai, the general, the prefect, and the sub-prefect, whose titles they bore embroidered on their cassocks, and whose might they represented in the eyes of the people.

Followed by the envious glances of those of our comrades who remained behind, we joyfully departed. At a few miles from the town we left the usual road, and entered the mountains by a narrow gorge. The route we followed had been travelled before only by Father de Guébriant, accompanied by MM. de Marsay and

Las-Cases, whom he had brought to his residence by this new road.[1]

Having crossed by a sunken pass, just the width of the torrent which had made it, the mountains which hem in the basin of the lake of Yunnan-sen, we journeyed through a series of charming valleys, which have an aspect very rare in China, for they exactly resemble our French valleys. Their sides are gently sloped, and their streams, gaily murmuring, roll their clear waters over shallow beds, here and there working a mill. The rice-fields which occupy all the bottoms, with their young stems of delicious green, look like perfectly kept lawns; numerous villages and farms, occurring at regular intervals, give the landscape a human interest and enrich it with foliage; for the Chinese worship trees, and the white houses can hardly be seen through the boughs.

Presently—to complete the resemblance—the mountain-crests, which since our entry into China had been denuded of vegetation, began to clothe themselves in trees like our own—birch, ash, beech, and especially pine. As in our own spring-time, the air was pure, the sky clear, and the light had a quality of youth and gaiety; nothing recalled the tropics, and it was with a feeling of astonishment that we saw the blue blouses of the labourers surmounted by yellow faces. We instinctively looked for features of a familiar type.

What a singular feeling obsesses one in mountainous China, once the high-road has been left behind! The traveller feels himself a thousand leagues from all that pertains to civilisation, organisation, and society. There is no road communicating with the rest of the world; every one remains in his own home; there is neither post nor telegraph to bring news; men lead a tranquil

[1] At the end of four days our itinerary crossed, and on many subsequent occasions doubled, that of Major Davies, an English explorer of great merit (1898); but his narrative has only just appeared (1909) and his passage through this region had remained unknown.

existence, without troubling about matters of which they know nothing; there are no visits of officials from the outer world, no policemen, customs officers, highway inspectors, foresters, schoolmasters, or tax-collectors; there is no one but the village headman, appointed by the inhabitants, if he is not—as is usually the case—the hereditary seigneur. All powers are concentrated in his person, yet he exercises none, for nothing is performed except by a common agreement, which is easily obtained.

It is an admirable thing to observe, in the China that we like to regard as inert, how everything is performed by private initiative and the voluntary co-ordination of individual efforts. For example: in two localities—Tao-Wen and Siao-Ma-Kai—we saw reservoirs designed to irrigate the countryside; each had been created by completely damming a deep valley by means of an enormous wall of earth. This method—it is common in India, but one which I had never seen elsewhere in China, and which has not, I believe, been recorded—naturally demands a very great amount of labour, and this labour had been spontaneously undertaken by the peasantry.

Similarly, the road by which we travelled, which was made only nine years ago, was built by the co-operation of the owners of the bordering land with the corporations of merchants and caravan-owners of Yunnan-sen and Kien-Chang. Several bridges have been built over dangerous rivers; a cornice has been hewn in the precipitous rocks which border on the Blue River; several bottoms, where heavily laden animals might have been engulfed, have been flagged with stone; and arrangements have been made with certain peasants to provide shelter for travellers. Thanks to these simple and economical measures—I heard mentioned the sum of 20,000 taels, or £2,600—the series of ill-kept tracks by which people travelled, as best they could, from village to village and from farm to farm, has been

THE WALLS OF YUNNAN-SEN.

CROSSING THE PU-TU-HO.

To face page 26.

transformed into a new high-road over 150 miles in length.

For a road exists so soon as you are no longer checked by a river—thanks to a bridge, a ford, or a ferry; nor by a mountain-peak—thanks to a cornice or a zigzag; nor by a bog—thanks to a few suitably placed stones; and so soon as you may find, at noon or nightfall, a shelter and a resting-place, and from time to time a market where provisions may be bought. Little matter though it afford no level surface, no certain foothold; even though it be too narrow for two men to pass or walk abreast, or even, at times, for a laden beast; the question of the surface does not enter into consideration; the soil is taken as it is. To appreciate a narrative of travel in mountainous China it is indispensable to become familiarised with this idea: the march is a perpetual gymnastic exercise, fatiguing even in the tamest valleys, a giddy and really dangerous affair in the precipitous gorges.

On the third day we scaled a mountain-chain, crossing a pretty forest of pines; and having reached the crest, we found ourselves at the brink of a precipice some 1,300 feet in height, at the foot of which flowed a wide torrential river.

We were now truly in China. To climb the approach to an important watercourse, and to find the latter not in a wide valley but at the bottom of an abyss opening in the actual substance of the dorsal ridge of the mountain: there you have the very type of Chinese orography.

The Pu-Tu-Ho, which was now before us, is an affluent of the lake of Yunnan-sen, by which the latter discharges itself into the Blue River. Its considerable volume of water has enabled it to erode a deep furrow in the friable schistous soil, and, in consequence, to capture over a considerable radius the rivers of all the more elevated valleys, to which Nature would seem, in the beginning, to have assigned a different destiny;

so that they now, so to speak, flow in the wrong direction. It is to such phenomena of erosion and capture that mountainous China owes its singular and at first incomprehensible aspect, to which I shall often have occasion to refer. Needless to say, these torrential waters, impeded by rocks fallen from the overhanging declivities, are impossible of navigation; no road can follow their narrow cañon, which consequently remains inaccessible and invisible, except at a few rare points where trails cross it by means of ferries.

The first exploration of this secret gorge was made in 1903 by Lieutenant Grillières, at the cost of abnormal fatigue, heroically endured, which resulted in his death at the very outset of a fresh expedition in 1905. It was with a pious emotion that we crossed this chasm, whose exploration had cost the life of our predecessor, who was my true friend.

On the mountains of the further bank live numerous Lolos, mingled with Chinese, whose fashions of clothing and of dwellings they have adopted; but for the costumes of the women, which have survived in a greater degree, their presence would hardly be remarked. Their houses, however, are set apart from the road, which they do not frequent, and on which one encounters only Chinese. Not having leisure at the time to leave the road, I then and there decided to return at a later time in order to study this population: a project which was afterwards executed.

Once we had crossed the ditch of the Pu-Tu-Ho, the valleys were once more gay and peaceful. The forests, however, grew more and more extensive, as is everywhere the case where no navigable river exists, nor one permitting of the floating of timber. These numerous valleys, small and verdant, half-hidden by the pines which carpet the gentle slopes of the hills, would remind one somewhat of the landscape of Thuringia, were it not that one sees, from the higher ground, a horizon-wall of majestic mountains, their flanks precipitous and bare, high as the Alps, yet snowless. They served to remind us that we were approaching Tibet, and that we were not far from the tropics.

It was towards these mountains that we travelled. But where was the Blue River? There was no sign of its proximity. Instead of flowing towards the north, in which direction the river lay, the streams we encountered were flowing southward, and we were continually ascending them. But I was forgetting that we were in China! To climb a mountain is the natural thing when one is looking for a river.

Suddenly we uttered a cry of admiration. Before us the earth suddenly fell away. We were overlooking the most frightful chasms; colossal walls of rock jutted out in all directions, the debris of foundered mountains; there was an inextricable chaos of gulfs, already filling with the shadows of night, prodigious pillars and splinters of rock red with the setting sun. A magnificent sight! We had not the impression of a motionless, definitive landscape; it was as though an irresistible force lay there in travail, destroying and re-creating at will; we had surprised the secret of one of those stupendous operations by which the crucible of Nature prepares the transformations of the globe.

We could not even guess, amidst all this upheaval, where lay the river that was the agent of this enormous cataclysm. We descended to seek it in the depths. It was no easy matter; we had to reach one of the pyramids which had remained erect amidst the precipices, and by zigzag paths cut in its side, to wind round it until we reached its base, and then to recommence the same manœuvre on some other mass lower down. Night fell when we were still only half-way down; fortunately two houses were at hand to shelter travellers.

On the succeeding day we reached the river, at an altitude of only 2,900 feet. Scarcely a hundred yards wide, enclosed between perpendicular walls, encumbered with rocks and rapids making navigation impossible, not even a footpath could have followed its banks. In 1898 Captain Vaulserre undertook to survey its course. As it was impossible to work along the stream, he was forced to travel across the mountains, bristling with obstacles which hem it in, without even obtaining a glimpse of it except at such points as he crossed in order to continue his work upon the other bank. An extraordinary fact, that the fourth river of the world should thus escape the human eye for some hundreds of miles of its course!

The passage of the river was negotiated upon a short tranquil reach by means of three large boats, which, when empty, had a great deal of freeboard. This was the first time we had occasion to marvel at the incomprehensible disdain which the Chinese profess in the face of certain difficulties; nowhere could we find the narrowest gangway to assist us in embarking the horses. They were forced to leap over the gunwale of the vessel, which was often more than forty inches higher than the bottom of the water through which they had to wade; they fell blindly headlong into the boat, colliding with baggage, thwarts, or running gear, at the risk of breaking their legs, or sometimes, giving an insufficient leap, a horse would remain suspended in equilibrium, its belly upon the gunwale, beating the air with its four hooves until it finally fell forward or backward by its own weight. The majority of the horses and mules are familiar, doubtless by age-long heredity, as well as by experience, with this singular proceeding; but many exhibit all the signs of complete rebellion. The result is sometimes hours of conflict between the unfortunate animal and the ferrymen; and the spectator is left amazed at the amount of strength, ingenuity, patience, and brutality expended to obtain the desired end, when a simple plank would suffice.

Once across the Blue River, we were in the province of Sze-Chuan. We had a sudden and abrupt climb—

THE BLUE RIVER AT HO-MEN-CHANG.

To face page 30.

and by what paths!—finally finding ourselves at a height of 6,500 feet, the same altitude from which we had descended the day before, in a series of little valleys like those I have already described. We were in a continuation of the same country, and the river, which comes from a distance and cuts it in two, running through a kind of subterranean passage, and receiving no affluents except by way of waterfalls or rugged gorges, never through a natural valley, seems a stranger to the country which it enters only to throw it into confusion.

One of the first effects of this upheaval is the revelation of the riches contained in the deeper levels of the soil, which appear in the eroded sections. The sides of the ravine facing the reach I speak of are full of coal and copper; five thousand workmen are employed in extracting them and in purifying the copper in tall furnaces. A mandarin directs the undertaking; and although the deposits are on the territory of Sze-Chuan, the profits, in virtue of ancient rights, are shared with Yunnan.

On the evening of this day—the seventh since our departure—we slept for the first time at an inn and in a town. The town, Tong-Ngan-Chu, we took to be a prefecture of the second order, from its name (Chu). What, then, was our astonishment on learning that it has no Chinese prefect, but a Lolo prince, and that the latter being in his minority his mother governs the country, although the population is partly Chinese. This princely family is extremely powerful and possesses six residences.

Thus in the heart of the Empire there are territories peopled by Chinese and crossed by commercial routes, which are governed by native princes, or even princesses!

It was only there that I learned that we had been travelling for three days through countries directly administered by Lolo chiefs; for although I was aware of their existence, I had supposed their power to be limited to the indigenous inhabitants ; I should never have imagined that they also governed the Chinese villages through which we had passed. These countries are therefore not Chinese territories, but simple protectorates. To be precise, the greater portion of Yunnan, of Sze-Chuan, and a large portion of all the mountainous provinces, as we shall presently see, are in a like case, even when the populations along the road seem purely Chinese ; so that European travellers have often no more suspected this curious situation than had we during the preceding days.

Crossing a region furrowed by the gorges cut by watercourses hastening to throw themselves into the Blue River 3,500 feet below, we went forward by forced marches in order to reach Wei-Li-Chu on the ninth day, where the principal Catholic mission of Sze-Chuan was established. This mission was in the district of Father de Guébriant, and there we should doubtless hear news of him. The missionary, however, was absent ; no one was expecting us. I was consumed with anxiety, and we resumed our march as speedily as possible, preceded by a fresh courier. Wei-Li-Chu was first visited by Francis Garnier (not counting the French missionaries). Passing through the city, we found ourselves on the well-known highway which connects the western portion of Sze-Chuan with Yunnan, Burmah, and Tonkin. The valley of the Kien-Chang, along which the road lies, is one of the richest of all the valleys of the Chinese mountains. Besides rice and cereals it produces silk and vegetable wax, and contains metals in abundance, notably the " white copper," a metal greatly prized by the Chinese, as it deserves to be by Europeans.

The chief characteristic of this valley, however, is that it is the only portion of Chinese territory in the midst of mountains peopled by Lolos. As one travels north the latter become more numerous and more aggressive, until the Chinese are veritably besieged in their valley. We heard of nothing but the exploits of these brigands, who fall upon the valley, kill travellers, and pillage the inhabitants. All the villages are fortified, and posts occupied by peasants armed with pikes, tridents, sabres, and sometimes with indifferent flintlocks, are permanently established along the roadside. A sight that one remembers is the gleam of the lances which the field-labourers have thrust into the earth while they guide the harrow or the plough in the immediate neighbourhood.

On the third day we reached the little town of Te-Chang. It is the home of a missionary—Father Dubois—and we were delighted to find him at home, and with him his colleague of Wei-Li-Chu, Father Castanet, a veteran of this country. These worthy Fathers, who live isolated from the world, accorded us the most touching welcome.

But the news was not good: far from it! Father de Guébriant was certainly at Ning-Yuan-fu, but I was not to hope anything from his presence; that he had not already left was because a delegate from the Viceroy had just arrived from the capital for the express purpose of investigating serious charges which he had brought against the prefect in the name of his Christians, and Father de Guébriant would be absolutely obliged to plead his cause, on which the fortune, the liberty, and even the life of many of his flock depended. As my Chinese interpreter would not consent to accompany me among the Lolos, there was nothing before me but to turn aside. But we should see!

Next day, at two hours' distance from Ning-Yuan-fu, in the village of Ma-Tao-Tze, we found a long line of richly clad personages drawn up, who welcomed us with all the signs of genuine pleasure; they were the Christian notables of Ning-Yuan-fu who had ridden out to meet us on horseback. They led us in great pomp to the inn; on the threshold Father de Guébriant awaited us with Father Bourgain, his assistant. It was a moment of genuine emotion in the midst of the general gaiety, which was expressed by the explosion of innumerable petards.

We took our seats in the palanquins which had been sent us by the general commanding at Ning-Yuan-fu, and our magnificent troop got under way. At the doors of the prefecture it was further increased by a hundred Christians and a superb Lolo chieftain in national costume : bare feet, a long cassock of brown felt, and a blue turban coming to a point above the forehead. He took, on horseback, the head of the procession, which with its four palanquins, its forty horsemen, and its hundred afoot, promenaded its pomp through the streets of the city amidst a formidable rattle of petards, the while the population were crushing to catch a sight of us. A noble entry, which will be remembered in the annals of the city ! I was well aware that in welcoming us thus the good Father did not wish merely to receive a French mission with due solemnity ; he hoped also to lessen the disappointment he was obliged to cause us. Hardly had the visitors departed when he took me aside and assured me that he could not quit his post.

I well understood the duties which his position imposed upon him ; but since I had come as a result of his promise, and since I had dispensed with the services of Lieutenant Lepage, so that I was left helpless by the lack of an interpreter, he surely would not desert me and thus lead to the failure of an expedition which ought to assure our native country of the prestige of an important discovery?

The good Father was deeply moved. It had so long been his own desire to penetrate the country of the Lolos, that to lose such an opportunity as had offered would be doubly painful. He determined to do his best to persuade Father Bourgain to replace him, and to convince the Chinese, the leaders of the

A PRIMITIVE IRON BRIDGE AT KIN-CHUAN-KIAO (VALLEY OF THE KIEN-CHANG).

To face page 34.

Christian community whose vital interests were at stake, that his presence was no longer indispensable; if he succeeded we should set forth in company.

For ten days there were discussions and interviews. The better to allay the suspicions of the Chinese authorities, the Father quietly continued his negotiations with the Viceroy's delegate. At the same time he invited a host of Lolos to visit us; and with their aid I prepared, from the information given, a chart of the country to be explored, so that I should not enter it blindfold; but as these were Lolos of the subject territory, through which Father de Guébriant had already led other travellers, there was nothing in all this to excite suspicion—rather the reverse.

However, the situation did not improve, and we were in great perplexity as to what we should do, when the Imperial delegate furnished us with an unexpected solution: he pronounced his judgment upon the affairs at issue, and this judgment was so extraordinary, excusing as it did in the most outrageous fashion the scandalous behaviour of the prefect, that there was no room to doubt that the latter had purchased his connivance.[1]

There was therefore no need for Father de Guébriant to remain in order to defend a lost cause: we should be able to go forward. He saw at once who was to be the indispensable instrument of our attempt—our future Lolo interpreter.

This is the moment to explain the situation and the procedure by which we hoped to succeed.

The state of war between the Chinese and the Lolos does not persist uninterruptedly; each expedition is terminated by a treaty of peace which defines their

[1] This is not a mere accusation: the fact was demonstrated at a fresh inquiry ordered by the Viceroy. The prefect was removed and degraded, the sub-prefect and the delegate dismissed, and the mission was accorded full satisfaction. Although there are corruptible judges in China, it would be absolutely unjust to suppose that such is the rule.

relations. However independent the Lolos may wish to be, they cannot entirely dispense with the Chinese: in order to resist them they must have firearms, and from whom can they buy them if not from the Chinese themselves?

The disturbed condition of the country does not favour industry; the culture of hemp is neglected, weaving is almost extinct, and the natives are forced to resort to the Chinese cotton-stuffs. On their side, the Chinese have need of the Lolos. The "Great Cold Mountains," as they call the great range, enjoy a singular monopoly—that of the wax-insect, a source of wealth for the Sze-Chuan.[1] This reciprocal need, combined with the independent humour of the Lolos, who wish to be masters in their own house, has given rise to the most singular organisation.

On the one hand, the Lolos may enter Chinese territory in perfect liberty; whether singly or in force, they come down bearing arms—always ready to leave them with the guard if they enter a town, and to resume them upon leaving; they come and go, trade, and deliver battle; in a word, they behave absolutely as they would in their own country. But each tribe which wishes to enjoy such liberty must undertake to respect the Chinese *on Chinese territory*, and must as guarantee give hostages, who dwell in the yamen of the prefect or sub-prefect.

The Chinese enjoy no reciprocity in the matter of entering Lolo territory; they are formally forbidden to enter it, under pain of being killed or reduced to slavery, and the Imperial authority cannot execute the

[1] Colborne Baber, the Lyons Mission, and A. Hosie have described this singular industry: a certain insect has the property of causing a much-valued wax to flow from certain trees by pricking and perforating their tissues; and the trees live only in the hot plains of the Sze-Chuan, while the insect is born and breeds only on a species of privet which is hardly ever found outside the country of the Lolos, at a distance of some hundreds of miles from the plains.

slightest measures of reprisal. This unless the Chinaman obtains a Lolo passport: in which case a Lolo of noble caste must consent to receive him and to answer for him to the clan. Now there are plenty of Lolos who are by no means reluctant to extend their protection in this way for the consideration of a suitable present. Regarding the men who hunt for the eggs of the wax-insect, and who come every year to the number of several thousands, there are established usages: the Lolos await them on the frontier, offer their protection for a price agreed upon, and take them in charge. The given word is never violated, and the Chinese return, safe and sound, the richer by their precious quarry, from a country in which they would be robbed, taken captive, or massacred were they to set foot in it without permission.

I must add that the better to persuade the Lolos to accept an engagement already so greatly to their advantage, China pays them an actual tribute,[1] each of the frontier clans receiving an appreciable sum yearly—namely, 75 to 150 taels, or £12 to £24.

We had to follow the accepted custom of procuring a Lolo to introduce us to his clan. The matter was not easy, for the advent of persons of our quality would give rise to all sorts of anxieties and heart-burnings; and only an influential chief would be prepared to receive us. We must select one well provided with alliances along our intended route, so that once our friendship was sealed and established it would recommend us to them also. Then—not as travellers, but as guests—we should be sacred. The main thing was not to hurry, not to refuse indirect routes or changes of itinerary, and to deal with honest men.

[1] The Lolos only make use of simple barter among themselves, never employing currency. All our payments without exception had to be made in merchandise carried for that purpose. However, they often accept silver from the Chinese, in order that they may purchase fire-arms when they have saved a sufficient sum.

Through his Christians, Father de Guébriant was able to procure the services of the best possible agent for the realisation of this plan. He was a young Chinese twenty-eight years of age, the son of an educated innkeeper who had settled at Ta-Hin-Chang, the last Chinese village on the frontier, which the Lolos frequent in large numbers. The innkeeper and his son did business with them as general purveyors; I should not be surprised to hear that they smuggled arms to some extent, arms being the form of merchandise chiefly appreciated by the Lolos. They also had friends among the principal tribes, and we counted on these to secure us an open road.

Three days later, at nightfall, the innkeeper and his son mysteriously arrived; they brought with them a Lolo with noble and regular features, who was one of the principal members of the great clan of the Ma, which occupies the frontier. Quickly won by the confidence we reposed in him and the reputation of Father de Guébriant, and perhaps to some extent by the reputation for friendliness which we had already acquired among the Lolos who came daily to see us, and also —need I add?—by a few presents, the Ma declared that he would answer for us in the name of his tribe. If we would solemnly assure him that our object was not the discovery of mines—a discovery the Lolos fear above all things, since the precious metals provoke invasion—we had only to go forward; all his kin would extend us a hearty welcome, and would contrive that their neighbours should do the same.

Our departure was fixed for two days later, as the Ma required time to advise his clan. On the following day the prefect scented something; his secretary hastened to Father de Guébriant's house to inform him that our intention of visiting the Lolos was being spoken of, but that his master would not credit us with so wild an undertaking; but in any case, if we had entertained any such proposal the worthy Father must

A CARAVAN TRAIL.

VALLEY OF THE KIEN-CHANG.

To face page 38.

use all his influence to convince us of its absurdity. Father de Guébriant listened to this invitation without a smile, and undertook to overwhelm us with counsels of prudence, as indeed he might very well, knowing that we should be deaf to every word.

We could not have hoped for better fortune. No doubt our secret was known—it could not be otherwise at the last moment—but it was not known that the missionary intended to accompany us, and that the expedition was a long-settled undertaking, not the mere whim of a traveller which a word would suffice to suppress.

On the following day, at the moment of departure, Father de Guébriant caused the prefect to be informed that his eloquence was in vain ; that we were hotheads who would listen to nothing, and that the only means left him of tempering our extravagances was to accompany us himself. The prefect remained unenlightened, but replied, like a good loser, that he admired the Father's wisdom and devotion, and would send us, to do us honour, eight men who would escort us to the frontier village, which lay at a distance of some six miles from the town.

To be escorted to the Lolo frontier by the very Chinese authorities who might have stopped us—what a successful issue to our stratagem! It was almost too good! It would not do to wait for a probable change of mind, so we took the road without losing another minute.

CHAPTER II

THE COUNTRY OF THE INDEPENDENT LOLOS

OUR expedition was greatly reduced. I had dismissed the temporary Chinese interpreter, sending him back to Yunnan-sen; and as we placed little reliance in our two Annamite boys—how badly we missed our military servants!—we did not even think of taking them with us. However we should require their services later, in order to return to Yunnan-sen, so we sent them, in the care of a trusty man of Father de Guébriant's, to Swei-Fu, in the lower Sze-Chuan, which we expected to make our destination, so that they would follow with our baggage, the highway which makes the circuit of the Lolo country. As we naturally needed men to cook our food, look after our horses, and carry our loads, we took three of Father de Guébriant's Christians, hardy mountaineers, who were so devoted to him that they would have cut themselves in little pieces for him, as the saying goes.

With a bed apiece, a canteen for two, containing an extra load of silver bullion, cartridges, rolls of photographic films, and medicines—in short, our whole personal outfit—there was little room for the rest of our goods. Two loads of salt, sugar, cloth, and small articles intended as presents, and a dozen boxes of preserved food for absolute emergencies—such were our impedimenta, and they did not promise us much comfort; but we could hardly add to their weight.

We skirted the pretty lake of Ning-Yuan-fu, and ascended the hills which hem it in to the east, which is the edge of the world as known to Europeans. Our new Ma friend was there awaiting us, accompanied by his squire—for every Lolo noble has about his person a confidential servant, chosen from among his serfs, who serves him as a steward or bailiff in times of peace and a squire in war. He would conduct us as far as Ta-Hin-Chang, where he would place us in the hands of three of his kinsmen, who would come to meet us and take us into their keeping.

Behind these hills, which had seemed the foot-hills of the high mountains, we were surprised to discover a small plain into which opened a number of gorges. This is the gateway of the Lolo country, and the outer ramparts of Ning-Yuan-fu and the Chinese Empire. No less than fourteen military camps or posts are huddled together there, walled and crenellated, containing, according to the gravity of the situation, from a thousand to three or four thousand men. Numerous hamlets, also fortified, are scattered about the fields, and in the centre is the village of Ta-Hin-Chang.

As soon as we entered it a multitude of Lolos, who thronged the streets, pressed about us in order to see us. It must be confessed that their appearance is "perfect gallows"; they have all the look of bandits meditating a crime, and we surprised many an exchange of smiles or glances which seemed to indicate that they already considered us their prey. There is no doubt whatever that if any traveller were to go among these brigands without the protection of a powerful chief he might be certain that his journey would end there.

However, we reached the inn. The host—we were rather surprised that he had not come to meet us—was not in the house; neither was his son. This was peculiar. But doubtless they were busied over our affairs; we should see!

One of the Father's Christians, who had arrived before we did, decided, after some little time, to find out how matters stood. It is a peculiarity to be remarked in the Far East, that no one will communicate even the most urgent news precipitately; it is supposed to be unmannerly. However, this is what we learned:—

A mandarin had preceded us, and had made it known that whosoever gave us the least assistance would incur terrible penalties. The innkeeper and his son were terrified, abandoned their plans, and went to hide themselves, not daring to face our reproaches. Our Lolo sponsors, having heard the news, had also disappeared.

Here, then, was the secret of the prefect's amiability: by threatening all those of whom we had need he counted on making it impossible for us to go forward, although officially he had furnished us with an escort of honour! A pretty trick, entirely in keeping with the best traditions!

The difficulty was serious. Nevertheless, by means of reasoning and promises we might perhaps succeed in restoring confidence. After all, a prefect was not omnipotent, and foreign lords of our quality could not be molested with impunity. But the innkeeper remained undiscoverable. At night, however, his son Siu was found. He, who had doubtless anticipated the payment we should have made him for services rendered, appeared broken-hearted by this dilemma. We assured him of our protection, dangling before his eyes the promise of a large reward as bait, and he soon entirely entered into our views. He would endeavour to convert his father.

Next morning the latter at last appeared. Nonplussed, he stammered that it was true that he had promised to help us, but could he have supposed that we were not in agreement with the prefect? How could he disobey the latter? We undertook the task of bringing him to a better frame of mind. A good sum in cash on our departure and another in case of success "put us square" with the rodomontades of the prefect, which were directed in vain against those who should be of service to us. The innkeeper's son and our Christians also took their turn at lecturing him.

He was shaken; but the mandarin was still on the ground, and him he feared. Learning that the official was present in the inn, we invited him to come to see us; and he dared not refuse, since we had arrived under the official ægis. Then, before the innkeeper, we asked him if it were true that the prefect was threatening the people we had engaged. He lied shamelessly. What was this? The prefect would be only too pleased that they should help us, and he himself had only come to prevent evilly disposed persons from offering us their services. There had merely been a misunderstanding (this was really capital!), and the innkeeper could no longer do other than second us.

All seemed arranged at last. But now the Lolos began to fail us. Warned by the mandarin that the prefect would put them to death if they reappeared on Chinese territory after having piloted us, they were not anxious to embroil themselves with their Chinese neighbours for the sake of a cause to which they were, on the whole, indifferent. It was impossible to get them to face us.

Happily the young Siu showed himself a resourceful youth. In the host of Lolos who populated the villages he could easily find some who would be willing to earn honest wages. He returned with a tall, determined-looking scoundrel who offered no less than to conduct us to Chao-Tong, the prefecture of Yunnan, whither he often went.

We could scarcely believe our ears. How did he know this city, which lay on the other side of the Blue River, and what would these savage Independents be doing so far from the refuge to which they are supposed to be confined? We pelted him with embarrassing questions which he answered with the greatest ease, describing very precisely the roads, the stages of the journey, and the points of crossing other itineraries which I had already noted. He went to Chao-Tong because it was a country full of Lolos of the same race as the Independents and in constant communication with them.

These facts were absolutely new and of the greatest interest. If this interesting scoundrel was speaking the truth, we should make some curious discoveries. He pressed us to accept his proposition, and Siu, who knew him, assured us that we might put our trust in him. We felt that we could not accept his offer except it were absolutely a last resource, for the route he proposed would lead us a long way from the heart of the Lolo country. However, it was good policy to encourage him, and to give him the idea that we found it difficult to choose among so many applicants.

At this juncture a new change of face was attempted. The prefect, doubtless warned by the mandarin, sent a thunderous letter to the innkeeper: "How, pitiful fellow, dare you flout the wishes of the Emperor and lead strangers among the revolted Barbarians? Remember that you will be charged with connivance with these rebels, and your race will expiate your offence with you."

Tut, tut! Our arrangements were all confounded. The terrified innkeeper declared that he washed his hands of the affair and would never permit his son to accompany us. Father de Guébriant, after reading the prefect's letter, sadly admitted that no Chinaman would dare to brave such explicit threats, and that nothing more was to be hoped for in that quarter; his opinion was that we could do nothing but return to Ning-Yuan-fu and there seek to induce the prefect to withdraw his opposition by threatening to complain of his proceedings.

It was clear, however, that the good Father's only object in proposing this course was to avoid confessing that he considered we had received a definite checkmate ; for how could we hope that the prefect would give way, especially after such a proof of our powerlessness as our return to the town? No ; if we gave way, if we took a single step to the rear, then goodbye to the Lolos—we should be forced to abandon our object.

Now was the time to act, without giving way an inch. I therefore wrote to the prefect, stating that the innkeeper, deceived by false reports, believed that he, the prefect, had forbidden our departure ; an obvious lie, since I had in my hands the letter in which he wished us a successful journey and offered us a guard of honour to escort us. Besides, how absurd to suppose that the prefect would consider a man guilty because he had assisted French officers, guests of the Empire and accredited as such ! Was not the man now in our service, and therefore as inviolable as ourselves? The prefect would know how to suppress statements so damaging to his reputation for intelligence and loyalty.

Night fell during these preliminaries. The sound of a violent dispute arose in the courtyard, and by the uncertain light of a few candles we distinguished the silhouettes of Lolos, who seemed to be on the point of coming to blows. The people of the inn ran out and finally induced them to depart. The subject of the quarrel? It was certainly unexpected. At the moment when the Chinese were forsaking us the Lolos were disputing as to who should have the honour of conducting us !

Our new friend had gathered his kinsmen before our door, and they had all together proceeded to swear by the sacrament of blood that they would lead us faithfully. This oath, the most sacred of all, is very like that of the ancient Germans : each participant pricks his arm, allowing a few drops of blood to fall into a cup of wine, after which all in turn touch their lips to the contents while repeating the words of the oath. Just as they were going to take the oath the Ma envoys, who had hitherto suffered a prudent eclipse, being informed that others were about to rob them of their honourable charge of conducting us, and reap the rich harvest of reward, rushed forward claiming their rights.

This episode came at a critical moment, and bade us hope on. Our tenacity had already won over the Lolos: why should it not succeed with the Chinese?

In the morning a whole troop of men made their way into the narrow room to which the negotiations had for two days confined us. They were Christians of Ning-Yuan-fu, sent by Father Bourgain. The missionary, whose sagacity and knowledge of the Chinese character is proverbial, had very wisely concluded that my letter—which I had sent to him in order to have it translated—to the prefect would not attain its object: the prefect would find some loophole of escape. He might openly protest his good intentions, while he would still adhere to his secret orders. The same arguments would apply to the innkeeper.

Father Bourgain therefore wrote two letters; in one the innkeeper replied to the prefect that he could not understand what offence he could be committing in serving honourable foreigners who had arrived with an official escort. Now that he had pledged himself, believing that he was conforming with the Emperor's desires, how could he break his word?

In the second letter I was made to declare that I had taken into my service the innkeeper and all his family, and that any one who sought to quarrel with them on that account should address himself to me, and that I was requesting the French Minister at Pekin to inquire whether any malevolent action had been taken against them (at a later date).

These letters, admirably expressed in the Chinese style by a remarkable man of letters who was the chief of the Christian community, were magnificent examples of caligraphy, and were embellished with vermilion with the happiest effect. Surrounded by all our retinue of Christians, we presented them to the innkeeper. Impressed by this ceremoniousness, his scholar's heart thrilled with admiration at the sight of so eloquent a letter, and with pride at the thought of signing it ; the guarantee of the protection of France seemed to him an invincible talisman ; and without further deliberation he affixed his name to the letter, which was immediately sealed and entrusted to the Christians. He then prostrated himself and saluted us as his masters. This time we had him fast.

Immediately the three Lolo envoys, whom we had not yet seen, came to present themselves and to prostrate themselves in turn—for they pique themselves upon not being barbarians, and on understanding the usages of polite society, and nowhere did we receive so many *ko-tiu* (prostrations of the face against the ground) as from this haughty race. Thenceforth they answered for us ; they were our *respondents*, according to the Chinese expression, which I will here adopt.

There was nothing to prevent our setting forth. "Eat before you go," said the Lolos : "here you have all things in abundance ; up above there is nothing. Save your provisions." Word full of wisdom. Alas, that wisdom is often a bad counsellor ! We breakfasted rapidly, and finally we left Ta-Hin-Chang, pushing our way with difficulty through the dense sea of people, whom our conflict with the prefect had greatly excited, and who were asking themselves what the reckoning would be for our triumph of the day.

Thus we had at last succeeded in casting down the first of the barriers which guarded the forbidden land. The Chinese authorities, taken aback, had not anticipated our manœuvres, nor prepared an efficient opposition ; their final measures, precipitate and incoherent, were easily parried. But what invaluable assistance we had received from the ability and coolness of Father de Guébriant, the filial devotion which inspired all his

Christians, and the diplomatic readiness of Father Bourgain!

Perhaps the reader will find the tale of this three days' negotiation rather long. Certainly falls over precipices, charges of horsemen armed with lances, ambushes, treasons, and heroic devotion speak more loudly to the imagination. Happily such subjects will not fail me; but I should have nothing to tell of such delights had not this obscure duel with Chinese authority, invisible though active, fought out as it was in one of the chambers of the inn, terminated in a successful result.

*

* *

But where were our Lolo respondents? They had lingered behind to drink a stirrup-cup; Siu had to leave us to get them started. We passed through several military outposts, the men mounted on horseback and stationed along the road, the better to bar it. At some distance from the last the whole garrison, consisting of a score of men, came out to present arms in our honour; by a happy chance the commanding officer was a Christian, who wished to salute Father de Guébriant. The little troop took the head of our column and accompanied us as far as a gate, the remains of a demolished fort, which marked the frontier. Before this gate, the gate of peril and adventure, it lined up again and once more saluted us.

At last the unknown was before us. Delicious sensation! One that, for the explorer, softens the rudest hardships. It is as though some spell has dissolved the magic wall which has hitherto set a term to the foot and the eye of man; a new world appears before him, and he finds it marvellous. An invincible confidence invades him; he feels as though under the protection of an omnipotent power; for has not Fate marked him out to reveal to the world this secret corner of the earth, which she has kept secret since the beginning

THE LOLO ENVOYS.
Lieut. de Boyve. Father de Guébriant. Lolo Noble. Serf.

FAREWELL HONOURS.

To face page 48.

of the ages? Now a charm protects him ; all will unfold before him. And how his senses are on the alert, how his attention, his receptiveness increase, the better to fulfil his mission, to present his fellows with the completest picture of what he has seen ! Not a blade of grass must escape him. Do not be surprised, then, if in his descriptions the blade of grass occupies too prominent a place.

Do not smile at this enthusiasm. I do not believe there is a single explorer, be he never so sceptical and apparently phlegmatic, who has not repeatedly felt it ; for to embrace a soldier's life without seeking the intoxication of victory, and an ascetic's without having in view the felicities of heaven, a man must have a vein of mysticism, must believe in his star.

We scaled the steep slopes of the mountain, whence we obtained an admirable view of the valley of Ning-Yuan-fu. A few Lolos, who were descending, threw us surprised glances, but the sight of our respondents' slaves, who were carrying our loads, assured them that we were not intruders, and they passed on. None the less, we were in a sufficiently annoying position, with neither sponsors nor interpreter. What were our men doing? As far as the village of Ta-Hin-Chang, down below at our feet, the road was empty. What if some unforeseen mischance had occurred? What if the prefect had invented some fresh move? That unfortunate breakfast ! A stupid precaution ! Why did we not start on the spur of the moment, profiting by a fit of enthusiasm which had probably now subsided?

If our reflections were gloomy, the sky was more so ; the sun, which had been radiant, suddenly disappeared behind the black clouds which surged up behind the mountains, and a terrible wind enwrapped us in its eddies. Our Lolo porters rushed towards a little valley which opened into the heart of the mountain, although we were at a considerable elevation ; and we hastened to follow them. We had scarcely time to notice, at the entrance, a dog hanging from a cross; a sinister warning to all intruders.

The storm broke with incredible violence; rain, hail, and snow, lashed by an infernal tempest, while the lightning flashed and fell on every side. We had to put forth all our strength to advance at all, although we had reached level and partly sheltered ground; had we been surprised a few minutes earlier, on the steep slopes of the mountain, our only means of safety would have been to lie down and cling to the rocks in order not to be carried away by the wind.

Happily we had only gone forward for some five hundred yards when we found two houses; we hurried up to them. Houses!—the most miserable hovels one could dream of. That which we entered had only one tiny room, and its gaping roof let in torrents of rain, while a thick smoke rose from the hearth and blinded us. To be smoked and drowned at the same time was truly the height of ill-fortune! We were astonished to find these cabins inhabited by Chinese women; they lived there by permission of the Lolos, one of whose villages, hidden by the lie of the land, was only fifty yards distant.

The tempest, always accompanied by snow and thunder, lasted all night. Truly the welcome of Lololand was not encouraging. "She wants to frighten the audacious creatures who dare to set foot upon her soil," smiled Father de Guébriant. But the torrents of water and the hissing of the tempest engulfing our hovel were not the only matters to keep us wakeful: we had no interpreter and no respondents—a fact which disturbed us more than the storm. Would they ever come? And what sort of a welcome should we get from the Lolos of the village, who had not given a sign of life?

Day came, and a glorious sun dissipated the clouds, but not our anxieties. Not until nine o'clock did we see, with a sigh of comprehensible relief, the approach

FORTIFIED FARMS NEAR TA-HIN-CHANG.

To face page 50

of the laggards. It appeared that on the day before the Lolos were so delighted at the idea of guiding us into their country that they had begun, while we were at breakfast, to drink our health, which they did to such effect that they ended by getting completely drunk. Now, however, they were entirely at our service.

This preliminary proceeding must not be allowed to give the reader an incorrect idea of our respondents: they were soon to raise themselves in our esteem.

It is time to describe them, for hitherto all descriptions have been properly diffident. Colborne Baber described the Lolos as *taller than any European race;* he had not seen "a single man who could be called short, even for an Englishman"; but Commandant Bonifacy, the best-known ethnographist of Tonkin, declared it impossible to tell a Lolo from an Annamite if they wore the same costume; and the Annamites, as every one knows, *are one of the smallest races in the world*. Such are the precise data of science!

"They are a right fair folk, but they are not fully white, but are brown folk." This picture, drawn in the thirteenth century by Marco Polo, is still exact. Two of our respondents were magnificent men: one, Ma-Hotse, was over 6 ft. 6 in. in height, with fine, reflective features; the other, Ma-Yola, who was barely 6 ft. 2 in., had one of the finest heads imaginable. There was nothing of the Asiatic; the complexion was not yellow, but swarthy, like that of the inhabitants of Southern Europe; the eyes, neither oblique nor flattened, were large, and protected by fine arched brows; the nose was aquiline, the mouth well cut. Above all, what a frank, open, soldierly expression! What an assured glance!—yet not provocative or challenging. A European head—yes, but with something of the Indian type. What superb redskins these men would make, with a plume of feathers or a war-bonnet on the head!

Photography gives a poor idea of the beauty of their type ; a little uneasy as to what we were going to do, they could not retain their natural expression, but screwed up their eyes and twisted their mouths. This, unhappily, is a pretty general peculiarity, so the reader must embellish in imagination all the portraits here given ; for the European photographer, even with those subjects most familiar with the operation, is obliged to take a thousand precautions, to retouch the negative, and often to repeat the exposure.

As for our third respondent, Ma-Walei, although of the same class, he was moderately ugly, and not nearly so tall, (he stood about 5 ft. 4 in. high) ; but he was greatly renowned for his courage and intelligence.

While we were posing them for their photographs there appeared above the wall which crowned the slope against which the cabins were built a whole row of curious countenances ; these were the Lolo women of the village, who, now that our respondents had arrived, so that we were by that fact introduced, wished to observe the palefaces, as they doubtless called us. They came just in time to furnish an interesting background, though none of them were pretty—we shall presently understand why.

Now, our numbers complete after so many alarms, it was time to be off. The climb was trying, for the road ascended in a straight line ; but although the slope grew steeper and steeper as we proceeded, it was far less trying than the mountains we had hitherto scaled ; however, we were already at a height of nearly 10,000 feet. When we turned round the view was marvellous. The snow had covered the summits in the night, and from this height we saw them gleaming against the infinite like waves fringed with foam ; it was Tibet, stretching for countless miles into the west.

A twisted, tormented country ! But here the summits were rounded, the rock hidden by the soil and the soil by turf ; we could ride, as we could walk, every-

OUR THREE RESPONDENTS.

To face page 52.

where. No need of road; a simple trail, at least ten yards in width; and instead of proceeding in Indian file, a necessary measure on the narrow roads of China, and keeping a careful watch as to where we set our feet, here we all went freely, halted, formed groups, chatted, laughed, and sang. It is a joy to march in such a country.

The region through which we advanced was little populated; so near Chinese territory the inhabitants would never be secure, the wars being almost continuous. We passed only a few huts of bamboo, mere shelters for shepherds, herds guarded by boys, and several bands of men—I cannot call them caravans, so little did these cheerful and unorderly companies recall the regular and methodical aspect which the word implies—who were going to Ta-Hin-Chang in order to sell horses, hides, and honey.

Usually the nobles were in the saddle, mounted on small, agile horses of a race peculiar to the country. Their feet, sure as a goat's, were not shod; their trappings were coloured red, and ornamented with little round plates of bone, which had a pretty effect. The stirrup merits a special mention; it has the form of a slipper or wooden shoe, with the hinder part cut away, while the fore part is solid, except for a quite small cavity which the toes alone enter, the rest of the foot having no support. This singular device resembles to some extent the stirrup of the old Japanese knights.

Each noble was accompanied by slaves bearing burdens, and a few armed serfs, their arms being a huge lance, some twenty-five to thirty feet in length, which is one of the characteristic Lolo weapons, a trident, a bow and quiver, and sometimes a gun; while the noble himself wore a sabre hanging from a baldrick which was covered by the same discs of bone as were seen on the saddles; these were evidently much in vogue.

All saluted us in friendly fashion, and halted a moment to inquire curiously of our respondents concerning this new species of guest. We took advantage of these halts to take photographs; they asked us to explain our intention, and, on this being known, posed themselves with their men-at-arms in decorative groups, which were even a trifle theatrical, just as a professional photographer would have arranged them. They have a sense of effect and the picturesque.

We crossed the range by a pass 10,400 feet above sea-level; but then, instead of redescending, found a wide plateau in form of a saucer, a place of abundant grass. "Be pleased to gallop, gentlemen; it is the custom here," said our guides; and indeed this plateau of Chaol, in which the Lolos hold assemblies, and concentrate before undertaking their expeditions, seems a natural race-course. We gave our horses the rein, and they set off as though possessed. In China every flat is a rice-field or poppy-field; nothing is left untilled but the steep slopes where nothing but grass could be grown; the roads are narrow and stony; never would you find the least room for such cheerful customs. Here was space, a plain, and the turf! Such a thing had never been seen within the memory of horse, and our mounts were as though intoxicated.

Another pass, 10,000 feet high; then we began to descend. Pines, box, and great bushes of azalea covered with white and pink bloom transform the turf-covered slopes into a lovely park. Suddenly, at a turning, Siu gave an exclamation of joy. "Success assured!" he cried, and showed us, on the horizon, a rosy shape lost in the sky.

It was Long-Tiu-shan, the mountain of the Dragon's Head, as the Chinamen call it, or Chonolevo, as the Lolos have it. No mountain is more famous. Its characteristic shapes—it has several, all remarkable, according to the side from which it is seen; it was now a regular, sharp-pointed pyramid, its prodigious

LOLO NOBLES WITH THEIR MEN-AT-ARMS.

To face page 54.

height—16,250 feet, according to my subsequent estimates—enables one to distinguish it from all other mountains. It is one of those manifestations of the power of Nature which strike the popular imagination and cause legends to spring from it; there is not a Lolo family that does not regard it as the cradle of its ancestors; not a story in which it does not play a considerable part, and when a story-teller takes up his tale you may be prepared to hear its name.

When seen as we saw it, upon entering the country, it is a certain sign that all will go well. I was very willing to believe this, for thenceforth one thing would certainly progress well—namely, my chart. Chonolevo was precisely at the opposite end of the Lolo country, so that I could at the very outset note the exact point at which we expected to end our journey, and thus, in spite of the alterations of route which the vicissitudes of politics or the accidents of the soil might force upon us, I could always obtain for my surveys a base-line of perfect precision.[1]

Further to the south another range, apparently as high, offered a second landmark; this was Shama-Swei-shan (the Snow Mountains of Shama), whither we also expected to go. It wore its name well, for its summits raised into the sky a vast field of snow which was reddened by the last rays of the sun, while Chonolevo, doubtless because of its pointed form, was not as yet snow-covered.[2]

Behind us the sun had already disappeared; a veil of darkness was drawn over the unknown country which we wished to explore; alone, almost unreal amid the

[1] This was all the more fortunate as from this time forward my guides, disturbed by my questions, observations, and notes, begged me urgently not to make a chart of their country. We had thenceforth to invent stratagems worthy of Red Indians in order to obtain and record such data as direction, &c., without exciting their suspicion.

[2] It never is covered on the southern face, which is too perpendicular—except in a few crevasses—but the northern face, which we saw later on, always retains a little snow.

clouds, the rosy peaks of the two giant mountains gleamed like the habitations of glory and splendour. Magnificent symbols! When we came face to face with the obstacles and the dangers that were now hidden from us by the shadows, we should have before our eyes the radiant vision of this goal, this gleaming apparition in the sky.

The home of Ma-Walei, where we were to sleep, was close by. It consisted of a fairly large house, without a courtyard, in which lived the seigneur, and at a short distance, on the farther side of a brook, an agglomeration of bamboo huts, surrounded by fragile wicker palings. Here dwelt the serfs. Another noble lived a little higher up.

I must hasten to explain that this was the only dwelling of a Lolo seigneur which we saw in the open and isolated; all the others were built in an enclosure, inside which were a number of families of serfs, ready to defend their lord against a sudden attack. Perhaps Ma-Walei had reckoned, in time of war, to install himself with his better-protected neighbours; however that may be, his confidence did not bring him fortune, for during my second journey to Kien-Chang I learned that he had been killed by a hostile clan. How many of our Lolo friends have already disappeared!

Like all the houses of rich Lolos, this had its walls built of planks disposed vertically; the roof was also of planks, which were kept in place by rows of great stones, as in the Swiss chalets; but the planks were very unevenly cut, and left gaps almost as wide as themselves. There were no windows, and indeed they would have been superfluous, as the light and the air entered only too freely already, as did also the rain and the snow, through the openwork roof. The house contained two rooms; the master of the house and his wife occupied the smaller, the other being the common hall.

No furniture, except a few coffers containing the clothing and all the poor wealth of the household. In the centre of the room, to abate the bitter cold that enters by so many chinks, was a hearth, with a fire always alight. It was a great circular stone, the centre slightly hollowed to hold the ashes, the circumference carved with rude arabesques. Three stones set in the middle helped the fire to draw and supported the great flat mortar in which food was cooked.

In the large hall, facing the door, was a sort of retreat in which some of the pigs and sheep were enclosed at night. In the corners were other such divisions, which served sometimes for storing arms, tools, fishing-tackle, or hunting-gear, and sometimes as bed-chambers for any who wished for isolation.

Such a case as this is rare; as a rule the Lolo has no bed nor fixed sleeping-place; all that he needs he carries on him: his great cloak or cassock. He crouches near the fire, and when sleep comes he stretches himself as near the fire as possible, his legs half wrapped in his mantle.

This garment, exactly like those worn by the shepherds of Limousin or Provence, is of felt, usuallv of a deep brown colour, but sometimes blue and often of the natural tint of the wool. This, together with hempen cloth, is the only textile produced among the Lolos; it is a rough and uneven material. Such as it is, however, this garment affords such excellent shelter against rain, snow, and cold that the Lolo regards it as invaluable. He never doffs it, winter or summer; thanks to it, he does not fear to be surprised by the night, for he will stretch himself out in the first hollow he can find among the rocks, and will slumber peacefully in this wonderful cape, which takes the place of mattress, blankets, and even roof. The true home of the Lolo is his cloak.

Late into the night we sat round the fire with Ma-Walei, his wife, his servants, and others, familiarly chatting. Unfortunately, they had more questions to put than we; for were not all our possessions marvellous? Of all things, what they most admired was our pocket electric lamps; the gleaming fire that each of us carried upon him without getting burned, which could at will be extinguished or relit, and pointed in all directions—was it not a miracle, a proof of the magic power with which we were surrounded? They were burning to examine our arms: we saw that we should have to let them witness their effect next day.

When the time had come to sleep, all save Ma-Walei and his wife, who retired, remained stretched out by the fire, in front of our prepared beds. This was for us a decisive experiment: if the Lolos were such brigands as the Chinese paint them, our last hour would sound that night, for they had only to stretch out their hand in order to strike us in the darkness, and all our treasures were theirs. If we were alive in the morning it would be because they did not covet them, and we should know that we were dealing with a loyal people.

Despite the instinctive sympathy that we already felt for our hosts, prudence bade us sleep with one eye open, our revolvers ready to hand. Sometimes the dying light on the hearth was extinguished, and the darkness was absolute; very soon we heard the sound of a crawling body. Quickly a jet of light sprang up; it was only one of the sleepers, who, waked up by the cold, was seeking to relight the fire.

Already a vague light filtered through the chinks in the walls; every one stretched himself and rose. As for us, we all three joyfully wished each other good morning, for we felt now that the battle was half over. To have none to fear but professed enemies—it was really almost too good to be true!

LOLO SERFS.

SERFS' HUTS.

To face page 58.

CHAPTER III

IN THE HEART OF THE "GREAT COLD MOUNTAINS"

BUT for those who wished to penetrate this country it was not enough to have loyal hosts. The division of the clans and their dissensions constitutes the most formidable obstacle, and the fact of having been well received by one tribe was merely a guarantee of the greater hostility of its neighbours.

We were going to learn this fact by experience without delay. We had to cross the valley of Lan-pa, which belonged to another clan, the Ngigai, cutting the territory of the Ma in two. The real patrimony of the latter is to the east, but a few remnants of the tribe, being too closely confined, had gone to settle in the hitherto desert zone which bordered on China. This was in conformity with the movement which has everywhere, for two hundred years, led the Lolos from the east to the west—the reverse of what was hitherto believed—and it was this new domain that we had been traversing for the last two days.

Now the Ngigai were on good terms with the Ma of the east, but hostile to those of the west, and our friend Ma-Walei, having led us to the frontier, had to refuse to escort us further, as this would expose us to attack. The respondents who remained even questioned whether the mere fact of having arrived under his ægis had not indisposed the Ngigai; for although the latter had promised to consent to our advance beforehand, there was no one on the frontier to receive us. This was a rather bad sign, for we had been signalled for some time: so we were asked to wait while Ma-Hotse went ahead to sound their intentions.

The valley of Lan-pa, which unrolled before us, contains many villages and rich pastures. The river which rises there runs towards the south, and for some distance waters the Lolo country; but it soon leaves it, and the lower portion of its valley is traversed by the great Chinese road from Kiao-Kia-Ting to Ning-Yuan-fu. It is a singular fact that the existence of this road remained unknown to European geographers, who prolonged the country of the Lolos far beyond this point. Father de Guébriant, in 1897, was the first to follow the road and record the general error. As to finding a Chinese road where an independent and inaccessible territory was charted, he had retained a certain scepticism in the matter, believing it to be a fiction invented by the mandarins in order that those in high places should recognise their merit in making themselves respected by a population so formidable. Great was his astonishment now to find that we were really in the independent country in which he no longer believed, and that we had left China behind us. How largely this immense country, which is supposed to be so well known, is really closed and mysterious even to those who reside in it!

Our guides pointed out to us a group of men ambushed in the rocks. Posted there or elsewhere, they were always ready to fall upon any who should enter the country without authorisation. Each tribe has such outposts always on the alert. Moreover, the least details reveal this permanent state of war; for instance, in attempting to depart a short distance from the trail I found that the whole of the ground, as far as the rocks which form the walls of the pass, was planted with little pegs, fixed with their points

VALLEY OF THE LAN-PA.

To face page 66.

upward, barely emerging from the ground ; it seems that these points were poisoned. They are, one guesses, intended for the bare feet of such as might seek to get by in the night, escaping the vigilance of the outpost which guards the road.[1]

The wait was a long one. A considerable disturbance was apparent in the valley : groups were forming and dispersing.

It appeared that we were threatened by an attack on the part of the Lomi-Loko, a neighbouring clan, and the Ngigai did not know whether we were worth risking that eventuality for.

This was the moment selected by Ma-Yola, the respondent who was guarding us, to witness the power of our arms ; and our interpreter also thought that a few projectiles falling from the other side of the valley could only improve the situation. We took their advice, and sent our balls successively into the river, where the water was thrown up by their impact, then across it, and finally against the opposite mountain slope. The range of our shots, the rapidity of our firing, and the apparently unlimited capacity of our arms—we had repeating carbines taking ten cartridges, and took care not to let it appear that they could become exhausted—excited transports of enthusiasm in our guides, and also among the people below, who raised shouts of admiration.

I do not know whether this little exercise counted for anything in the decision arrived at, but we were almost immediately told to advance, and a Ngigai "respondent," followed by a numerous crowd of sightseers, came forward to meet us. A magnificent young man, 6 ft. 2 in. in height, carrying a modern rifle, he prostrated himself before us in the most courteous manner. Our guides were delighted ; for this was the nephew of the *nzemo*, or prince of that region, and

[1] This is a means of defence used wherever men go barefoot. I have often seen it used in Africa.

with him we had nothing to fear from the Lomi-Loko. Nevertheless, we were asked to keep our carbines in our hands, and to take care that they were plainly visible; and even Father de Guébriant, who had warned us that he would never make use of those murderous weapons, decided to take part in this martial demonstration.

The reader must pardon me if I break the chronological thread in order to make my narrative more intelligible. I will now explain the social organisation of the Lolos as we came to understand it only after the lapse of some months, for it is difficult to understand the laws where there is no written constitution and where exceptions, while confirming the rule, only too often conceal it.

The independent Lolos live under the feudal system. All the soil belongs to the seigneurs. The latter esteem and practise the art of war before all else; but we shall see that they do not neglect letters. Agricultural skill they do not appreciate. Agriculture, to them, is the work of the serfs and slaves; slaves and serfs they must therefore have, and the Chinese are at hand to furnish them; they raid them and carry them into their mountains. Is not this a paradoxical situation? The vast Empire of China cannot, on her own territory, prevent her children from being enslaved by the Barbarians.

The slaves are not ill-treated—provided they are obedient and do not run away. They form several stereotyped classes—usually three. At the end of several generations of good service, the slave is customarily freed and becomes a serf. The class of serfs, which has also its own hierarchy of classes, sometimes contains at the summit broken nobles, generally those who have been defeated in war, and who, refusing to accept the yoke of the conqueror, go elsewhere to seek the protection of some powerful seigneur. Such was the case in a village we passed; it was inhabited by exnobles of the Loko clan, who had taken refuge in the territory of the Ngigai and become their serfs.

Finally, right at the top of the heirarchy are the nzemo, or princes. Their power, I believe, is not defined by any charter ; it depends, as in all monarchies by Divine right, more especially on the worth of the person who yields it, and on his personal resources ; one nzemo, rich and active, can make his nobles respect his power, while another will enjoy no influence beyond his private estate. These princes exercise only the rights of suzerainty, as we Europeans used to understand them, over their vassals ; they do not in any way govern them.

No union is allowed between one class and another The nobles are so jealous of the purity of their blood that if illicit relations between one of themselves and a serf woman are discovered, the two offenders are expected to commit suicide. These classes are thus actual castes, like the castes of India. As a result there are no ties of race between the nobles, who are the true Lolos, and the serfs and slaves of foreign origin who form the great majority of the population.

It must be understood that this rule is fundamental, and that any account of the Lolos that does not refer to it can only lead to the utmost misunderstanding.

These four classes are not represented everywhere. Noble families will often, feeling themselves sufficiently powerful, cast off their bonds of loyalty to the nzemo and live in complete independence upon their lands. At other times serfs, discontented with their lords, will shake off their yoke either by force of arms or by placing themselves under the direct authority of a prince; in such a case the noble will be left out of the hierarchy. Finally, among the subject Lolos of Yunnan and Kwei-Chu, the princes have often been overthrown by the Chinese, and the majority of the noble families have perished in wars which have ended in conquest, or they have emigrated, and their serfs and slaves have become free. From all this it follows that no traveller has ever seen the complete social edifice; and observations, however exact, upon individual and accidental cases have naturally given rise to entirely erroneous conclusions. This is not the place to discuss in detail the highly contradictory data which have hitherto been accepted, but the statement already made will allow us to reconcile them all.[1].

The nobles are divided into clans, each sprung of one single family. Sometimes two clans have amalgamated, in which case their names are combined. Of such are the Lomi-Loko, whose attack our guides were even then fearing; and such are the Alu-Ma, whom we met at a later time.

Certain clans have at their head a nzemo, like the clan of the Ngigai, with whom we were now travelling, whose prince was a kinsman and a vassal of the powerful nzemo of Silo, Tu (or Atu). The greater number, however, have no direct rulers; the nzemo is merely a suzerain who dominates several clans, but does not enter into the private affairs of any, which are settled by a council formed by the heads of all the noble families. Thus the clan of the Ma has no prince at its head, but admits the suzerainty of the nzemo Len, the most powerful of all the Lolo princes, whose nominal authority extends from the spot at which we stood as far as Ta-Tu-ho, some 160 miles farther north

We were riding through the magnificent prairies which occupy the whole of the valley floor, and are transformed into a lake at the rainy season, so nearly level is the soil. Catching sight of a couple of bustards, I was preparing to fire at them when, "What are you about?" cried our interpreter; "those are the sacred birds of this region! They bring happiness to those who see them, especially when they are seen together. We saw the Dragon's Head yesterday, and to-day we

[1] Readers interested in such questions will find them completely discussed in Vol. V. "Ethnographie," of our scientific publications.

meet a couple of bustards; you are men beloved by Heaven. But beware of offending Heaven by killing these divine birds." Less the music, this was almost the speech of Gurnemanz to Parsifal. Moved to repentance, I did not break my bow—that is, my heavy automatic rifle, which I might well require some other time—but I bowed myself devoutly.

This respect for bustards is not peculiar to the Lolos; I encountered it later among the Chinese. It is not the sort of respect which we entertain for swans or swallows, for these great birds, which are extremely rare—we met with only four couples during the whole of our journey—are not the familiars of man. I could not discover precisely what the Lolos believed of them, but the Chinese regarded them as spirits (*Shen*).

This beautiful valley of the Lan-pa, which communicates by secondary depressions with the territories of numerous other tribes, is one of the arteries of the Lolo country. Having crossed it, we left the territory of the Ngigai and entered the actual heritage of the Ma.

First of all we crossed a range, the Soso-leang-tze, which is famous for two reasons. It bears on its crest, whence a magnificent view is visible, a forest, small but extremely dense, which was the only forest we saw in the Lolo country.[1] The Lolos, indeed, like all pastoral peoples, are great destroyers of trees, as they have need of the land for pasture; directly they settle in any part they begin by setting fire to the neighbouring forest. If the space thus cleared is sufficient they respect the rest, but they will burn that also if the increase of their flocks demands the sacrifice. For the rest, without disliking trees—they often have near their villages a sacred grove, in which the dead repose—they do not love them as do the Chinese; you will see none around their houses, as you will in the courtyard of every Chinese dwelling.

[1] Except in a few desert nooks of the Shama mountains, shortly before our exit.

The second notable fact concerning this range is its strategic position, which has made it play an important part in all the wars between the Lolos and the Chinese. In the last campaign, in 1905, which ended in a disaster for the Chinese, the latter would have been slaughtered to the last man had not a rear-guard, left by them upon this mountain during their march forward, successfully resisted the attacks of the Lolos, who wished to cut off the retreat of the principal body.[1]

The valley of Su-Kwei-pa, into which we now descended, is the headquarters of the Ma clan. We passed, without halting, a number of walled villages and seigneurs' dwellings—little fortresses perched on the tops of the lesser hills.

Before one of these a large number of people were awaiting us, and when we had at last climbed up to its level they prostrated themselves. The group consisted of Ma-Jeijei, one of the best-reputed chieftains, surrounded by his people. He bade us welcome to his country in terms full of affability, assured us that all was prepared to receive us, and informed us that he would visit us on the morrow.

As night was falling already, we hastened towards the shelter awaiting us; not on this occasion a Lolo dwelling, which I regretted. Our hosts, in their hospitality, thought we should be far more comfortable in a Chinese house, so as there was one in the country they reserved it for us.

But what were these Chinese doing in a country forbidden their countrymen? Their presence there, as at our first halting-place, pointed to a mystery which we should have to resolve.

This Chinese house, which for the rest was extremely wretched, stood at a central point of the beautiful valley of Su-Kwei-pa, which was covered with Lolo villages. The woman who dwelt there alone with her

[1] The Chinese officer who was the hero of this engagement entered our service later on as our chief of convoy.

THE CREST OF THE SOSO-LEANG-TZE.

To face page 66.

children lived by the coming and going of the Chinese admitted to visit the clan. All lodged at her house; it was there that they discussed business matters with the Lolos of the district, and the landlady kept a small store of merchandise. This tolerance is thus extremely useful to the Lolos, who, without leaving their territory and without turning merchants themselves, are able to obtain the majority of the goods they require, such as cloth, sugar, and salt. This Chinese woman was not a slave, but she paid the clan a considerable rent, could not leave the district without permission from the chief, nor enter the country of another clan save in the care of a respondent—in other words, she was a captive, although her actions were free.

We were obliged to stay some little time at this place, as we now intended to enter the territory of another clan, the Ashu, a step which necessitated further negotiations.

On the morning of the following day we saw Ma-Jeijei approaching, accompanied not only by his kinsmen, friends, and servants, but also by his wife, who was surrounded by a numerous retinue of servants.

This was the first occasion of our coming into actual contact with the feminine element; the wife of Ma-Walei, an insignificant creature, had scarcely noticed our presence. As for all the other women we had seen, they were serfs or slaves; and after the explanation I have already given of the method of recruiting the different classes, it will be understood that they had little or no Lolo blood in their veins, and, as will be seen by the photographs, they formed a great contrast with the women of the noble families which we thenceforth encountered.

Ma-Jeijei's wife at once attracted and retained the attention. She was really handsome, of a noble and regular type of beauty, and her poise and all her movements were instinct with perfect grace and dignity.

She wore most becomingly the national costume, which is quite unlike that of the Chinese. Instead of a tunic falling to the mid-thigh and a wide pair of trousers, the Lolo woman wears a bodice with a high, close-fitting collar, which comes up to the chin, and a long skirt or petticoat which is pleated and adorned with flounces. Like the man, she covers her shoulders with a mantle, but the woman's mantle, which is precisely like the fashionable mantles with high gathered shoulders that were worn a few years ago in Europe, is commonly not of felt but of fine lambswool.

The head-dress is varied. There are forms reserved for young girls, for married women, for mothers, for noble or serf women, &c.; but the fashions also vary from tribe to tribe, and, in spite of the assertions of certain travellers, I do not think any general statement can be given. The turban, formed of a flat band of thin material rolled upon itself an infinity of times, is certainly, as far as I have been able to see, reserved for the women of the nobility; and Ma-Jeijei's wife was wearing such a head-dress. She also displayed earrings of silver, and her collar was fastened by a brooch of the same metal.

The costume of the men is extremely simple. In addition to the mantle already described, it consists of trousers and a vest buttoned at the side, like those worn by the Chinese, both commonly made of blue cotton cloth of Chinese origin. However, one also sees garments of white hempen cloth of Lolo weaving, but these are usually worn by children, serfs, and slaves. The lower part of the leg, as among the Chinese, is gripped by a narrow band wound round it; but the latter does not confine the wide trousers, which always hang loose on the calf. The Lolo likes to wear a single silver earring in the left ear.

The mantle, however, is not the only peculiarity of the Lolo costume; there is also the famous "horn." The Lolo wears no pigtail; neither does he shave the

LOLO NOBLE AND LADY.

To face page 68.

fore part of the head; on the contrary, as though he wished to emphasise the contrast between himself and the Chinese, he gathers all his hair together on the front of the crown and makes a twist of it above his forehead. When he wears a turban he rolls it round this twist in the shape of a pear, the end of the piece of stuff sometimes escaping in a little peak. This original form of head-dress is known to the Chinese and to European travellers as the "horn" of the Lolo; but it must be remembered that this is only a "show" head-dress. When at home among themselves, the majority of the Lolos, even the princes and the nobles, go bare-headed or roll their turbans in the ordinary manner. Their heads are sometimes shaved, sometimes with a little lock in front; but as a rule they wear their hair of a moderate length. Men and women go barefoot, but in winter they often wear sandals of straw or short felt boots.

While her husband was making us a present of a sheep, Lady Ma-Jeijei offered us—and how gracefully!—a fowl. In return she received a few knick-knacks, which gave her the greatest pleasure, and most willingly allowed us to take her portrait. The whole morning was passed in agreeable diversions.

I think the most agreeable in the eyes of the Lolos was the ceremony of the "wine of honour." Travellers have given the Lolos a quite undeserved reputation as drunkards. It is quite true—and I myself have recorded a characteristic example—that the Lolos readily get drunk when they go down into China. They have in hand the price of the goods they have just sold, and the innkeeper is there to tempt them with his "fire-water"; but they go into China very rarely, and at home they have no alcohol. Yet they know how to distil it; we must suppose that they do not greatly value it. It is the rule to offer it to notable guests; wherever we went the chiefs had to send out men to beat up the country for a day's march around in order to obtain two or three pints, which as often as not did not arrive until the next day.

The ceremony of offering the beverage is extremely curious. Everybody sits in a circle. The cup-bearer—a slave whose privilege it is to act as such—holds two goblets in his hands. One of these he fills from the pitcher of alcohol; then, approaching the guest, he bends his knee before him, while at the same time both hands are employed in making extremely rapid and complicated passes with the two cups, the liquid being poured from one to the other. Finally, he checks himself in a very singular slanting position, almost that of a boxer, whose attitude expresses not pugnacity but gratitude and respect, and whose hands, instead of being clenched, hold toward you the two goblets full of alcohol.

When the guest has drunk, he himself points out to the cup-bearer the person whom he wishes to honour, and the same ceremony is repeated before the latter.

Such are the rites of Lolo hospitality. It is difficult, however, to give any idea of the nobility and gravity expressed by the manners of the chiefs, together with a familiar simplicity. Although nothing in their simple costume distinguishes them from their serfs, they may be distinguished at the first casual glance; moreover, there is nothing servile in the respect and obedience which surround them, but a deferential and almost filial attention. We were back in the days of chivalry, and the lord was master only because he was the strongest, the bravest; because he led the others into combat, gave the mightiest blows with his sword, and paid the most with his person. We felt that the serfs admired their suzerain.

But now the Ashu were coming up. It appeared that they had required some pressing to receive us; living far from the frontier, they had scarcely heard of Europeans, and took us for men like the Chinese mandarins, with careful and mealy-mouthed manners. Our interpreter, Siu, therefore coached me in my behaviour; I must assume a decided and energetic air, showing that we were men of war who were afraid of nothing, and did not fear to show their strength.

The Ashu introduced themselves, and their chief, Sia-Moudjei, certainly appeared a fairly rough customer; he barely saluted us. As I was advised, I assumed a rough and almost bullying tone, informing him of our desire to enter his country, and requested him to receive us. Father de Guébriant translated my words in the same key, and really, to hear us, you might have thought we were addressing an ultimatum and were on the point of joining battle. Sia-Moudjei vouchsafed us a few words under his breath and withdrew with his people. We had blindly followed the advice of our interpreter; we could only hope he had not induced us to commit a solecism!

But no, he returned delighted: the comedy was entirely successful. Sia-Moudjei had changed his opinion of us; he recognised us for men with whom a hero of his reputation might have dealings without dishonour. But would we not give him some idea of our talents. They brought us a fiery horse and ironically invited us to mount him; but it was not for nothing that Boyve was a sergeant-major and future officer of cavalry, and this Bucephalus was subdued by this new Alexander. Rapid fire at long range, raising spurts of dust on the mountains opposite, excited transports of enthusiasm, redoubled by the discharge of our revolvers, the presence of which in our pockets nobody had suspected. On this occasion no one could deny that we were warriors, and warriors no one could resist; Sia-Moudjei was our friend!

His tacking about was both comical and touching; for now he came to give us the full salute, bowing to the ground, and offered us a ewe and a living pheasant; then, having doubtless learned from our interpreter that the Father baptized infants, he presented his only son, who was still quite a child, to the latter, and begged him to give the boy a name.

The Father, whose dearest ambition would be the conversion of the Lolos, was profoundly touched ; a Christian name was already almost a profession of faith ; was this child destined to propagate the Gospel? And the Father, not, I fancy, without addressing to God a prayer for the salvation of the child and all his people, conferred upon the child his own name, Jean, in Latin Johannes. "Yoha, Yoha!" repeated the Lolos: "Yoha! a magnificent name!" And they ran to proclaim everywhere the fine unknown name in which the Father had just baptized the child. Such was the apostolic effect of our improved firearms!

Next day we regretfully left our excellent friends the Ma, who had so hospitably opened for us the gates of the forbidden country, and under the protection of Sia-Moudjei we set out in the direction of Kiao-Kio.

We crossed a small range full of coal measures, which cropped out everywhere but were worked by no one. Then we descended into the valley of the San-Wa-ho, a river which is joined by that which waters Su-Kwei-pa, after flowing through a narrow gorge which divides the mountain.

This plain is covered with villages and rice-fields ; the Lolos do not make fields in terraces on the mountain-sides, but they do not neglect to utilise the waters for the irrigation of the bottom of the valleys. The mountain, where the slope is not too steep, is planted with oats, barley, buckwheat, and potatoes.

All these villages are, of course, fortified. The houses are arranged in little parallel streets, and give one quite the impression of military barracks.

The amazed population gathered to see us pass. Their attitude was not everywhere the same, for in the same clan all were not in perfect agreement ; and although the friends of Sia-Moudjei acclaimed us, his adversaries

A FORTIFIED VILLAGE.

A LOLO NOBLE WITH HIS SERFS.
(The figure in the centre is our Chinese interpreter).

To face page 92

affected to look sourly upon us. This gave rise to a comical incident.

We had just passed a village whose inhabitants had held aloof, when Boyve took a photograph of the site. We had already resumed the march when shouts broke out behind us, and a crowd ran forward summoning us to stop. What was the matter? What had we done to them? What did they want? They wanted to be photographed—nothing else! How could we carry away the image of their valley if they were not in it? After this I could not have the heart to fail to give the public the portrait of these good people, who were so anxious to offer it to them.[1]

We then scaled a range of considerable height, which separated us from Kiao-Kio. It appeared that we were probably running some risk then; a section of the neighbouring Paki clan was at war with the Ashu, and often attacked passers-by. Most unfortunately, during a moment's halt, my horse escaped and made off at a full gallop; our men did their best to pursue it, but it evaded them and got farther and farther away. An animal lost, and there was I on foot! Boyve leaped upon his horse and set off in pursuit, and very soon both had disappeared. We were decidedly anxious; the Paki prowlers might well be in ambush thereabouts; besides, what would happen if any Lolo, no matter

[1] The reader may be surprised by this readiness to pose before the camera; many travellers have stated that the Lolos manifested the greatest objection to allowing themselves to be photographed. No doubt, if one did not explain to them the object of the apparatus, work the shutter, and show them proofs already printed; but as soon as they saw portraits of other people and were able to distinguish what they represented—the flat, black and white image of a solid coloured object is at first sight unintelligible to people unaccustomed to see such things—their keenest desire was to offer themselves also to the admiration of their fellows. Afterwards the marvellous apparatus became famous, and its fame, preceding us, brought crowds before the lens. I have never seen this patient method fail in any African or Asiatic country.

who, were to meet a stranger alone, without a respondent? It was only after an hour of anxiety that we saw Boyve reappear with my horse ; it did not seem to occur to him that he had run a very real risk. So real that Sia-Moudjei, before resuming the climb, begged us to keep our carbines in our hands ; then all his men, brandishing their lances and their sabres, rushed forward with strident shouts to the sound of the Lolo national march, which was led by a flute-player : an original melody in a short, accented rhythm, which we heard from one end of the country to the other. There were no enemies, and our heroes halted triumphantly upon the crest.

Between ourselves, I suspected them of having somewhat exaggerated the danger in order to try us ; but the picturesque spectacle of a charge of Lolos was worth it. It was truly impressive. They took the mountain at such a pace that our horses could scarcely follow them, and what with their piercing cries, which freeze the Chinese with terror, the clashing of their arms, which they beat against one another, and their windmill gymnastics as they pierced imaginary enemies, they exhibited a savage eagerness and impetuosity, served by muscles of steel, which accorded well with their terrible renown.

From the summit of the mountain we saw at last the plain and fortress of Kiao-Kio, which would mark a decisive stage of our journey. As we were hastening to descend in order to reach them before the night, a numerous group advanced from the entrance of a village and prostrated themselves ; at their head was Shuka, the most influential seigneur of the clan of the Ashu. He thanked us for the honour we did him in coming to him, and we were at first sight won by the uprightness and nobility revealed by his countenance and his words.

And the Chinese depict these people as savages ! To be sure, they are poor, and, to judge by appearances, primitive ; but nowhere more than among these Barbarians have I felt how factitious is the superiority which our limited knowledge gives us, and in presence of these intrepid warriors, loyal and good-natured, I began to admire and love them as the heroic folk deserved.

Kiao-Kio rises not precisely from a plain, but from a sort of irregular basin formed by the union of several wide valleys. The ramparts of the little town rise from a low hill which stands between two almost parallel rivers, which come together about three-quarters of a mile farther south. The principal stream, which we had to cross in order to reach the town, was none other than our old friend the Su-Kwei-pa, which had rejoined us by crossing the range through a perpendicular gorge. Thenceforth—it had already changed its name at least three times, for the streams take the names of the districts they run through—it is called the Kiao-Kio. Through a narrow ravine opening towards the south it goes to rejoin the Blue River. To the north rises one splendid mass of the Paki mountain, which for two days had been our goal; 11,700 feet in height, it is rarely that its peak is not crowned with snow. At its foot another plain, that of Chu-Hei, prolongs that of Kiao-Kio towards the north-east, a slight rise of the ground dividing the two.

Kiao-Kio and Chu-Hei are called "the heart of the Lolo country." These valleys are the most thickly peopled and the most fruitful of the whole region, and to see the closely packed villages, the well-irrigated rice-fields, and even—for there are Chinese here—a few fields of poppies with blazing flowers, one might well believe oneself in one of the most populous country-sides of China. Here are held the general assemblies that decide upon the greater wars. "Here it is," say the Chinese books, "that the Barbarians rush together in order to carry havoc into the countries round about, destroying the habitations and leading the people into captivity."

Yet, being a town, Kiao-Kio is more exposed than the almost nomadic and inaccessible tribes to the attacks of China, and the latter had recently succeeded in establishing a mandarin there at the head of a garrison. This is why Father de Guébriant, without having too much faith in our final success, had hoped that we might at least succeed in travelling so far.

When we arrived the whole population came out before us, and we were taken to a lodging already prepared—two very small rooms with a little court. But where, then, was the mandarin? and why had we not seen a single Chinese soldier? The people regarded us with astonishment; did we know so little of events as the question implied? We certainly did not know much, and it took a long inquiry, both then and on the occasion of my second journey to Kien-Chang, to arrive at the facts. I will summarise these facts at once, as they will help the reader to understand the situation.

Formerly the country contained many Chinese; in 1523 the inhabitants of Kiao-Kio addressed a petition to the prince of the country informing him that their houses were now sufficiently numerous to deserve rank as a city; in consequence the prince ordered that a wall should be built around the whole. In China, that "pacific" country, every city is girt with ramparts, so that the same word signifies wall and city—a capital symbol of the state of the country, for no wall, no city; it would be sacked and destroyed by the rebels or brigands. The Chinese at that time were exploiting the whole country, which was full of mines of gold, silver, copper, and wood.[1]

It seems that the Lolos did not begin to be formidable

[1] "Wood-mines" is the name given to whole forests which are found buried in the earth, and the wood, being marvellously preserved, as a result of conditions I do not understand, is imperishable, and therefore has a considerable value. There are numerous wood-mines in the Kien-Chang.

LOLO WOMEN.

ARRIVING AT KIAO-KIO.

To face page 76.

until the last century. In 1868 General Chao, surnamed the Great Warrior, who wished to reduce them, suffered a complete defeat at their hands near Niu-Niu-pa, two days' march north of Kiao-Kio ; this was the Granson of the Lolos, and the Chinese were forced to recognise their independence. From that time dated the organisation of the network of forts surrounding the Lolo country which marks the frontier, and also the system of hostages which I shall refer to again later on.

However, the victorious Lolos neither expelled nor despoiled the Chinese owners of the soil, contenting themselves with enforcing their authority and the payment of a tribute ; they even tolerated the appointment of a mandarin, who came from time to time to Kiao-Kio in order to try such cases as arose among the Chinese ; and provided he obtained a respondent and rewarded him suitably, and was careful to meddle in nothing that did not concern his compatriots, he was as free to come and go as a humble buyer of wax-insects.

But the state of perpetual warfare in which the tribes existed prevented any commercial relations, and exposed the Chinese residing on the territory of a clan to the risk of being carried off and reduced to slavery by a hostile clan. Gradually the exploitation of the mines ceased, the farmers abandoned their fields and returned to China ; yet even to-day, so great is their sense of equity, the Lolos recognise their right of property.

The Chinese Government has made a score of attempts to regain this lost country, but all have ended in disaster. The last took place in 1905. Convinced that only a Lolo could ever make any impression on the Lolos, the Government confided the command of its troops to the Lolo prince Lu-Chaowu, the nzemo of Wei-Li-chiu and other places, assisting the Chinese commissary Chang. The army advanced without meeting with any great resistance as far as Poussa-tang (so named on account of the great statue of Buddha, or Poussa, formerly erected there by the Chinese), a day's march south of Kiao-Kio. But there it found itself blocked in a defile by superior forces, which overwhelmed it, from the rocks above, with arrows and stones. Cut off from their convoys and threatened with death by starvation, the Chinese made a sortie by night. The majority perished, but Lu-Chaowu and Chang escaped, and thanks to the heroic resistance, already mentioned, of the rear-guard left on Mount Soso-leang-tze, they were able to regain China.

Since then the Chinese have almost completely disappeared ; scarcely any are left save the two families of Chiu-Sen-pa (our first halting-place), our hostess of Su-Kwei-pa, a dozen families at Kiao-Kio, and eight at Chu-Hei. Finally, last year the Lolos, embittered by the memory of the ancient Chinese domination, burned the yamen and the pagoda of Kiao-Kio. The great enclosing ramparts now shelter only two small streets, themselves walled at their extremities, and some fields in cultivation on the site of the razed buildings.

Such is the brief history of the last struggles between the Chinese and the Lolos, terminated by the victory and independence of the latter. It shows us that far from being a decadent race in process of disappearance the Lolos are in full ascension ; and later on we saw signs of this progress everywhere. We must not study them as a peculiar variety of savages, destined to disappear upon contact with civilisation, and presenting no points of interest save to the anthropologist, but a people that will one day play a part in the destinies of the East.

For us it was the greatest good luck that there was no longer a representative of China at Kiao-Kio, for he would certainly have received an order to stop us ; and even as it was we were about to find it sufficiently difficult to proceed. We had now to enter the territory of the Paki ; now this clan was in conflict with the

Ashu, and the cause of the quarrel was Kiao-Kio. This city used to belong to the Ashu, who sold it to the Paki, but the latter had not yet paid the price agreed on. The tension was so great that it was quite impossible for our friend Sia-Moudjei to come to Kiao-Kio; this crabbed old gentleman, who had, no doubt, expressed his opinion a little too frankly, would be killed if he crossed the river which bounded the debatable land.

Luckily Shuka had as son-in-law one of the principal seigneurs of the other clan, Paki-Muka. It was on him that we relied for an introduction.

All the following day was spent in palavers. Hitherto things had, on the whole, gone smoothly; thanks to his mercantile connection, our courier and interpreter Siu had, without much trouble, induced his Ma friends to receive us, the latter had passed us through the Ngigai to their allies Sia-Moudjei and Shuka, who were, by the way, the only nobles of the Ashu with whom they were on friendly terms. All this had resulted from the initial pact, and except to win the friendship of our guides and ensure ourselves a favourable welcome, our diplomacy had hitherto scarcely found an opportunity to display itself.

Now matters were different; Siu had no more friends, and we had to find some plausible motive in order to obtain permission to go forward. We had declared that we were on the way to visit the prince of Shama, in the hope that the intermediate tribes would not dare to risk embroiling themselves with him by stopping us. However, we had only Shuka to plead our cause; happily the good impression we had received of this worthy seigneur was reciprocal, and he had conceived a real friendship for us, which we only had to cultivate. He brought before us, in succession, all the notable Paki, for needless to say the little city was full, quite a crowd of Lolos having hastened in from the surrounding parts, to whom we had to exhibit all our possessions and explain their object and the method of handling them.

No more than the fiery son of Peleus could the Lolos dissimulate their true character. The most perfect apparatus or instrument only excited their discreet approbation ; what they awaited with impatience was the exhibition of our arms ; for already the fame of these marvellous engines had preceded us. But they could not believe that objects so small could possess so great a power, and all begged to see them in use.

We had perforce to give the usual exhibition. The whole population was massed at the foot of the ramparts to see us fire, and as we lacked targets the men offered their mantles. In eager emulation the young men, rushing out into the country, spread their mantles on the soil, and in order to prevent jealousy we had to fire upon each of them. Immediately they all rushed out to see the result ; and what cries of admiration and triumph when they brought back their mantles perforated ! If we had listened to them we should have transformed their mantles into sieves—and very quickly exhausted our provision of cartridges ! It is true the effect was as great as if we had killed one man at every shot : and how much better to have demonstrated the power of our rifles on mantles only !

On the following morning our friend Shuka, followed by his notables, entered our house and invited us to come and see some equestrian exercises ; he led us in a troop to the other side of the river, into Ashu territory. We there found our friend Sia-Moudjei and a considerable crowd of people gathered before a vast circular race-course, evidently much frequented ; and we were surprised to learn what we afterwards saw for ourselves, that in the outskirts of almost all the villages there were similar enclosures, where the young horsemen exercised the noble art of equitation.

Then began the most astonishing acrobatic feats.

Several young men galloped at high speed into the circular enclosure, where they threw themselves back until the head was almost touching the crupper ; but instead of keeping the legs down, as would be done in Europe, they lifted them right up, thus combining the two exercises known in French equitation as " Flexion of the loins backwards " and " Elevation of the thighs." They had, of course, no grip of their mounts whatever, and kept on the backs of their animals only by the exercise of the most extraordinary suppleness, which enabled them to keep their equilibrium at a giddy pace, as though their bodies were one with their horses. The great mantles, held only by a running string round the neck, and streaming backwards with the wind of their flight, prolonged the outline of each horse by at least three or four feet, so that it seemed an apocalyptic monstrosity. The riders made several circuits of the course, giving an extraordinary exhibition of skill.

In order to understand how astonishing this high development of equestrian sport really is the leader must reflect that the Lolos inhabit a mountain country, and that the Chinese who surround them only use the horse as a beast of burden. It is thus neither in the example of their neighbours nor in the facilities offered by nature that we must look for the origin of this deeply rooted love of horsemanship. I may be wrong, but I incline to think their tastes in this direction are atavistic, and that they form a valuable indication as to the origin of the Lolos. It is a fact that vast plains unfit for agriculture, like those we crossed later in Tibet and Mongolia, form pastoral peoples who ride on horseback ; and we shall find that Lolos of pure blood know nothing of and look down upon all agricultural labour, which is left to slaves of Chinese origin. The rearing of flocks and herds, almost unknown to the Chinese, is, on the contrary, the speciality of the Lolos.

This unexpected fantasia and the reflections it gave rise to did not prevent our noticing that a very numerous body of unknown Lolos, all armed, among whom we had been asked to sit in order to watch the riding, were sustaining a cold and hardly friendly attitude. These were the principal members of the Paki clan, through whose territory we wished to travel. Presently Shuka, in the most gracious manner, came to ask us to take advantage of this excellent race-course to enjoy a good gallop; and Siu, in translating the request, did not conceal the fact that was a polite manner of packing us off for a short time.

It was easy to see that this great assembly had not really convened itself for the purpose of watching a tournament: the latter was merely a pretext for bringing us thither. It was evident that our affairs needed a little assistance. But since we had friends, what better could we do than allow them to act for us? We set out, therefore, at a hand-gallop, and profited by this moment of liberty to visit the valley.

At the entrance of the gorge by which the river Su-Kwei-pa issues from the range we came upon two enormous dogs, which were crucified back to back. We had already seen two others on the opposite side of the Kiao-Kio.

As a general rule this custom, which is one very widespread among the Lolos, signifies that there is a grave dispute to be settled: in this case, that dividing the Paki and the Ashu on the subject of the territory of the Kiao-Kio. It is impossible to express the wild and sinister impression, the sense of something threatening, produced by the spectacle of these powerful beasts, with their tawny coats and their size apparently doubled by the tension of their limbs; they evoked in a striking manner the savage scene of the crucified lions in "Salammbô."

When we returned the assembly of the clans did not seem to be agreed: quite to the contrary. Siu had been requested to retire, and we entered Kiao-Kio without any Lolo accompanying us; we had all the appearance of being in quarantine. On the way Siu gave us the news. Unfavourable rumours had arrived from Ta-Hin-Chang; from one it appeared that we had been sent by the Chinese to prospect for mines, draw up a chart, and take pictures of the country with our cameras; from another we were persons by no means to be commended, who had fled Chinese territory in order to escape punishment for our crimes, and the Imperial Government would only be grateful if rid of us. These contradictory accusations, whether they had been fabricated by emissaries of the prefect or by enemies of Siu, who were jealous of his good fortune, resulted in a dilemma, both horns of which pointed in the same direction: we must be suppressed. A solution which would have the advantage of enabling the Lolos to help themselves to our marvellous arms and the other treasures that our boxes contained. Siu did not conceal his uneasiness, all the greater in that he could not refute these calumnies, being excluded from the assembly.

This was the crisis, the inevitable crisis. Hitherto all had gone too smoothly! As after several days of heat under a steamy sky it is prudent to look out for a thunderstorm, so the explorer should recognise that the calm which envelops him for the moment is that which precedes the tempest. Let him meditate on the impression which his passage must produce in a country all of whose forces have hitherto been directed towards the exclusion of strangers! The rumour of the event spreads in every direction; tongues wag; imaginations grow heated; opposing parties are formed. While he goes forward, profiting by the impulse which has carried him over the first obstacles, eddies are produced all round him, and suddenly he finds himself enveloped in a whirlwind. If he is unceasingly vigilant he will be able to put down the helm in time, and to pour the calming oil upon the waves; and he will profit by this calm passage to gain the land—until a fresh hurricane springs up.

Happily Shuka had not forsaken us; he sent one of his men to tell us that he and Sia-Moudjei were faithful to their word and were defending our cause. By the same messenger we sent him word of a few arguments that might be effective; did those who said we were brigands pursued by the Chinese authorities know that we arrived at Ta-Hin-Chang with an escort, a guard of honour? and as for believing that we were Chinese spies, had not our Ma respondents related that the mandarins had done their utmost to keep us out of the country?

So the day passed; from the top of the ramparts we could see the assembly, the leaders seated in a circle, their men a short distance behind them with their long lances thrust into the ground. Incessantly messengers detached themselves, bringing such news of the state of negotiations as was passing from mouth to mouth; they had decided to massacre us; we were to be allowed to pass; we should be led to the frontier and delivered to the mandarins.

All these rumours aroused the liveliest excitement around us. The whole town was full of Lolos, and when the news was bad we knew it at once from the hostile expression of certain faces. Around us was a crowd of serfs and slaves, the seed of goodness knows what races, with basely cruel faces; there were also some nobles with the heads of brigands; one of them in particular, a giant more than 80 inches in height, with a brutal, evil air, a true beast of prey. It was fortunate that he was not called to the council.

It must not be thought, because I have complained of the injustice of the Chinese opinion of the Lolos, that they are all plaster saints. Quite the reverse; it is obvious that in a people who live by war, without

THE GATE OF KIAO-KIO.

To face page 85.

government and without courts of law, there must exist a certain number of violent, knavish, and covetous characters, whose evil characteristics there is nothing to control. The surprising and admirable fact is that there are not more of such.

Only at five in the afternoon was the palaver concluded, and a messenger ran to tell us the good news: the Paki would make us welcome. Shuka returned in triumph; he assured us that it was the good impression we had caused which had finally tipped the scale; but we knew very well, from all our informants, that he and Sia-Moudjei had had to throw in the weight of their swords, threatening war if we were not received. Brave Ashu! We shall never forget him, that loyal and worthy Shuka, nor the surly old Sia-Moudjei, whose manners, it is true, were not urbane, but who, once his word of honour was given, did not hesitate to stake his life in the service of his passing guests, whose thanks he could not even come to receive, being forbidden by reason of his vendettas.

There was an outburst of joy. Paki-Muka, who became our respondent-in-chief, brought us a sucking-pig. We offered in exchange a kid given by Shuka, and to Shuka we gave an ewe given by Sia-Moudjei. Thus, with the exception of the pig, which we should eat with enjoyment, we disembarrassed ourselves of these inconvenient animals and gave presents munificently without making ourselves the poorer; and these ingenious combinations took me back eight years, into the impenetrable forest of Cavally! It was to me a continual source of satisfaction and confidence to find how far, in spite of differences of climate and race, the situations I had already encountered would recur in identical detail, and would be resolved by the same means. The simple man is everywhere the same.

In the evening we were preparing to go to rest when Shuka came into the house. It appeared that the blackguardly giant who had produced such an unpleasant impression during the day was resolved to settle our hash that night. He was ambushed with his men in a neighbouring house; to climb the wall dividing our courtyards, to throw down the door with a blow of the shoulder, and, without even entering, to pierce us with their long lances in our mouse-trap would be but a game. Shuka had warned him that he would have him to deal with, and, accompanied by three of his people—all, unfortunately, that he had kept in the city—he came to pass the night beside us. But the brigand had a numerous band; we must hold ourselves in readiness! Shuka showed us the proper manœuvre: electric lamp in the left hand and revolver in the right, and then up at the brigands and kill them! Good riddance to the country!

Was it the fear of Shuka and the revenge that his clan would take, or respect for our revolvers and the magic light? The night passed peacefully.

Next morning the Paki came in search of us. Shuka had had a small jar of alcohol brought, and offered us all the stirrup-cup with the ceremonial I have already described.

The whole population of Kiao-Kio came out to escort us. To these unfortunate Chinese, prisoners and serfs of the Lolos, who had renounced all hope of ever being rescued, our coming had brought a ray of hope; so Kiao-Kio was not forgotten—people still came thither! If our journey succeeded it might be the dawn of a new day for them. The chief of the community, a venerable old man, wished to accompany us as far as the frontier of the territory, and gave us his son as baggage-porter—an adroit idea, for with us the young man could go everywhere without paying, and would bring back information and form connections which might be useful to him.

Nothing could have been more picturesque than our departure. Before the gate of the city, at the foot of the crumbling but still lofty ramparts, a crowd of people

NOBLES AND SERFS.

LEAVING KIAO-KIO.

To face page 86.

were massed upon the slopes; the pacific faces of Chinese ; Lolos, recognisable by their " horns " and draped in their mantles ; women ; children perched in some gap in the wall; men-at-arms with glittering tridents or lances—one of those pictures which, across the centuries, lead you back to the earliest civilisations. Was this not one of the gates of Jerusalem?

CHAPTER IV

THE LAST OF THE INDEPENDENT TERRITORY

OUR march was a festival; from one hamlet to the next, the whole population escorting us; cheerful and active as young pullets, the children bounded along on the flanks of the procession, raising piercing cries of "Iou, iou, iou!" after the fashion of the Arabs. From all the manors and villages we saw files of people, who rushed upon the little dikes of earth which separated the rice-fields, or impatiently waded across the mud in order to take a short cut. Many dames of high lineage, mounted on their palfreys, hastened to examine these strangers of unaccustomed appearance; and, in spite of the freedom of their carriage, they were a little taken aback to see the glass eye of the kodak insistently staring in their faces.

What a difference between these and the Chinese women! The Lolo woman, if she is not the equal of the man, none the less holds an important place in the family. The Lolo can only marry one wife, except in case of sterility. The young girl, who goes about freely, has perfect liberty of choice, on condition, of course, that she exercises it in her own caste and in the interests of her clan. After marriage she frequently returns to her parents, and each time her husband must exercise all his fascinations to induce her to return to the conjugal roof; if he does not succeed in pleasing her, the woman remains indefinitely with her own family, and no one can criticise her action.[1]

The woman has absolutely equal rights with her brothers over the fortune of her parents; yet, curiously enough, she does not inherit; only the sons may share in the inheritance. But the young girl receives as a dowry, upon marriage, precisely the equivalent of what should come to her in the partition of the estate; it is an advance inheritance by which she benefits. If she is unmarried when her parents die her brothers become owners of the property, but will give her her part when she marries, and until then are obliged to provide for her support. Community is the rule in the household, but on the death of the husband the woman resumes the full enjoyment of her dowry, as in cases of divorce pronounced "on the faults of the husband" by the family tribunal.

Even by the accounts of the Chinese living in the country, the moral code is extremely severe, in spite of the liberty enjoyed by the women. The contrary assertions which may be heard on the confines of the independent territory apply only to slave women who are Lolo only by name.

Widows whose sons are minors exercise all the powers of the head of the family, including the political powers. It is said that women take part in battle; and it is natural enough that they should do so, for night surprises are frequent between hostile clans, so that the women, who are not usually spared, are forced to defend themselves. To the north-east of the territory, however, near Ma-Pien-Ting, there are clans in which women are respected by belligerents; so much so that it is they who are sent as envoys to treat for peace.

[1] Many erroneous statements have been written in respect of these customs. As they may vary from one district to another, I am willing to believe that each observer has been right in the particular cases which he has witnessed among the subjected Lolos; but all the generalisations which have been drawn therefrom are somewhat rash

This custom, which is by no means general, is the more worthy of remark in that Father Huc has recorded it as existing among certain tribes of Tibet.

Our first march was not a long one. We had barely gone seven or eight miles when our Paki guide introduced us to new respondents, for we were entering the territory of Chu-Hei, which belongs to the Alu-Ma.

Chu-Hei is a hollow in the continuation of the valley of Kiao-Kio, but its waters flow in a contrary direction; plunging through a narrow breach, they run northward into the River Magou or Mai-Ku, the most important watercourse of the northern portion of the Great Cold Mountains. The depression in which Chu-Hei and Kiao-Kio are situated is therefore a means of communication between the two portions of this territory, one being watered by the Mai-Ku and the other by the river of Sze-Kwei-pa and Kiao-Kio ; hence the preponderating part which it plays in the life of the country.

Our respondents led us to a village, the remnant of a small ancient town, in which eight Chinese families vegetated in the deepest poverty. We were to pass three miserable days there. During the night a violent storm broke over us. Under our imperfect roof we were flooded and frozen. Next morning we saw all the mountains covered with snow, but in the valley a diluvian rain fell without ceasing. In the recesses of our miserable lodging we took refuge in the corners in which the water poured least vigorously; we were reduced to impotence and inaction; there was no one to see, for even the Lolos kept in their houses in such weather.

Only our respondents, whose houses were near, came to visit us, and we passed the time in asking them questions. Our chief respondent, Ma-Muka, was a charming young man of twenty-one—unhappily much maligned by the photographer. He was the son of the most influential chieftain of the clan, one Thetsu, who

PAKI AND MA-MUKA, OUR RESPONDENTS.

IN THE KIAO-KIO VALLEY.

To face page 90.

generally lives with the prince of Shama, whose firmest supporter he is. Ma-Muka was to take us to his father, who would introduce us to the prince.

Chu-Hei was formerly subject to the nzemo Len, suzerain of all the north-west of the Great Snowy Mountains; but the latter, having given Chu-Hei as appanage to his daughter, who married the nzemo of Silo, the Alu-Ma refused to recognise the new prince and declared themselves independent. In order to obtain a moral support, they allied themselves with the prince of Shama, who was himself threatened by his terrible neighbours, the Tamuka, who dwell beside the Mai-Ku, to which alliance Shama contributed his prestige and the Alu-Ma their warriors, of whom Shama was greatly in need; for which reason we should be certain of the best of welcomes if introduced by him.

The prince of Shama was shortly to visit the nzemo Len, his brother-in-law, and it was Ma-Muka who was to introduce him to his friends the Paki; for the princes themselves need respondents among clans which are not subject to them. Each of his hosts must, on account of his dignity, present him with a bullock, a sheep, and a fowl, and will himself receive presents of proportionate value. Between ourselves, I have strong reason for suspecting that this exchange of magnificent presents is managed something like this: "'Noble prince, I offer you a bullock, a sheep, and a hen," the host will say, and he will duly present the fowl, or perhaps the sheep; as for the bullock, it is in the pastures, at some little distance; it will be driven in on the morrow. The prince will thank him warmly. "And I, worthy seigneur, offer you a turban, some cloth, and a horse," he will say, and he will give him the turban immediately; as for the stuffs, he has none good enough; he is going to buy some from the Chinese; and he will send the horse as soon as he gets home. There, needless to say, matters will remain, and, as we say after a harmless French duel, honour is satisfied But it is a charming ceremony, and it is much better to exchange presents than bullets.

Ma-Muka had been married a short while. He received from his father a village, and his wife brought him two as a dowry. Now he is chief of a little clan and free of parental authority. Here is a characteristic entirely opposed to the Chinese custom: with them the power of the father over the son lasts all his life.

The rules of inheritance present some notable peculiarities. The serfs and vassals are divided in absolutely equal shares; so much so that if their number is not exactly divisible the surplus is held in community. Thus a slave may belong to several brothers at once; he serves them all in turn, or if he is attached to the land the produce of his labour is shared. But in the case of all the rest of the inheritance—herds, houses, and lands—an advantage is given to the *youngest:* a generous custom which is also found among the Mongols. The eldest son, none the less, enjoys a pre-eminence over his brothers; it is he who inherits the political power of his father; but in cases of minority the widow exercises them, seconded by the younger brothers of the deceased.

On the third day the rain at last ceased, and we received numerous visitors, notably some members of the great confederation of the Tamuka, which comprises numerous clans of the basin of the River Mai-Ku, and some Alu, of whom the Alu-Ma are a detached branch, grafted on a branch of the Ma. From them we receive data respecting the northern region.

The fine weather having at last returned, we left on the morning of the fourth day, in the midst of the same concourse of people and the same piercing acclamations as at Kiao-Kio.

The mountain of Wu-Po-Chang, which lay on the left and divided us from the Mai-Ku, is full of copper; mines to-day abandoned were exploited by the Chinese, and of old made the fortune of Chu-Hei.

We were travelling at altitudes of 9,000 to 10,000 feet, over the very gentle gradients which form the northern slope of the watershed of the Mai-Ku and the Kiao-Kio. No rock; a turfy soil which feeds numerous flocks; one would never have guessed the altitude, nor suspected the abrupt and rugged aspect of these mountains as seen by those who inhabit the low-lying valleys. However, from time to time we came to a depression of one of the spurs which limited our view to the left, and were amazed to see a profusion of precipitous mountains with snow-covered peaks, springing from abysses which seemed of prodigious depth. Then once more the view was cut off, and we continued to march over gentle ascents and descents; but thenceforward the sense of the invisible depths which surrounded us gave to the most ordinary places a sense of something solemn and affecting.

Through one of these openings we could see the mountain, of a very striking shape and easily recognisable, at the foot of which lies Niu-Niu-Pa, the scene of the great national victory, which was pointed out to us with pride. It was formerly the principal residence of the nzemo, whose nominal power extended over almost the whole of the north of the Great Cold Mountains; but this prince had sided with the Chinese against his insurgent clans, and their defeat ruined him; now his successor lives always in the two yamens which he possesses in Chinese territory, and he exercises only a fictitious suzerainty over the independent country, although he is still powerful by reason of his numerous serfs and the extent of his private domains.

However, the present nzemo, the Prince Len, whose name I have already mentioned more than once, is young, active, intelligent, and a keen nationalist, and is contriving to restore his prestige. He belongs to a new dynasty, which usurped the throne of the ancient family, the Ngan, after the battle of Niu-Niu-Pa. The Ngan have not abandoned the hope of regaining their principality. A number of nzemos who belong to the same stock have lent them their support, and it is by no means unlikely that a War of the Roses may be added to the numerous quarrels which have already stained the region with blood.

Even more than the vistas which revealed the horizon, these glimpses of Lolo history aroused my passionate interest. But to be truthful, although the Lolos fascinated us by their proud bearing, their frank, handsome faces, and a mingling of physical and moral qualities which distinguish them from the yellow race, and seem to bring them nearer to our own, it must be confessed that in the matter of "civilisation" they lag very far behind. No architecture, no statues, no paintings, no industry; people barely clad dwelling in unfurnished cabins; my friends the cannibals of the Ivory Coast were more advanced!

Yet the Lolos have possessed a civilisation: they have invented a peculiar mode of writing, and a score of their books, as yet indecipherable, have been brought to Europe; a long inscription was discovered in Yunnan, and although it remains unintelligible, a Chinese text, engraved beside it, and dated 1533, informs us that it concerns a prince whose mother had been received in audience by the Emperor and favoured with notable honours. Various Chinese texts speak of the sumptuous life and ceremonial of the ancient Lolo seigneurs of Yunnan. Since the independent country was regarded as the cradle of the race, I had hoped, not without logical excuse, to find the ancient civilisation intact there. It was a profound disappointment when I found neither inscriptions, nor arts, nor industries, nor religion.

Was this the effect of decadence? No; for there was not even a trace of civilisation; moreover, the very aspect of these rude mountaineers, devoted to war and to violent exercise, told of the vigour of a young race. I began to ask myself whether the race before our eyes was really the same as that which was formerly described by the Chinese in Yunnan; there was not even an identity of name, for "Lolo" is only a nickname, and the natives nowhere employ it. Here was an ethnographical and historical enigma to be solved.

Thus all data relating to the past had for me a peculiar importance, and for that reason, even at the outset, I had decided to bend our journey through the territory of the nzemo of Shama, whose house was particularly famous. It seemed impossible to me that the prince should have no archives, however rudimentary, nor records, however summary. At the same time I intended to return to the Kien-Chang, where both the rivals, Len and Ngan, reside, in order to look into their titles.

The road we were now following was almost deserted; there was only an occasional hamlet; sometimes a peopled valley opened in a fold of the mountains, but we passed without descending thither.

However, we encountered one young and handsome knight, attended by his squires. He was a great friend of Ma-Muka's, and we halted to exchange salutations. Suddenly Ma-Muka informed us that this noble knight was famed for his address with the bow, and that he wished to see which was the better, his weapon or ours! We accepted this naïve challenge.

All dismounted. The Lolo took his bow from the hands of a squire, and invited me, a little ironically, to bend it; but recollecting in time the confusion of the suitors when Penelope gave them the bow of Ulysses, I declined the test, and took my revolver in hand. I acted prudently, for to judge by another Lolo bow, which I obtained at a later date and brought to Europe, I should have been utterly incapable of bending it an inch. The Lolo strung it almost without apparent effort. He chose an arrow from a quiver carried by a page, took a long look at a little patch of brown earth which showed at some fifty yards' distance in the midst of the green turf, and, to the applause of the Lolos, shot his arrow into it, the weapon sinking far into the soil. But a ball followed it immediately; then others, out-distancing the arrow more and more, raising little clouds of dust which in a moment hung in a regular line between us and the summit of a neighbouring hill. The archer contemplated with stupefaction the rapidity and range of a weapon that demanded no effort. He owned himself beaten, and asked the price of so extraordinary a weapon. "Four hundred taels" (about £60), replied Siu, who wished to impress him by this formidable figure. "I would willingly pay them," said the warrior, without hesitation. "But," he added sadly, after a moment's reflection, "where should I get the cartridges?"

He was so full of admiration that he could not tear himself away. Turning his horse, he escorted us until the following day, inquiring eagerly into all our marvels, and exhibiting a sincere friendliness, as was proper between true men of war.

The Lolos had no knowledge of anything like our weapons. Although such as possessed muskets or rifles loved to make a parade of them, we had seen only a few in their houses, and of these the majority were captured from the Chinese troops at the time of the recent expeditions. None were repeaters, and it is probable that they scarcely ever used them, for as a rule the cartridges, which were extremely expensive, the trade in weapons being prohibited in the Empire, and which were obtained from the Chinese of the frontier, were not of the same calibre.

The prestige which our weapons gave us had certainly much to do with our success. At the same time, it is certain that they evoked among the less scrupulous Lolos a violent desire of possession; and we conjured this peril only by continually surrounding our-

BOW *versus* REVOLVER.

To face page 96.

selves with the most honourable notables of the country. Proof of their envy was furnished in a tragic fashion by the death of Mr. Brooke in the following year.

In March, 1908, I met this English traveller at Cheng-Tu ; he was then returning from Tibet, where he had attained his object. He asked me, as was natural, and without allowing me to guess his plans, for information concerning our journey through the Lolo territory : information I willingly gave him. In December of the same year he arrived with another Englishman at Ning-Yuan-fu, and almost immediately leaving his companion, who was not anxious to tackle the adventure, he entered the independent territory with sixteen Chinese servants. He followed our route exactly as far as Chu-Hei, everywhere making use of our names in order to obtain a passage ; for the rest he asked for no other services, had no respondent, lived on provisions he had brought with him, and slept under his tent. Evidently there was not much at fault with the reputation we had left behind us, since no one hindered him as long as he was with our friends.

Unhappily, encouraged by this fortunate commencement, he wished to explore a new region. Hardly had he left our track when matters were different. A noble of the Arho clan, a little to the north of Chu-Hei, ordered him to surrender his magnificent repeating rifle, which excited the general admiration and envy ; upon his refusal the Lolo attempted to strike him with his sabre. Mr. Brooke killed him, as well as several other Lolos who had flung themselves upon him. He then attempted to beat a retreat, but the Lolos pursued him. He took refuge in a house, where he continued his heroic resistance, firing his last cartridge and killing a dozen of his aggressors ; but at last he was massacred with fourteen of his men. Two of these only were spared and reduced to slavery ; but they succeeded in escaping, and it was from them that the details of the catastrophe were learned.

Despite the demands of Great Britain, the Chinese Government denied all responsibility ; " it was not the master in Lolo territory." All that could be done was to promise a reward for the body of the unfortunate explorer—which amounted to an actual premium on assassination. This offer was successful, and the remains were despatched to the British consul-general ; but only after endless negotiations, *for it was necessary to find and pay respondents to conduct the body* through every clan whose lands it had to cross ; and—a grim detail—while the trunk was brought to the fortress of Yu-Hi, in the west of the Lolo country, the head came out through Ma-Pien, a stronghold on the eastern frontier !

China, however, organised a fresh expedition, and five thousand men concentrated at Tong-Mu-Kiu, on the southern and most accessible frontier, and marched upon Kiao-Kio. According to their usual tactics, the Lolos gave way before the troops, then fell upon and captured their convoys. The column, in a state of destitution, had to beat a retreat, and was soon in full flight.

Perhaps these dramatic events will help the reader to understand the actual state of the country. We ourselves saw few but smiling faces ; crowds pressed about us to welcome us and escorted us with shouts of joy ; the chiefs, on receiving us in their homes, prostrated themselves and offered us the first-fruits of their flocks. All was apparently idyllic, and I do not think I have omitted any detail of this cheerful picture—except the fact that nothing could be more deceptive.

Alone in the midst of a nation, the explorer is powerless ; on the day when a decided enemy stands up before him, he is done for. He who has succeeded in passing has seen only smiles ; otherwise it is probable that he would not have returned. But it must always be remembered, must be kept in mind at every moment,

A SHAMA DONJON.

LEN AND TAMULEI.

To face page 98.

that these smiles are not spontaneous, and that the whole art of the explorer consists in evoking them on faces ordinarily savage. To dissimulate, even out of modesty, the latent peril which has surrounded him would be, in the leader of a mission, to fail in his duty and to run the responsibility of the catastrophes which might fall upon his successors.

*

* *

We lodged in a village belonging to Ma-Muka. Next morning, about eleven o'clock, we met another horseman; this time a man of ripe years and grave aspect. At the sight of us he stopped, disconcerted; Ma-Muka rode out to him and doubtless explained who we were, but we must suppose that the new-comer was not enthusiastic, for he pretended not to see us. Making a semicircle with his men-at-arms, he followed us at a distance of fifty yards. "Who is he?" we asked. We learned that this ill-disposed personage was none other than Ma-Muka's own father, the powerful Thetsu, chief of the clan of the Alu-Ma and mayor of the palace of Shama. He was highly displeased that Ma-Muka had taken it on himself to conduct us without consulting him, and he refused to make our acquaintance.

We were somewhat abashed to learn that Ma-Muka had taken such a step without being certain of the consent of his father: the irritation of the latter, on whom everything really depended, was a serious matter.

We stopped for lunch near a spring, at the bottom of a ravine with outcrops of coal; the sun poured down its burning vertical rays, and when on resuming the march we had to reascend the slope, the heat was overpowering; the more so in that we had been suffering from the cold for some days past. Boyve, who in spite of his vigorous constitution was not broken in to these sudden changes of temperature, was suffering severely from dysentery; of a sudden he was taken ill and slid from his horse to the ground, unconscious. Father de Guébriant and I ran to his assistance. Fortunately it was only one of those accidents most familiar to an officer, the "heatstroke" so common during military marches; a vigorous whipping of the face and chest with a handkerchief dipped in water, and the circulation, interrupted by a failure of the digestive organs, resumes its natural course.

But the treatment was slow to act, and we had to take turns in continuing the application, which enabled us to remark the peculiar attitude of our Lolo companions. Ma-Muka had cut a twig, made a certain number of notches in it, and squatting on his heels was reciting some prayer or incantation while counting his tally. Thetsu and his spearmen had drawn near, and were observing the scene with passionate interest. Obviously a struggle was going on in their minds; we were all three at their mercy, one of us unconscious, the two others on their knees and supporting him. It would have been enough to lower their lances!

But Ma-Muka rose. "All goes well; he is saved!" he said. The faces of the Lolos relaxed, and they regarded us sympathetically. A few moments later Boyve opened his eyes, stretched himself, and in a few minutes was on his legs. General rejoicing! Ma-Muka and his men felicitated us, and even Thetsu's followers shared discreetly in the general delight.

But what would have happened if Fate, consulted by Ma-Muka, had given him an unfavourable reply? It is very possible that she would have been a true prophetess, and that none of us would have stood up again; for who shall protect the accursed ones whom Fate has condemned?

Ma-Muka felt that this incident had diminished the distance between his father and himself. Like a true Lolo, he knew how to complete the reconciliation; he invited me to fire a few shots from my revolver. It was enough to wake Thetsu from his pose of immobility, and make him stare with admiration. Then Ma-Muka conceived a master-stroke ; he asked me to lend him my revolver so that he in turn might fire the wonderful weapon. I had always refused such requests, for it was as well that the management of our weapons should remain our secret. Yet here the conquest of Thetsu demanded an abrogation of the rule, and briefly explaining to Ma-Muka what he must do, I consented to let him fire three shots and no more.

Although he had never touched a pistol his three shots carried truly, striking a spot of earth I had pointed out to him. Thetsu was delighted, congratulated his son, congratulated me, and we were friends! But what do you think pleased Ma-Muka the most? "This weapon obeys the foreign lord," he told Siu ; "he told me to fire only three shots, and when I tried to fire a fourth the little pistol refused!" And in fact I discovered that by some extraordinary chance a jam had occurred after the third shot. Not a very reassuring incident, yet this accident, transformed into a sudden manifestation of our superhuman powers, was still further to increase our prestige.

All day we had been marching in a parallel line to the formidable mountain of the Dragon's Head. Its form revealed the origin of the name ; it did really resemble the back of an enormous beast, lying east and west, with the head abruptly raised. This head, which from a distance appeared as a single pyramidal peak, has really three summits, one of which rises, by a dizzy, perpendicular cliff, thousands of yards above the gorge of the River Mai-Ku. The two others, almost hidden by the first, are still loftier. It is a curious fact that when we afterwards arrived at Lei-Po-ting, on the eastern slope of the same mountain, we found its form almost identical, but this time it was headed south.

As for the Snowy Mountains of Shama, since the day before we had frequent glimpses of them between the almost perpendicular buttresses of the great range which we were following. By a final pass 10,000 feet in height we crossed the third buttress and were face to face with the vast mountain-range, whose peaks reach a height of 15,500 feet, and which stretches from north to south an impregnable barrier. Only to the south is there a depression, and through this depression we saw—oh, so distant!—the mountains of the Yunnan which represented safety.

At our feet lay outspread a long valley, very different in aspect from all those we had seen. It was, to be truthful, sinister-looking; the high mountains which encompassed it gave it the appearance of a ditch; the soil was of a dirty yellow and the rocks black; above them even the snow had the look of funereal trappings. Happily the architecture of the great range is extremely fine; there is a breach in the very centre of the crest, and curiously symmetrical peaks on either side. Pines climbed the slopes to a height of some 12,000 feet; above them was the bare precipitous rock.

Thetsu, now our friend, went before us to prepare for our reception; our interpreter, Siu, went with him, bearing a magnificent watch which we sent as a present to the nzemo. We passed through several villages of noble vassals, serfs, and slaves, and at last arrived at the princely residence. It could be distinguished at a distance by its donjon, or keep, which was the only structure of the kind I had seen among the mountaineers, who disdain the arts of building.

We were shown into a large courtyard, surrounded by buildings of wooden planks like those I have already described, and were requested to wait until our lodging was prepared. A crowd of Lolos were there, crouching opposite our party; silent, or exchanging a few occasional words below their breath.

There was one man there dressed in white hemp like a slave, but wearing on his feet a sort of Turkish slippers in red leather, which were tied on for greater security. This was the first Lolo I had ever seen shod ; the slippers he wore were of unknown origin ; there was also a boy of some fifteen years wearing Chinese garments of silk and walking to and fro in a similar pair of red slippers. Surprised at this luxury, we discreetly made inquiries, for the ice was not yet broken nor the introduction effected, and learned that this was the prince himself, with his son, who had come out among his councillors to observe us. The prince had fairly good though not handsome features, and a shifty expression which made us uneasy ; he had not the vigorous, soldierly aspect which is characteristic of the nation as a whole. But this perhaps was only a first impression.

As for the son, his features and pale complexion were almost Chinese, but his gaiety and petulance were entirely Lolo. It was the hour when the herds and flocks returned ; the cattle and sheep entered the gate and invaded the courtyard, threatening to submerge our noble assembly ; whereupon the little prince, armed with a switch, rushed at them and commenced to drive the recalcitrant animals to their byres. A scene of Homeric times ! [1]

However, it was decided that we should be taken to our lodgings : surely a palace, by the time it took to prepare them ! It was one of the side-buildings in a second courtyard, the end of which was occupied by the dwelling of the prince. Our accommodation was one of the most miserable hovels that could be imagined ; the planks of the roof in particular exhibited the most discouraging intervals, for already it was beginning to rain. The prince was gracious enough to have us informed that he would have had us installed in his own quarters, but that his wife had been brought to bed the previous night ; and what he offered us was certainly

[1] We were not to see the fine red slippers again. As soon as the rain came the prince and his son went barefoot in the mud like other people. This also was exceedingly Homeric.

the best there was in the place next to the central pavilion. So it was really a palace, after all!

Night fell, and a torrential rain, which commenced almost immediately and lasted until daylight, literally soaking us, prevented the establishment of further relations between ourselves and our hosts. However, the prince sent to ask us if we preferred that he should offer us cooked meat or live animals. Distrusting Lolo cookery, we voted for livestock, and the prince sent us a pig. Ignorant fellows that we were! we were to learn later on what a feast we had missed.

Our apprehension, however, was excusable. No one is more frugal and sober than the Lolo, nor more indifferent to good cheer, as to all comfort. His usual diet consists of a broad cake of buckwheat, made of badly kneaded, unleavened dough, and containing little or no salt, as salt, which comes from China, is rare and expensive. These thick cakes, or rather balls, are often stuffed with potatoes, for the potato is cultivated everywhere. It must have been imported from China, for it has no special designation in Lolo, but is known by its Chinese name.[1] To this buckwheat cake is added, according to the wealth of the individual, rice, potatoes boiled or roasted in the ashes, and sometimes meat. Wheat is also used, being made into unleavened bread or gruel. There are no vegetables, not even the haricots so beloved by the Chinese. We never saw any use made of milk, which is extraordinary in the case of a people owning great herds and the habits of a pastoral rather than an agricultural people.

[1] This name, *yang-yu*, signifies foreign root, or European root, which shows that the Chinese imported the potato, though no one knows where or how. Is it not curious that this vegetable spread spontaneously throughout China, which we choose to think refractory to every innovation, while in progressive France the most determined efforts and the intervention of royalty were required to persuade the people to eat them!

"And you—what did you eat?" the amiable reader will ask me. I am sure this important question has long been on the tip of his—or her—tongue, to judge by the number of times it has been put to me verbally. Well, we ate very ordinary food: potatoes, rice, eggs, bacon-fat, fowls, and the meat of the animals presented to us. It is a little shameful to own it, but in no country does the explorer make his daily diet of crocodiles, pythons, and monkeys, nor even of swallows' nests, and even when he does taste them occasionally he has the bad taste to prefer to base his diet upon exceedingly commonplace dishes.

Next morning the rain was still falling, particularly in our house with the breezy roof. One of the slaves to whom we showed in despair the cascades spurting through the openings gazed in astonishment at people who concerned themselves about such trivialities, then went out and returned armed with a lance. It was our turn to be surprised; but he, very naturally and simply, raised the planks of the roof with the point of the lance, made them slide one against the other, and thus contrived a small square of roof which was almost watertight—needless to say very much to the detriment of the rest of the room. A system our builders might take note of!

The palace people began to come to see us in spite of the rain, and among them the little prince, Tamulei, who offered us a living pheasant. We were friends with him at once; and a very pleasant child he was. Having passed some time on Chinese soil at the house of his uncle, Prince Len, and his cousin, the nzemo of Lei-Po-ting, he had learned a little Chinese; he was therefore able to converse directly with Father de Guébriant, and, at a pinch, act for us as a second interpreter. He was the only Lolo we had met in the whole of the independent country who could speak a word of Chinese. As for the slaves of Chinese origin, they are absolutely forbidden to speak a word of their native language, as their masters prefer to understand what they are talking about. The boy was thus delighted to show off his superiority, and took us under his especial protection, which was lucky for us, for the nzemo did not appear particularly anxious to see us.

It was a great advantage to us to have two interpreters; the assistance of Siu was only too often required in material difficulties, so that he could not ask questions for us. I profited immediately by the circumstance to inquire into the matter of Lolo writing, and I showed Tamulei the specimens of Lolo characters published by the Abbé Vial, missionary in the Yunnan. The little prince could not read them, but there were three *pimos* in the palace, and he went to call them.

The pimo is a personage not easy to define; indeed I was unable to place him exactly until a much later period. He is not a priest, for he has no sacred character, but he can read the books in which are recorded the formulæ of the prayers and ceremonies which constitute religion among the Lolos. He is therefore the only person who can perform these ceremonies, and this is one of his functions. Moreover, since he is able to read and write he will act as public writer; very often he is employed by the prince or seigneur of the place as chancellor, and as tutor to his sons; for these rude warriors—although we scarcely suspected as much—have a real reverence for their national writings: an irrefutable testimony of their civilisation.

The three pimos arrived. Confronted in turn by the Abbé Vial's book, they began by holding it not as it was written by its author, but in a perpendicular position, so that the vertical lines became horizontal; then they read certain characters, but attributed quite different sounds and meanings to them; finally they declared they did not know the others; in short, they could not understand the text at all. Only the prince, they told us, might be able to make something of it, for he was far more learned than they, and only Prince Len surpassed him.

A considerable crowd had gathered to enjoy this interview. One of those present stepped out of the ranks and took up the book as though it were a familiar object; but, having turned over the pages, he declared in a low voice that he could make nothing of it either. "It is the prince," whispered Siu; and sure enough we recognised the characteristic face that had struck us the night before; the desire to show his knowledge had made him break his resolve to stand aloof. Since he was there, we kept him. "Is it not the illustrious prince of Shama?" we said to him aloud. The nzemo, finding his incognito discovered, bowed to the ground. He had not dared to introduce himself, not having any wine to offer us; he had sent to a distance to find some, but the messengers had not returned; would we deign to excuse him?

The introduction once effected, he was entirely at our disposal; but in the meantime he wished to re-habilitate his reputation as a scholar, which had suffered from his inability to decipher our book; and one of the pimos respectfully brought him a Lolo manu-script. This was no less than the Genealogy and History of the Dynasty of Shama. The prince read us certain passages; it was a true revelation.

The Lolos are not indigenous to the Great Cold Mountains; they come from the southern Yunnan and from Kwei-Chu. The ancestors of the prince, the Ngan, were of Chinese origin; it was the great Emperor Kang-He who gave them the hereditary government of a number of Lolo tribes in the neighbourhood of Wei Ning, in Kwei-Chu, in 1713. The Emperor Yong-Cheng wishing to consolidate the Chinese suzerainty, which until that time had been purely nominal, the Lolos took up arms in 1727, but were crushed. A great number of them abandoned their country, flying to-wards the west, crossing the Blue River, and taking refuge in the wild ranges of Chonolevo and Shama, then covered with forests, to which they set fire.

The Ngan took no part in this exodus, but remained subject to the Emperor. But their sometime subjects, after fruitless attempts to reconquer their domain, and wishing at least to secure recognition of their new state, appealed to their princes and asked them to obtain terms of peace. The Emperor K'ien-Long consented to this, and confirmed the Ngan in their dignities by giving them a seal.

At each succession, however, this seal must be returned to the Chinese authorities, who confer it upon the legitimate heir. Now the prefect of Lei-Po-ting, in place of returning to the prince the seal of his father, gave it to a cousin who had no title to it. The tribes refused to recognise the usurper, who was forced to take refuge in the Yunnan; but the legitimate heir no longer possessed the seal of his father. Although the seal was not, as among the Chinese, the instrument of his power, which was founded only upon the consent of the Lolos, its possession gave him a decided prestige, as proving that he was recognised by the Emperor: its loss did him sensible damage; several tribes profited by it to refuse him obedience; his enemies redoubled their insolence, and without the alliance of the Alu-Ma his position would have been critical.

All this was explained to us in a much less logical fashion, in answer to our astonished questions. While retracing the illustrious past of his race the prince's voice was full of melancholy, but also of pride; his notables, seated around us, nodded their heads in token of acquiescence. At each reply it was as though a curtain were withdrawn: the vestiges of a previous Chinese occupation, the complete absence of any traces of an ancient Lolo civilisation, the family traditions, all of which made them come from the west, the survival of relations with Chao-Tong and the north of

Yunnan, and the maintenance, despite the hostility of the peoples, of good relations between China and the princes—all, in short, that had so greatly surprised us was now made clear. A light was thrown on the present, and a phase of unknown history emerged from the darkness.

How I should have liked to possess that book of Lolo annals! But it was not to be hoped that the prince would part with it. He assured me that in their ancient territory the Lolos, although submissive, had retained their feudal organisation, their customs, and their writings, and that there I should find documents in abundance. Thus a whole field of research lay open before me.

But not the road thither! To the north of us the road to Lei-Po-ting, which we wished to reach, was intercepted by the Tamuka, at a distance of only a mile and a half from where we stood. Moreover, the River Mai-Ku, which we should have to cross, and its tributaries, which flow into the Blue River, have worn the most frightful abysses in their journey thither; these can only be crossed by means of a cable stretched across the river, on which runs a pulley supporting a leathern sack, in which the passenger is fastened.[1] No horse can pass. To the east no one can cross the crest of the range who has not his hands free to cling to the rocks; to the south-east the nzemo could pilot us as far as the Blue River, opposite Ho-Kyu; this was the only direction open to us.

It vexed us greatly to return southward—a proceeding that would uselessly add to the length of our journey to Lei-Po-ting and Swei-fu; and we were not convinced of the reality of the difficulties which the prince described to us as besetting the northern and eastern routes, when an unexpected proof of his assertion was afforded us. A Lolo woman made her entrance on

[1] Except for the leathern sack, this procedure is well known on the confines of Tibet.

horseback, followed by several men-at-arms and two Chinese soldiers! She was the wife of the nzemo of Lei-Po-ting, to whom we wished to present ourselves; and she came to assist at the accouchement of the princess of Shama, her aunt; and she, precisely on account of the obstacles which intercepted the northern route, had been forced to travel over Chinese territory from Lei-Po-ting to Ho-Kyu—whence the presence of the two Chinese soldiers, placed at her disposal by the prefect, to escort her upon her return to Imperial soil. Before this proof we could only bow our heads.

Suddenly our affairs went badly. Next morning we heard that the prince and his councillors had passed the night in discussing the treatment to be meted out to us; the prevailing opinion was that we ought to be kept as prisoners. Here was a new storm, easy to foresee after the period of calm enjoyed since we had left Kiao-Kio. But whence had it arisen?

Thanks to the amiable Tamulei, who was greatly troubled at our disgrace, we learned the cause. The two Chinese soldiers, foreseeing the displeasure of their mandarins if we were to succeed in crossing territory forbidden to themselves, had declared that we were certainly criminals who had broken our ban; otherwise the prefect would have known of our coming, and would have advised the prince; let the latter think before incurring the Imperial wrath!

The argument was plausible, for no one can travel in China unless all the authorities are advised beforehand of one's advent; and the mandarins would certainly be annoyed with the Lolos if the latter allowed us to pass. Our attempts at diplomacy, notwithstanding the good offices of Ma-Muka and Tamulei, had no appreciable result.

Happily there was the argument to which no Lolo is insensible: the reader will have guessed already what I mean. I had only one "turn," but that was a good one. Ma-Muka, who knew that by experience, led us out to practise firing just at the foot of a terrace whither the prince and his notables had retired in order to hold a council out of the reach of indiscreet ears. The usual effect was produced, and the prince, upon seeing our bullets reach the pass whence he feared every moment to see his enemies the Tamuka appear, and where he had constantly to maintain an outpost, was filled with envy of the owners of such weapons. They could not be reprehensible persons! Suddenly our argument, which was that if the prefect of Lei-Po-ting had not warned him of our coming it was because he did not know that we were coming by way of Shama, appeared sound and convincing.

Scarcely had we returned when the prince entered our lodging, prostrated himself, and declared himself our vassal. The arrival of the famous "wine of honour," which had taken him three days to find, sealed our friendship, and the prince invited us to visit his dwelling. It was the building which occupied the bottom of the courtyard; in front was a verandah, whose columns were connected by a kind of ogive of original design. In the interior were three apartments; of these two were closed; one served as a treasury, the other was the sleeping-room, occupied then by his wife. In the centre was the reception-hall, a large apartment some thirty-two feet long by twenty feet wide and over thirty feet in height. It rose to the roof, which was of the usual type—of planks kept in place by stones, but carefully made and almost waterproof. This residence was new; the old castle of Shama, a day's journey to the north-west, was inhabited by two younger brothers of the prince. We were told that it was much finer, and that it had a roof of tiles brought from China, which represented the acme of luxury.

When the time came for our departure, the prince begged us to leave him some personal souvenir. Father de Guébriant gave him his chaplet, and I my French visiting-card, on which I recommended the nzemo to his future visitors. This little courtesy appeared to touch him, for he asked me for another card, on which he wrote two lines in Lolo characters, which, so he told me, were also a warm recommendation. Later I had this precious autograph translated. The prince declared that he had offered us two pigs and two sheep—certainly a highly original form of recommendation, but one proving his high esteem and suggesting an excellent example.

These are the men whom the Chinese map, with a concision worthy of Tacitus, describes in these words: "The Barbarians of Shama, at indeterminate periods, cross the Blue River to kill, pillage, burn, and make captives."

*
* *

We were now *en route* for the last stage of our journey, accompanied by the major-domo of the palace and a number of serfs. Since we were going to follow the best road, we supposed it would be passably good, in spite of the prospect of descending from the heights of the Snowy Mountains of Shama to the bottom of the gorge of the Blue River. The first part of the journey was certainly easy, lying as it did through a pleasant valley. We slept in a village of serfs, where two drinking-cups were stolen from us at the moment of departure. I mention this theft because it was the only one we ever suffered on Lolo territory, or even while in China—Tibet excepted—although we had always been surrounded by a crowd of people who used to examine our treasures, and on whom we could not possibly keep an eye. Yet the Chinese are always called thieves!

Next day we crossed the principal range without effort, by a pass 11,400 feet high, where, under the falling snow, we gathered ripe strawberries among the thickets of azalea and rhododendron, both in bloom, in the midst of a forest of pines which unhappily were damaged by fire. This was almost the counterpart of the pass of Shaol, through which we had entered the Lolo territory.

We thought we had only to climb down. A deep valley, containing numerous villages, was at our feet; we would follow it as far as the Yang-Tze. Alas! arrived at the bottom, after an exceedingly difficult and precipitous descent of 4,000 feet, we were invited by our guides to climb the opposite side of the valley, which was as steep as the wall of a house! As for the valley, it belonged to the Nilei, who had revolted against Shama, and very soon narrowed to an impracticable ditch.

We climbed, often helping ourselves with our hands, up a path of unimaginable difficulty. There was a dense mist, which hid even the mountain we were climbing. Our horses, although so accustomed to acclivities, were constantly in difficulties; we had to pull at their bridles to help them over some difficult bit; several times we had actually to rope them up, and the Lolos, with astonishing strength and skill, would haul them up some rocky wall. As for us, we were utterly "done": the rarefaction of the air at that height made our breathing most painful, and one cannot run up a perpendicular cliff; but apparently the Lolos could, even carrying our loads, and they assured us that if we loitered ever so little the icy night would surprise us on the mountain-side.

To complete our misery, we had several cases of sickness. Boyve's dysentery was becoming more serious; he could not nourish himself properly and was losing all his strength; and our Chinese, although robust mountaineers, were all exhausted—one of them was really at the end of his tether, stopped at every step, and would never have started again if Father de Guébriant had not sustained him by his encouragements. For a moment the path appeared less steep, and we got upon our horses, excepting Father de Guébriant, who gave his to the unfortunate Chinaman. Almost immediately we heard shouts behind us. Hastening back, we found the Father's horse hanging over the abyss, holding only by its fore-feet, with which it desperately clawed at the path ; as for its temporary rider, by a marvellous chance he was caught by a tuft of dwarf bamboos which grew beside the path. We helped him out of his perilous situation, but all our efforts to support the horse were in vain; its strength gave out, it relinquished its hold, and fell like a log. From time to time we heard the sound of its body as it struck upon a crag and rebounded.

Only then, thanks to the hole in the bamboos and the black coat of the horse, which was visible through the mist, were we able to realise our actual situation : we were on a narrow, almost vertical, ridge, with precipices behind us and on either side. I am sure none of us could have scaled this giddy track if the mist and the bamboos had not wrapped us in their reassuring mantle.

The loss of a horse was a real misfortune in our state of exhaustion. The loss was a double one, for strapped to the saddle-bow was one of our automatic pistols, enclosed in its holster. But what was to be done? In the first place, the pistol must be broken; secondly, we had no time to climb down and up again before nightfall. Scarcely, however, had the Lolos heard that one of the wonderful fire-arms was on the saddle than two of them rushed head-first through the very breach which the fall of the horse had made in the bamboos!

We lost sight of them at once, and shuddered. Twenty minutes later they reappeared, carrying the saddle, which was broken and useless, and the pistol, most wonderfully intact; the horse lay dead at the very foot of the precipice, 1,600 feet lower down. As for the two men, they were smiling with satisfaction, not in the least out of breath, and barely noticing the bleeding stripes on their hands and naked bodies—for they had thrown off their mantles and had absolutely nothing on but a pair of short cotton breeches resembling bathing-drawers—made by the spines of the bamboos through which they slipped on their downward path, seizing them with half-shut hands to check their descent. How splendidly tempered are these men for warfare!

After reaching a height of 10,000 feet, we still had to descend about 1,300 feet, and then again climb to the previous height before reaching shelter. We were absolutely played out.

Next day the programme was the same: down into a deep, populated valley; then a perpendicular climb. The mist was still all about us, and we only perceived the true nature of this savage country by the efforts it cost us to make the slightest progress. Descending into the depths of giddy chasms, scaling vertical walls, we seemed to be entrapped in some mysterious fortress of giants. In the hands of the mountaineers, who laugh at these abysses, this country is absolutely impregnable. Here is the very citadel of Lolo independence; and the white, inviolate peaks, which are visible from the extreme frontier, gleaming among the clouds, are its glorious standard.

Full of these thoughts we entered, always climbing, a forest which the mist and the falling snow had concealed; and we suddenly uttered exclamations of surprise. We were in an absolute fairyland; around us, above us, all was a world of marvellous flowers, gleaming through the snow like globes of fire. Overhead were giant rhododendrons, over thirty feet high, their boughs laden with white or bright red blossom; below them were arborescent azaleas, raising their rosy calices to a height of fifteen feet. Mossy lianas, glistening with moisture, hung like garlands from tree to tree, while the white flakes of snow fluttered down like butterflies. It was a dream-picture in which nothing seemed real: these blossom-laden trees, the petals opening in the snow, this scene of beauty and splendour burning through the mists on the summit of the wildest mountain of a strangely wild and desert country. Were we the victims of a hallucination, and would the Flower-Maidens come forward from the thickets of blossom to lead us into captivity?

Twenty minutes this enchantment lasted; then, on the crest of the ridge, the forest suddenly terminated, as though to hide from the enemy, China, whose mountains now appeared to our front. The descent into the depths, this time definitive, began once again; but our hearts and eyes were still full of the unforgettable vision. Country of the Lolos, we shall never forget you: country of the terrible renown and the hospitable welcome, whose indomitable warriors conceal warm and simple hearts, and whose girdle of precipices defends, like a priceless treasure, the flowers that open amidst the snow.

On the following day we continued our descent towards Yunnan, whose mountains we saw before us, now close at hand. In a lofty valley, at Ukulokio, dwelt a petty prince, a nephew and vassal of Shama; but we had exhausted our provision of presents, and since, thanks to the representative of the suzerain who escorted us, we could go forward without his permission, we left the valley on one side. We saw there an abundance of privet, which nourishes the wax-insects, a kind of yellow-spotted ladybird, which were just then clinging in bunches along the twigs in order to lay their eggs.

The appearance of the population was now entirely different. We saw the same bandits' faces as at Ta-Hin-Chang, on our entrance into Lolo territory; the offscourings of Chinese who had fled their country in consequence of some offence, and of Lolos who had come thither for no good purpose; the frontiers are the home and refuge of brigands.

The country here was most remarkable. The valley

in which we were marching, through which ran a stream, was more than 6,000 feet above sea-level ; at a distance of a couple of miles or so the wall of the Yunnan range had all the appearance of closing it ; yet we knew that on the hither side of the mountain the Blue River, although invisible, was flowing at a height of not more than 2,300 feet, to which level both we and the stream should have to descend. Yet the brook had the air of ignoring this fact, for it flowed calmly over an almost imperceptible slope, without appearing to suspect that an abyss was waiting to receive it. As for us, we shuddered in advance.

For, as was inevitable, at the end of the valley was a perpendicular drop. The river was not, as at our first crossing, hidden amidst a chaos of crumbling peaks ; here it ran between two walls more than 3,000 feet in height ; seeming, at that great depth, only a slender yellow ribbon, streaked here and there with the white of a rapid. Here and there the walls of the gulf gave way a little, leaving room for a few rice-fields of a tender green ; but between these oases the chasm narrowed, and we wondered how the road communicating with these level spaces found room to pass.

And now, to climb down ! The stream should by rights have taken a leap of 3,000 feet ; but instead of doing so it entered the earth ! This was one of the most curious phenomena produced by the work of erosion performed by this great river. When the small affluents, which have not sufficient force to erode their beds, draw near to the river at an enormous height above it they infallibly encounter some fissure caused by some landslip, some fall of rocks into the river ; such falls producing in the substance of the walls all manner of crevices and "chimneys." The subterranean sheet of water, of which the stream is only the outward manifestation, drains into these crevices, and the stream dries up. In this manner a large number of valleys watered by streams terminate in a terrace thousands of feet above the river, yet not a drop of water flows over the edge.

But what were we to do, who could not creep into some crevice of the rocks? For the Lolos the matter was simple: they merely ran down the almost perpendicular cliffs. But we, alas! were poor Europeans, clumsy, and subject to vertigo. And as we were negotiating the slope, summoning up all our courage and clinging to the rocks with our hands, some of the amiable bandits who had surrounded us a little while before, began to cross the rocks above us, armed with their long lances, with which they could so easily have sent us flying into the void. We drew our revolvers, and intimated that they had better vanish, if they did not wish us to fire then and there.

At a height of some 2,500 feet above the river were terraces, on either side of the gorge, which evidently marked the old level of its bed. These terraces, covered with excellent alluvial soil, were thickly peopled and highly cultivated. From this height we could see that the same structure obtained all along the valley, so that these mountains, which from below look so precipitous and desolate, are really fairly well populated.

On the terrace which constituted our last halting-place on the independent territory we had the astonishing good fortune to see for the first time a Lolo occupied in writing. He was a young man, who, sitting before his door, was finishing a copy of an ancient book: the genealogy of his family, from which he read us some passages. We then learned that all the Lolo nobles, and even serfs of the higher ranks, keep their genealogies by them, in which they inscribe, or cause to be inscribed, the names of new members of the family, their alliances, and the principal events. To prove this, a number of Lolos ran to find their books and show them to us. These are, of course, patents of nobility with which they would not part at any price; but the young man was quite willing to let us have his copy, which he could replace.

Thus, at the last moment, we acquired our first Lolo book! A happy chance, but one that proved to us that we had—for lack of a second interpreter—missed many similar opportunities. We should beware of so doing in future.

Finally, after a last terrible descent, we reached the bottom, and stood on the banks of the Blue River. On the further side was China. The country of the Lolos had been crossed, and our success was complete.

CHAPTER V

LOLOS AND MIAO-TZE

IT was high time! We were exhausted, half dead of fatigue, utterly done up, both our men and ourselves. How we should rest in a good inn! And we joyfully hailed the Chinese ferryman across the water.

The ferryman did not budge. Yes, he did presently move, but it was to make his way towards the village of Ho-Kyu, some little distance away. Astonished, we ourselves went abreast of the village, and all, together, or singly, Lolos, Chinese, and Frenchmen, shouted with all our might, launching appeals, promises, threats, and imprecations. No answer: the Chinese were deaf. We fired a few shots to show, by our improved fire-arms, that we were not Lolos—a fact which our white helmets should have demonstrated sufficiently. It was all wasted; the argument of the rifle, irresistible beyond the mountains of Shama, was here of no value whatever.

We were plunged into utter consternation; for how should we leave the country if the Chinese refused to come for us with their boat? Our Lolo respondents, who had faithfully fulfilled their task, were now anxious to return; and here were some of these evil brigands' faces, come from goodness knows where, mingling with us and incessantly increasing in number.

By sentimental discourse and the promise of our last knick-knacks we persuaded our respondents to remain until the next day, which would protect us from malefactors during the night. We ate a few fragments of food which had been kept by chance, for we had all counted on a luxurious Chinese meal. We slept on the sand, under a rain that was happily only light, facing the village whose roofs sneered at us. And we were the guests of the Empire!

At daybreak fresh appeals, fresh summonses. In vain! Should we end our lives here? We had *nothing* left to eat. This time our Lolos thought they had done enough, and took their leave. And we were left alone—except for the blackguardly faces, which reappeared. By day we could instil respect into these fellows, but at night!

With any companion but Father de Guébriant I do not know how we should have escaped. He had learned that at a distance of nine miles up the river there was another ferry, the keeper of which dwelt on the Lolo side of the river: he, at least, could not refuse us passage. Yes, but there was no road thither. No matter; Father de Guébriant, in spite of the crushing fatigue from which he was suffering with the rest of us, would do his best to reach it; once on the other bank he would soon contrive to find some person in authority who would put an end to this murderous boycott.

So it was. Father de Guébriant, in crossing the pathless rocks which bordered the stream, must have put forth the most extraordinary efforts, must have risked his life incessantly. Although there was no mandarin on the other bank, when once he arrived there, he handled the notables of the village of Ta-Kin-Pa so skilfully that they sent to their colleagues of Ho-Kyu begging them to cease their opposition to our crossing, which opposition was due to the xenophobia of the head of the village.

Finally, as the night was falling, after twenty-four hours of discomfort—we had not even eaten since the pretence at dinner the day before—the boat which puts the two countries into communication hailed our shore and ferried us over. With what delight we once more trod on the soil of the Empire now that our success was an accomplished fact!

The gorge of the Blue River, which we were now to follow, is one of the most picturesque and at the same time one of the wildest places in the world. On the Chinese bank a track has been made: more often than not it is hewn out of the perpendicular cliff; sometimes, owing to wear and tear, or a fall of rock, it is less than twenty inches in width, and it was only by creeping along and holding by our hands, and refraining from looking at the river boiling a hundred yards below us, that we managed to advance. Our horses went forward only with the utmost difficulty, and we were forced to rope them; however, they were sure-footed as goats and untouched by vertigo.

This savage gorge had only been visited previously by Colborne Baber in 1877, and in 1898 by Captain Vaulserre—His Excellency Vou, as the people call him, who remember him very well; and it was pleasant to notice the effect produced by our countryman in these remote and inaccessible localities.

The villages were fairly numerous. Each affluent, in making its way to the river, has disintegrated the mountain-side, which has crumbled and fallen; so that the valley is wider at all such places, and the soil fallen from the top of the gorge has collected there, forming fertile rice-fields.

At the same time the bed of the river is at such points obstructed by rocks, so that rapids are produced. I believe it is safe to assert that the impossibility of navigating this immense reach of the Blue River is due solely to these obstructions; the gradient of the river is low—as far as Swei-fu it falls only some 300 yards in nearly 300 kilometres, or only five feet per mile. Its depth is certainly considerable, for its bed, which is more than a hundred yards in width here, and often narrows to thirty, expands to a width of 200 yards directly it emerges from the mountains, although its depth is never less than thirty feet. I believe a comparatively insignificant amount of labour would open channels through these obstructions, which would not re-form, as they are extremely ancient, and their cause no longer exists; when the whole river would be navigable by steam-boats, which would then serve more than 500 miles of the western territory of Sze-Chuan, Yunnan, and Tibet, which are at present entirely without communications.

All these villages hidden in the wider portions of the gorge present the same peculiarity, one which I have already mentioned in speaking of the western territories of the Lolos: many of the houses possess towers, so that aggressors may be fired at from above. When these towers are high—and we saw some of seven stories—they have a very singular aspect, which I have seen nowhere else in China; they are splayed at the bottom, and diminish in width as they rise, the wall forming a curve, so that their general style is that of the towers of the old Japanese castles.

Although the attacks of the Lolo brigands, who cross the river on floats formed of bullocks' skins, have been fairly frequent, there are no longer those great irruptions of many thousands of armed men which desolated Yunnan forty years ago, and in the course of one of which Mgr. Fenouil, the first missionary of this province, was taken, stripped of his clothes, and forced to turn a mill; for such were the first relations of the Lolos with the people of Europe, and the gracious manner in which they became known to the civilised world. The warlike activity of the Lolos has decreased on this frontier, while it has increased on the other, which agreed with all we had learned of their march from east to west.

Hoang-Ko-Chu is a little fortified town in an amazingly picturesque site. It dominates an acute angle described by the Blue River, and, thanks to the vistas opening down two valleys, enjoys a wonderful view over the Snowy Mountains of Shama and the Dragon's Head, while in the foreground three torrents fall in great cascades between great pagoda-crowned rocks, which are surmounted by ruins like those of a Salvator Rosa landscape.

Here several roads meet and the routes of our predecessors diverge, and we ourselves, having marched for two days in their footsteps, struck off in a fresh direction, which would repeatedly lead us across the route traversed by Vaulserre.

Starting from the level of the river, at a height of 1,800 feet, in two days we reached the little town of Kin-Ti, by a pass 10,000 feet in height. The whole journey was prodigious. We traversed a sort of peninsula surrounded by the Blue River. Beyond the neck, and from 5,000 to 8,000 feet above sea-level, was a sort of inclined plateau, covered with hills, villages, fortified farms, copses, and terraced rice-fields, which suddenly ended on the brink of gaping chasms hundreds or thousands of feet in depth, at the bottom of which were torrents rolling towards the river. All this was in the centre of a circle of giant mountains of striking form with snowy summits. Thus in the very midst of the fields one felt, as it were, suspended in the surrounding space—a sensation which Semiramis, I should imagine, hoped to obtain from her hanging gardens.

Scarcely had we entered the inn at Kin-Ti when a tumult arose at the door. Boyve and I ran out, to find Father de Guébriant arguing with a swelling crowd, while two of our servants held a young Chinaman. The latter had begun to rouse the people against us, saying that we were evidently vagabonds, as we had no escort, and that they ought to hack us in pieces. If our men had acted less energetically, and if Father de Guébriant had not been present to tackle the crowd, proving his knowledge of the laws and demanding the presence of the mayor and the chief of the street, who were responsible for good order, the matter might have ended seriously.

This little brawl and the opposition to our crossing the ferry at Ho-Kyu were the only adventures we ever had in China. During the whole of our journey through these supposedly xenophobic populations we were invariably welcomed affably and without a word of discourtesy.

As a general rule, it is true, we had a few soldiers with us as escort. They were indispensable; not to inspire fear, but because it is the custom that persons of quality—such as foreigners who cannot travel without passports—should be accompanied by an escort; so that the mere fact of not having an escort is a sufficient excuse for suspicion and distrust. Hence it was an easy matter for one of those rogues who abound in every town, organised by the secret societies, and always on the alert to commit a crime, to profit by the fact in order to excite a popular disturbance. It would also be absurd to pretend that one has nothing to fear in China so long as one does not provoke the mob, or to pretend that the latter professes a hatred of Europeans. The essential thing—which is not always easy for an explorer—is to observe the customs of the country.

Crossing the Blue River, we re-entered Sze-Chuan, and proceeded to Lei-Po-ting, a Chinese stronghold which watches the east of the Lolo territory. At the very gates of the town resides a powerful nzemo, formerly visited by Vaulserre, and the nephew of the prince of Shama—the very prince whose wife, by her untimely arrival, had been the cause of our being held as prisoners. The town is full of Lolos, and the prince possesses a yamen there which he visits daily.

Here we suddenly resumed, or rather recovered, our

official splendour. All the authorities—colonel, prefect, commandants, intendant—fell upon us to congratulate us upon an exploit which they found rather disconcerting, as they themselves could not cross the mountains. At our departure more than twenty soldiers attended us to protect us on the highway, although we had just crossed the lair of the Barbarians alone!

Lei-Po-ting boasts, I believe, of the finest view in all China, with the terrific Dragon's Head above it, the winding gulfs of the Blue River below, the populous plateau of Kin-Ti opposite, and the beautiful mountains of Shama in the background. As we journeyed away from it we often turned, on the summit of each hill, in order to gaze on those peaks which from the other side had so long appeared as an almost inaccessible goal, and which were now fading into the distance and the past.

Blockhouses, with garrisons of variable numbers, were strung out along the whole of the road. A whole brigade is massed on this frontier, which protects the rich plains of the Sze-Chuan; the Chinese have not forgotten that fifty-three years ago the Lolos came down as far as Chu-Hi, only eighteen miles from the large city of Swei-fu. This defence was finally organised after the great defeat of Niu-Niu Pa. A general of division, who resides at Ping-Shan, for which we were bound, commands two generals in the east, at Hoang-Leang, and in the west at Ning-Yuan-fu, whose forces occupy the circumference of the *t'ing*, or military prefectures, and innumerable fortified posts, which encircle the Lolo country throughout the whole territory of the Sze-Chuan. The gorge of the Blue River only, by which we had emerged, and which forms a part of Yunnan, is abandoned to the raids of the Lolos; but fortresses on the brink guard the passes which give access to the inhabited plateaux.

We were completely crippled with exhaustion. At Hoang-Leang we learned that a boat descends a rela-

AMONG THE RAPIDS OF THE BLUE RIVER.

To face page 126.

tively calm reach of the river, some twelve miles in length, at indefinite periods, when the stream is not too greatly swollen by the rains. We were warned that there were some dangerous rapids, but fatigue made us indifferent to a danger that went hand in hand with repose, so we chartered the boat.

This boat, some fifty feet in length, carried an immense sweep at the stern, which served as the principal rudder. There were two other rudders, one on either side ; oars with very large paddles, contrived in such a way as to offer a large amount of resistance to the current.

The river was very calm—where there were no rapids. It was at once a delicious and imposing experience to glide between those majestic cliffs, as red as porphyry. The rapids would not have been more dangerous than those of the lower Sze-Chuan, which have been described a hundred times, and which I had already run, had not a special danger existed here. The river often narrowed to a width of thirty yards ; in the right-angled turns, which were frequent, a boat fifty feet in length was each time in danger of striking the banks. Moreover, at almost every sharp turn a torrent flowed into the river, and a torrent, as I have already explained, means a natural dam and a rapid, so that the violently rushing waters surge against the perpendicular bank, and, being rejected, fall back upon themselves in an endless whirlpool. To the ordinary perils of rocks and rapids is added the danger of sudden changes of direction, in a narrow bed, and that of the whirlpools, which drag the boat under the falls or throw it against the rocks.

All these dangers are united in a remarkable degree at the place called Nosu-Kyu, "the Lolos' Gullet," a rugged gorge through which the Lolos used to emerge in order to attack passing travellers. One cannot imagine that any other motive would have induced them to venture a boat on these waters. The minutes we passed there were certainly the most anxious of our life. Once the rapid was crossed, three times did the long boat make a vain attempt to surmount the ridge of the whirlpool, and three times was it hurled back towards the centre and flung at full speed towards the fall, which would have filled and overturned it in a moment; and when at last the frantic strokes of oars and rudders had driven us from the fall, it was a miracle that we were not dashed against the cliff, so close was it. One of the rudders broke with a sinister crash, the boat whirled on its own centre like a wounded bird about to fall, and it seemed to all of us that our last hour had come, when, at a sudden order from the pilot, a desperate effort bore us over the ridge of the whirlpool where a back-wash had depressed it.

The stern of the boat had not yet emerged from the fatal gorge, and our throats were still contracted with the suspense, when our boatmen, throwing down their oars like one man, drew out their pipes and stretched themselves out on the baggage. We were still whirling round and round, and apparently about to dash against the banks; but our men, lying on their backs, contemplated the sky through the smoke of their pipes. And this was the precise moment chosen by their leader to demand the passage-money! Infallible instinct of the Chinese boatman, which makes him put forth, when he must, with an admirable coolness and discipline, the maximum of effort of which the human body is capable, and also informs him of the precise instant when the danger is past, when he can husband his forces until the next struggle!

Next day we resumed our journey by land, as our boatmen did not wish to go farther from their own town; and it was a mystery to us how they could ever regain it. Although the boat was absolutely empty, it would take them five days of prodigious efforts. Three hours later, below the rapids of Tseng-Yao-Tan, through which no boats are taken, although it appeared

THE GORGE OF THE BLUE RIVER.

MAN YING-TZE.

To face page 128.

to us extremely easy of navigation, we once more chartered a boat and finally reached Man-Ying-Tze.

This large village is extremely picturesque, with its houses raised on piles on account of floods. It has hitherto been spoken of as the terminal point of the navigation of the Blue River, and it is certainly the last commercial port. The sight of the numerous boats moored along the creek, which is formed by the mouth of a large tributary stream, sent a thrill through our hearts, for we should only have to stretch ourselves out in one of those boats and allow ourselves to glide down the stream, and in twenty days we should find ourselves in Shanghai. Truly this was the terminus of civilisation!

It is not, however, the last navigable point, as we ourselves had proved; and once more I will express my conviction that a very little modification of the river would open it to steamboats for a distance of five hundred miles, as far up-stream as Ta-li-fu.[1]

From this point I may be permitted to abridge the description of this route, which is already known. Rapids, which some travellers have described as terrible, but otherwise we should scarcely have noticed them; Ping-Shan, the residence of the commander-in-chief, where the Lolo hostages are kept, and where a French gunboat, the *Olry*, arrived a month before, beating all the records of steam navigation on this river. As we continued to descend the current, and as the ramparts of Swei-Fu came into sight, the same emotion affected all three: the French flag was floating before us, and the *Olry* was there to welcome and to fête us. To set

[1] These lines, the summary of a special report addressed three years ago to the Minister for Foreign Affairs, were already in the press when the news arrived that Captain Audemard of the navy, accompanied part of the way by the Comte de Polignac and M. Jacques Faure, had descended the whole length of this immense and supposedly unnavigable section of the river. A wonderful feat of strength and courage under present conditions, but one which goes to prove the truth of my contention.

foot on a scrap of French territory while so far from France—what a pleasant reward at the end of our troubles! It was as though our country had come to meet us.

Swei-Fu, which we reached on the 10th of June, is a fine town of fifty thousand inhabitants, admirably situated on the confluence of the Blue River and its magnificent affluent, the Min, which the Chinese regard as the main stream, and whose source we discovered afterwards in Tibet. This town, which contains no less than three Catholic parishes, with a seminary, a house for the aged, a magnificent hospital, and a college on the European model, created and managed by the French missionaries, is the seat of the bishopric of western Sze-Chuan.

The bishop, Monseigneur Chatagnon, a venerable old man whose goodness and simplicity have charmed all those who have had dealings with him, together with all the missionaries, gave us an affecting welcome. They busied themselves in ensuring that we should enjoy the rest and attention we sorely needed—Boyve especially. It was wonderful to witness the energy with which he met and endured such fatigues as I have never before experienced, although he had suffered from dysentery ever since leaving Kiao-Kio, and was consequently unable to assimilate ordinary food. He had to go straight into hospital.

At the end of a fortnight Father de Guébriant left us to go to Cheng-Tu, to demand and obtain an inquiry into the behaviour of our enemy, the prevaricating prefect. Our common trials and experiences had created between us a tie that could not be broken, and the admiration which his noble character and heroic and unselfish life had awakened in all those who knew him was in our case wedded to a sincere and respectful friendship. It was a real joy to think that I should see him again on returning, with my whole staff, to resume and enlarge our researches about Kien-Chang.

In the meantime Boyve was hardly improving. I could not wait longer, although neither of us had wasted time, for he was plotting our journeys while I was collecting abundant information relating to the regions I now wished to explore. I should have to return to Yunnan-sen to rejoin my lieutenants, exploring on the way the unknown mountain-ranges which separate the two great official routes which all travellers have followed, studying the half-subjected Lolo and Miao-tze populations which inhabit them, and searching for traces of their ancient occupation by the Lolos of the Great Cold Mountains, the surprising revelation of which was one of the principal results of our journey.

I was about to decide to send Boyve home to France, but he begged me to take him with me, despite the state of his health. Knowing by experience that there is nothing like activity to cure a man of action, I consented, and had no reason to regret it, for by the end of a month he had completely recovered. It must not be supposed that Boyve was a man of delicate constitution ; on the contrary, his strength was Herculean ; he was accustomed to every kind of sport, and in Europe was impervious to fatigue. He rendered us invaluable service in occupying himself with a thousand details of existence in countries where nothing is organised ; and if the reader can supplement the insufficiency of my descriptions by contemplating a series of photographs the like of which have never before, I believe, been obtained in these portions of China, it is to his zeal and his talents that they are due, as well as to those of Captain de Fleurelle. This, I may explain in parentheses, is why I so often, despite my protests, figure in the midst of these photographs : they were taken by my companions.[1]

*

* *

[1] I must apologise to the reader for the rarity of photographs in this chapter and the end of the last : the heat and humidity of lower Sze-Chuan were fatal to them.

On the 8th of July, accompanied by a new interpreter and our Annamites, who had rejoined us at Swei-Fu by the route which encircles the Lolo country, we resumed our wandering life : firstly travelling by boat as far as Li-Lo-Cheng, and thence, by a new route, marching to Lu-Wei through a delightful country-side, scattered with low pine-covered hills. At Lu-Wei we began to encounter the Miao-Tze, sometimes isolated in their villages, sometimes mingling with the Chinese. By the agency of the amiable Father Chinchole, who lives there, I was able to effect relations with them which were to lead to unhoped-for results—if there is ever anything which the explorer does not hope!

The Miao-Tze are universally believed to know nothing of writing. Profiting by the fact that one of them, who had a law-suit, solicited my protection, I asked him to expound the affair in Miao-Tze writing, which he did without difficulty. He assured me that the Chinese, having destroyed, at the time of the conquest, all the works they were able to discover, the Miao-Tze had hidden what was left and had, from that time forward, pretended to know nothing of the art of writing ; but in reality they possessed numerous books containing the annals of their race, and he named the owners.

As may be imagined, I was bursting with delight. An unknown writing, books relating to an unknown history—here was a discovery which would revolutionise our knowledge of these peoples. Before all else I must have the key to this writing ; so I installed my Miao-Tze at a table, and for two days, keeping him captive lest he should not reappear, I drew up with his help a vocabulary of some four hundred characters with their sounds and their sense. Thus equipped, I had only to visit the possessors of these books, to whom he would give me letters.

Another important discovery was that of an inscription in unknown characters. The interest of such documents will readily be understood, for they are records of vanished civilisations of which we know absolutely nothing. This inscription was carved in a rock some thirty miles to the south of Yong-Ning, the capital of the whole of the region of the Sze-Chuan south of the Blue River.

The "Mountain of Celestial Virtue," on which this curious inscription was discovered, is a most extraordinary site. Imagine a huge rock, three-quarters of a mile wide and one and three-quarters long, and rising to a height of from 160 to 320 feet, completely isolated, and with perpendicular sides, which can only be climbed by ladders fixed laterally to the face of the cliff. On the top one is amazed to discover a plateau covered with a magnificent forest, in the centre of which rises a beautiful pagoda. One only had to withdraw the ladders, and here was a perfect hermitage! China is full of natural curiosities of this kind.

At Yong-Ning we had joined the official highway from Sze-Chuan and Yunnan to Kwei-Chu; but we left it immediately to enter the enormous mountainous mass which straddles over three provinces and separates Kwei-Chu from the town of Wei-Ning, and was quite unknown.[1] Its geographical interest is considerable. Situated in the middle of an enormous arc of a circle described by the Blue River between Swei-Fu and Han-Kow, it contains the sources of a multitude of affluents which flow in almost every imaginable direction, finally discharging themselves into the Blue River at points as much as six hundred miles apart.

It is an unimaginable labyrinth of inter-tangled valleys which run in every direction. The soil is formed

[1] Or so, at least, we were justified in believing; and it really was unknown as far as relates to the first two-thirds of the route we followed. In arriving at Chen-Hiong, however, we learned that the English officers Captains Hunter and Pottinger had reached that town from the south nine years earlier: a report confirmed by the narrative of Major Davies, which has only just appeared.

of a very soft limestone, which is quickly eroded by running water. A frequent result is that the stream sinks too low, cannot find an escape from the valley it has entered, and finally erodes a subterranean passage and disappears into a cavern. What becomes of it then? More often than not it is impossible to say; for although a large number of streams vanish underground an equally large number emerge from caverns, and in order to discover their identity one would have to undertake a methodical exploration of the sink-holes, a procedure which the celebrated speleologists of France have not yet completed in their own country. It is probable that many are lost in faults and fissures, and go to feed the considerable streams which one sees, at a distance of some hundreds of miles, emerging fully grown from some cavern or grotto at a much lower altitude. This range, in short, is like a gigantic waterworks, whose underground conduits distribute mysterious supplies to the whole of the region lying to the south-east.

The caverns are innumerable. Very often they are fitted up by the inhabitants in order to serve as a refuge in case of trouble, which is frequent; for this purpose they are selected in places difficult of access, and having two openings, which are furnished with ramparts; the water, which is always entering by infiltration, is collected in cisterns; wood and provisions are stored there from time to time, and a guardian is installed in the fortress. The requirements of the soul are also attended to: for nothing is more contrary to the truth than the pretended irreligion of the Chinese. Sometimes a population of statues slumbers and dreams in the mystery of these caverns, and the visitor experiences a feeling of religious awe as the torchlight shows their forms emerging from the shadow, like the very spirits of the earth. Alas! why are they only of loam, which quickly crumbles in the damp and shows the hempen stuffing? If they were all of stone—as are

RIVER IN A CAVERN.

A FORTIFIED CAVERN.

To face page 134.

some, but a very few—thus evoking by their very material the idea of durability which the place demands, these caverns would be counted among the most imposing temples of the world. Such as they are, they are magnificent natural curiosities.

In this rugged region the autochthonous races, as may be imagined, have had every advantage in resisting the Chinese domination. Miao-Tze and Lolos occupy the whole country-side, the Chinese possessing only the road which formed the axis of our explorations. Yet the natives are no longer independent, and we obtained here the confirmation of the historical data gathered in the Great Cold Mountains.

The first conquest was effected by the Ming dynasty about 1380, and another more serious one by the Manchu Emperor Yong-Cheng in 1727; and it was then that the irreducible populations sought an inaccessible refuge beyond the Blue River. We now saw the country-side which was once the home of the tribes we had already visited, the battle-fields where they often held their conquerors in check; we also found remnants of the same tribes which had preferred surrender, and which still preserve continuous relations with their fellow-clansmen across the river. This was why the Lolos on the other side knew Chao-Tong and offered to lead us thither; the independent clans had not forgotten their native country. Their former invasions in force were solely with the object of recovering this territory, and neither the Chinese nor the submissive Lolos have ceased to fear or to hope that they will eventually succeed.

The Lolos and the Miao-Tze are still governed by their hereditary princes, but the latter recognise the Chinese authorities, who give them a patent and seal as though they held their power from China. The Lolos have a complete hierarchy of four castes; but the nobles, freeing their slaves at the end of a certain period, and unable to obtain more by means of raids, are far less wealthy and powerful than of old ; the class of slaves, thanks to these liberations, has largely disappeared and been replaced by that of the serfs, so that at first sight one is apt to see only freemen and equals governed by chieftains nominated by China. My experience was different, yet it was with difficulty that I realised that I was mistaken.

Since this was the cradle of the Lolos it was here that we ought to find what we had sought in vain in the Great Cold Mountains—the vestiges of their ancient civilisation. At first our persevering inquiries were absolutely without result ; we were everywhere assured that the Chinese at the time of the conquest destroyed everything that could recall the ancient Lolo domination.

Happily experience has taught me this—that the natives of all countries will often declare they know nothing when questioned about their own neighbourhood, because they are interested in keeping outsiders in ignorance of it ; but ask them of distant things or places, and if they know anything they will tell it, precisely in order to allay your suspicions. By this method I finally learned that the tombs of the princes were at Yang-Kai-Tze, at a distance of about sixty miles.

Of course, when I approached the place no one knew what I was talking about. Oh yes ! they had heard tell of a tomb with a Lolo inscription, four days' march away. . . . Good ! we would see about that later ; but now we must begin by finding those which were close at hand. An ingot of silver in one hand and a revolver in the other, I summon an inhabitant to choose between my money and his life ! As the money is to be received, not surrendered, the choice is quickly made ; his memory returns, and he leads me to a spherical hill covered with pines which he states is the burying-place. It was impossible, however, to get him to approach any closer ; the Lolo prince of that region would have him killed if it was known that he had led us to the tomb. I sent forward to verify his statement. The inscription was really there, at the base of the mound. I released my prisoner, who fled.

This time I had the long-sought treasure, a Lolo inscription! A Chinese text, which occupied half the stele, allowed us to divine its meaning and the name of the prince who reposed under the tomb.

Now it was the turn of the other inscription, which was described as being at Chao-Yui-Yei, twenty-four miles east of Wei-Ning. There I met with the same obstruction. However, I finally found a native who consented to guide, not me myself, but one of our men, who would attract less attention.

But the poor devil I sent, discovered as he was completing a rubbing of the inscription, had only just time to take to his legs with his precious booty. Hampered by his personal baggage, which he was carrying on his back, he threw it away; and it was only at the end of twenty-four miles that he was able to shake off his pursuers. Having no provisions and forced to make a long detour to rejoin us, he had to sell everything down to his shirt and his sandals, and rejoined us at the end of eight days, his whole costume a torn pair of drawers, having begged by the way. He was dying of hunger, but he had brought the inscription!

I could go on for ever relating the incidents of this hunt for documents; our visits to the mighty princes of Sôka and Tuwhei, the discovery of the tombs of some very ancient nzemos (these without inscriptions, and quite cyclopæan in character): on the summit of the mountains were three spacious circles of rocks, and in the centre of each circle was a circular depression, in which the deceased was burned and his ashes buried.

The admirable point about these tombs, whether ancient or recent, whether they are situated on the summit of a mountain or in some mysterious valley, is that they are set in surroundings of landscape that are at once secret and magnificent. They are enough to reveal the artistic nature of the race, which has never yet fully realised itself.

As for the Miao-Tze who had been named to me as the owners of books, we went to seek them at the tops of their mountains, but one and all energetically denied that they had the slightest acquaintance with any kind of writing whatever. It is true that I was escorted by Chinese soldiers and a delegate of the prefect, which was doubtless enough to quench any desire on their part to divulge their secrets. Happily the vocabulary I had secured contained intrinsic proofs of its own authenticity, and the Chinese scholars declared that it contained ancient characters abandoned in the year 213 B.C., which opens up the most interesting hypotheses concerning the past of the Miao-Tze race.

The Lolo manuscripts were less inaccessible, and I was able to acquire several, while at the same time I drew up a dictionary of characters with the aid of a Lolo scholar.

But the books I especially desired were historical records; and the search for such led to indescribable scenes. One of my Chinese agents, in order to induce me to pay £40 for a manuscript—which was certainly very fine and ancient—imagined a series of impostures that would have made a Scapin jealous. Finally he presented to me, as the owner, a colleague who was simply the leader of an association of criminals. Threatened with denunciation, both thief and agent thought it prudent to disappear then and there, so that in spite of myself I was left, without paying a penny, in possession of this superb manuscript, one of the finest jewels of our collection.

To sum up, our researches led to this result: that this country is still only half-subjected to the Chinese, and that it still contains the autochthonous races in a relatively pure condition. The independent Lolos are thus balanced by tribes of the same blood on the right bank of the Blue River, which is the ancient cradle of the race ; and these latter tribes, despite the apparent submission of certain sections, still form a formidable mass of people conscious of their worth and proud of their party, which one day will doubtless again play an important part.

At Wei-Ning we rejoined the official highway. Although we still had many happy finds without departing too far from the track, consisting especially of steles commemorating the stages of the Chinese conquest, I will not dwell upon them here, as it is high time to relate the adventures of my two lieutenants during this long separation of nearly five months.

CHAPTER VI

THE INDEPENDENT MIAO-TZE

THE instructions I had left with Captain de Fleurelle directed him to seek out all the archæological monuments in the neighbourhood of Yunnan-sen, to study the Lolos to the east of Yunnan, and finally to attempt the exploration of the unknown and supposedly inaccessible region inhabited by the independent Miao-Tze of Kwei-Chu.

Although the latter task, which was an extremely hazardous one, was to him the most seductive, Captain de Fleurelle had the good sense to defer it.

It must never be forgotten that China is not an open country; that the foreigner can only travel by permission of the Government, and that the latter can always take advantage of a momentary difficulty to refuse the authorisation to go where one desires. Even without manifesting open opposition, there is a very simple method of paralysing the traveller; all the machinery of transport—mules, horses, porters—are directly dependent on the administration, which has the absolute control of all traffic, so that your carriers and drivers will desert you at a word from a mandarin and you will be unable to replace them. Nothing is easier than to pick a quarrel which will serve as an excuse for such behaviour.

Now at the time of which I write the important French undertaking, the construction of the Yunnan railway, made the goodwill of the Chinese administration a necessity, and any unpleasant incident might be prejudicial to the national interests. Our arrival, on account of our military rank, had caused some uneasiness ; the Chinese journals had referred to us as the advance-guard of the French troops ! Fleurelle, who would be travelling in the two provinces of Yunnan and Kwei-Chu, subject to the authority of the Viceroy of Yunnan-sen, judged it prudent clearly to demonstrate beforehand the purely scientific nature of his duties.

With Lepage he then proceeded to undertake a methodical search for archæological monuments. This was by no means an easy thing. In China everything is dilapidated, but scarcely anything is old. Whereas we live in the belief that the Chinese venerate their antiquities, they really know nothing about them. Certainly they are nearly all mentioned in the monographies which have by order been compiled in each province and in every city, but these books are extremely rare and scarcely any one has read them ; still less has any one taken the trouble to verify their assertions. Moreover, during the many centuries that have passed since these books were written, many monuments have been thrown down, others have been transformed, the steles have disappeared, broken, buried, or carried away, and scarcely anything is as it was. If you ask the inhabitants, they will not know what you are speaking of.

Moreover, the Chinese pay little or no attention to matters relating to their great men, and the history of other nations is of no interest to them. Anything that concerns the indigenous peoples or the Mahommedans is ignored ; the steles of the Mongol dynasty have almost everywhere been broken ; the Tibetan inscriptions are regarded with contempt.

Yet millions of steles encumber the pagodas, stand at the cross-roads, and border the highways. They celebrate the benefactors who have restored a temple, repaired a road, or built a bridge ; or, like those placards of the Touring Clubs which, having warned the traveller of a "dangerous corner," add the name of the generous donor of the notice, they indicate the distance from this or that locality, and then, inevitably, the name of the munificent person to whom this precious information is due.

Unfortunate archæologist! He has to decipher all this nonsense in order to find a few inscriptions worth the trouble of impression, which will throw a little light upon the history of those non-Chinese regions which have intentionally been left in darkness.

Nevertheless, our comrades gathered a rich harvest. Among others they found several Tibetan inscriptions, witnesses of the ancient influence of Tibet, which even extended its suzerainty over the Yunnan; two inscriptions in Mongol characters, the first of such to be discovered; the tombs, with a Sino-Arab inscription, of the first Governor of the Yunnan, who was a Mussulman descendant of the Prophet, the Seyyid Edjell Chams ed-Din Omar; the Mongols having entrusted him with the organisation of the province, which he had just conquered; for it was the Mongols that incorporated this country with China.

But the discovery of these precious documents was less exciting than the discovery of a truly artistic monument, of which no record has ever been made, although it was known to a few Europeans in Yunnan-sen. This is an octagonal pyramid of seven stories, in granite; it is covered with figures and bas-reliefs carved in the most exquisite detail. The plinth is covered with an inscription in Sanscrit, the first yet unearthed and the execution of this marvel would seem to have been due, at least in part, to the chisel of some Hindoo artist. This monument is contemporary with the Song dynasty (tenth to thirteenth centuries); there are few in all China to be compared to it for beauty.

Once it was thoroughly established, by their very success, that their interests were of the scientific order,

THE GRANITE STUPA.

ROCKS IN THE PLAIN OF LU-NAN-CHU.

To face page 142.

our comrades were able to take the road and commence their study of the Lolos of the east.

These are the Lolos, subject and accessible, who have been visited by numerous Europeans ; and it is chiefly they who have been written about, while the observations made among them have been extended to the whole race. But in all these descriptions there is no point of resemblance between them and the independent clans. Abbé Vial, who has devoted several volumes to them, assures us that "the Lolo is to the Chinaman what a dog is to a tiger," which is a truly unfortunate remark to make of the formidable warriors of the Great Cold Mountains. The rest is in keeping with this remark. To speak of this race with authority, it is essential to compare all its various elements.

Several missionaries being engaged in the evangelisation of these Lolos, the best means of overcoming their distrust of strangers was to profit by their position in the country. Crossing the region of Lu-Nan-Chu, which is as weird as Karnak, for the rocks rise out of the ground like the crests of breaking waves, so that the plain is not unlike another Along Bay emptied of the sea, our companions reached Tudza, a little village lost in the mountains, where the natives would certainly be of purer blood than in the plains. There resides Father H. Maire, who placed himself, with his Lolos, at the entire disposal of the travellers

The physical aspect of these Lolos, as revealed by photographs and anthropometrical data, together with all the characteristics of their social organisation and their character, seems to be absolutely different from that of the independent tribes. No princes, no seigneurs, no slaves ; one class, of free and equal peasants. The chief is nominated by them to the Chinese authorities, who ratify the choice. Their type is not purely Chinese, but neither is it in any way precise or determined ; in different individuals it approaches the types of all the races of the region, and notably that of the Tai; it is a half-breed type.

Most assuredly, to study the Lolo race from these samples could only lead one to the very reverse of the truth; these people are anything but Lolos. However, even among the independent clans we found two analogous castes, the serfs and the slaves, which were recruited from outside. Bearing this in mind, does it not seem probable that the Lolos of the Yunnan, who are subject to the Chinese, are simply the descendants of serfs or slaves whose masters have disappeared, either killed in resisting the invaders, or reduced and dispossessed, or having fled? As a matter of fact, one does sometimes find a few Lolos of a well-marked type, the same as that of the Great Cold Mountains. The Chinese infallibly call them Black Lolos, the very name given to the nobles in the north. They marry only among themselves, and, although they exercise no power, enjoy unusual consideration and respect. If there were in these parts descendants of the ancient seigneurs, deprived of their power and their estates, would they not appear precisely thus?

These discoveries were of great interest, and by comparing the manners of these ancient serfs with those of the independent Lolos it became easier to determine what was due to the pure race and what to extraneous influences.

Among such characteristics I will cite one as being particularly curious. Instead of the children living with their parents, they inhabit two large houses, one for the boys and one for the girls, and there they sleep until their marriage, although they eat and work with their parents. It may be supposed that such a custom does not tend to increase the power of family ties, and that the extreme liberty accorded to the children may lead to certain excesses.

The end of the harvest is the signal for numerous marriages, but it would seem as though these were

TAI WOMEN.

LOLO WOMEN OF TUDZA.

To face page 144.

to some extent merely the pretext for luxurious feasts; for after the wedding-night the young wife usually returns to her companions in the girls' house, leaving it only from time to time in order to visit her husband. Finally she remains in his house or ceases to see anything more of him, just as she pleases.

The costumes worn by the women on ceremonious occasions are highly original. They are adorned with horizontal stripes of many colours. As in the Great Cold Mountains, the women do not wear the Chinese trousers, except where the influence of the Chinese is particularly strong; the petticoat is triumphant, but is worn rather short, and falls over buttoned leggings. The head-dresses are particularly curious. The men, although dressed like Chinese, do not wear the pigtail.

Continuing their study of the Lolo populations which cover the whole of the eastern portion of the Yunnan, our comrades turned their steps towards Kwei-Chu, in order to proceed to the exploration of the country of the independent Miao-Tze.

On the way they passed through the most wonderful landscapes, such as that in which the peak of Pei-La-shan, 8,800 feet high, rises in the midst of flooded rice-fields, which have the appearance of a lake on which the villages float like islands, and which is bordered on the east by a multitude of isolated or piled-up rocks; rocks of those extraordinary shapes which Chinese painting has made familiar to us, though not life-like. But what horrible roads ran through this dreamland landscape!

Or else there would be a long series of basins without outlets; the waters, distributed on the surface through the rice-fields, and retained by dikes, being eventually entirely absorbed, without forming any current which could excavate a valley; sometimes, at the lowest point of the basin, there would be an orifice which would absorb the surplus water, if there was any. Nothing could be more singular than these gigantic funnels, whose sides are formed by series of terraces, of rice-fields glittering like the facets of mirrors, or covered with the finest growth of green. They furnish the typographer with all the contour lines he could need all ready traced; but, by a singular irony, they will only serve him to reproduce the most surprising and unusual formations. In the long run the culture of irrigated rice-fields exercises a considerable influence on the level of the soil, and gives rise to phenomena of the greatest interest to those who wish to study the configurations so peculiar to China.

Our comrades decided to make Hing-Yi-fu the base of their operations among the independent Miao-Tze, as according to the maps their country begins there.

But what a surprise awaited them! There were no Miao-Tze! The whole population belonged to the Tai race, or Dioï, according to the local pronunciation.

This race is, with the Lolos and the Miao-Tze, the most important of southern China, and extends over a great portion of Indo-China, notably over Siam; its future may be judged by the prosperous state of the latter kingdom. All the data collected in Siam as well as in Tonkin agree in pointing out a northern origin for the Tai populations settled there; and while in Yunnan the Tai are mixed with other indigenous races and largely with the Chinese, in the neighbourhood of Hing-Yi-fu they appeared to be settled in groups and of a strongly accentuated personality. This, therefore, was the region in which to study them and determine the characteristics of the race.

Hing-Yi-fu, entirely surrounded with ruined forts and towers, presents a most picturesque appearance. These ruins are souvenirs of the great insurrection of the Tai, who forty years ago united with the Mussulmans and the Taiping in an attempt to throw off the Imperial yoke. They entertain a most lively hatred of the Chinese, so that it is the more singular that they should originate, according to their traditions, from the seemingly purely Chinese region of the Kiang-Si.

In the year 941 A.D. a Chinese army, composed of troops levied in this province, took possession of the country. According to the usual procedure, these soldiers were settled on the soil by distributing the land among them, and their descendants constitute the present population of the country. The name by which they are known has no other origin; they are called Chong-Kya—"heavy cuirasses"—for the soldiers of the conquest wore cuirasses of buffalo-hide. At that time the country was populated by various indigenous people; the soldiers having espoused the daughters of the conquered inhabitants, their descendants were of very mixed blood, so that the Chinese, pronouncing the name Chong-Kya with a different intonation, gave it the injurious sense of "son of all races," or mongrel.

From this it results that the Tai language brought by these victorious soldiers originates from Kiang-Si; which still further reduces the domain of the pure Chinese! What will be left of it if researches of this kind become more general, and what will become of the belief in the homogeneity of China?

It is not generally known that Hing-Yi-fu had its period of splendour. At the time of the conquest of China by the Manchus, 250 years ago, the last emperor of the Ming dynasty took refuge there and made it his capital; and for many years he held the invaders at bay, still being recognised as emperor by a number of provinces. We know that this prince allowed his mother and his wife, the Empresses Anne and Helen, to become Christians, and his son to be baptized in the name of Constantine. His victory would have been the victory of Christianity. The city contains numerous vestiges of this extremely interesting period.

This unfortunate prince had so far won the affection of the native population that even to-day they proclaim their attachment to the vanished dynasty; and mysterious representatives of it still exist, though no one knows where. Whoever should engineer a rising in the name of the Mings would be certain of a following. Thus the survival of the prestige of the ancient Chinese dynasty is found oddly combined in the country of the Tai with their hatred of the Chinese.

For the moment the native populations are not at war with the Imperial Government—so long as the latter does not obtrude itself. Between Hing-Yi-fu and Kwei-Yang, the capital of Kwei-Chu, there is no direct road; but there are two roads each of which makes a considerable detour, one towards the north and one towards the south. These enclose a piece of territory that the Chinese never penetrate. This was the country my companions wished to explore.

It was not an easy undertaking. The conductors of the convoy, although chartered for the whole journey, had never ceased their protestations against the savage countries and the execrable roads across which they were led; and when they heard of the proposal to cross the country of the Miao-Tze their complaints redoubled. Fleurelle, justly suspicious, very wisely took every precaution; he gave the men only the smallest advances on the promised sum, and at night he had the pack-saddles put in his room. In this way he was assured against any attempts at flight.

At the last Chinese village his first care, at daybreak, was to see that the animals were in good condition to undergo the trials which awaited them. There were no mules! The terrified muleteers had deserted in the night, abandoning their pack-saddles and the money which was due to them!

Our companions were apparently checkmated. Fleurelle, however, soon came to a decision. Leaving the baggage in the care of Lepage, who would occupy himself by gathering his usual harvest of information, he made for one of the towns on the border of the

Miao-Tze territory: Tze-Heng, where he knew he would find a missionary, Father Willatte, who would certainly serve as his interpreter; and he demanded a new caravan of the prefect.

The mandarin refused. He could not allow them to enter that country; for "the Chinese do not go there." Fleurelle, however, was so firm, stated so positively that I was awaiting him on the other side, and that he could not disobey my orders, that the mandarin gave way; let them go if they would, but at their own risk and peril! Finally, as they set out, seeing that nothing could reduce their obstinacy, and fearing that he might be reproached for a dereliction of duty, he decided to send two soldiers with them.

Two soldiers! A poor escort, to be sure, if there had been any danger; but Fleurelle was about to learn, with astonishment, and even with regret, that there was none. Or rather there was one, and a grave one: the danger of slipping to the bottom of the ravines. They were leaving the "mountains of stone" and entering the "mountains of earth." In these ranges of slippery, sliding clay *there is not a single road;* only a few tracks barely practicable to a traveller on foot. Fleurelle, who knew this, had tried to obtain porters, but in vain: for at that season all the inhabitants were busy in the fields. No muleteer was willing to follow him, so he had to get the sub-prefect to requisition them; and it was before that official that their engagements were signed, with threats of the most serious punishment should they break their word.

Marching over these mountains of earth was a terrible business. It was the middle of the rainy season; the sodden clay gave easily under the weight of the laden mules. At every moment almost the animals had to be unloaded in order to lead them across some slippery slope or morass; and then the muleteers had to carry the items of the load, one by one, until as far as Pei-Tseng, two days up-stream. No less than fifty junks passed before him in the course of two hours.

This, however, was merely a moral satisfaction, as there was no ferry nor ford; why should there be since there was no road? Fleurelle hail d the boats, but no one replied. He ordered the two soldiers to get on a fragile raft made of three bamboos which happened to be lying to hand, and to requisition a junk; the two soldiers, who were not particularly courageous by temperament, seemed extremely embarrassed at the idea of such a task.

Happily the guide was a long-headed individual. He took the tunic of one of the soldiers—which of course composed his entire uniform—and thus transformed into a representative of the Imperial authority he boarded the raft, which sunk deep under his weight, gained the middle of the stream, leaped aboard a boat, and forced the boatman to approach the bank. The boat would only hold two beasts at a time, but the soldiers, fired with emulation, leaped upon the raft themselves, and requisitioned four junks in succession: quite a flotilla, which allowed of a comfortable crossing

Finally, after a further two days' march over indescribable paths, my comrades reached Wang-Mu, a little town regarded as the centre of the non-Chinese country. There they were rewarded for their pains by learning that the "independent Miao-Tze" *are neither Miao-Tze nor independent*.

Since leaving Hing-Yi-fu there had been no change either of language, habitations, or costume; the people were always the same Tai. Why the Chinese, who call them Chong-Kya at Hing-Yi-fu call them Miao-Tze beyond that town is difficult to explain, unless by the fundamental observation that they attach no importance to ethnography so that the same name often serves them to distinguish peoples who are perfectly distinct, while the same race is often called by several different names. For this reason no importance must be attached to their classifications. A typical example of this peculiarity is the fact that in Kwei-Chu they distinguish forty-six tribes of Miao-Tze, among which are enumerated the Chong-Kya and the Lolos!

Neither were these natives independent. It is true that they only obey their seigneurs; but that is the case in almost all the mountain populations of China. These seigneurs, however, recognise the authority of the mandarin, and pay him the tax which they collect from their subjects. At Wang-Mu resides a Chinese under-officer with an escort of *two* men: he has no power, but he represents the Imperial authority. It is therefore quite incorrect to say that this country is independent: it is autonomous, to be sure, but as many others are; its real peculiarity was happily expressed by Fleurelle, who called it "the country which the Chinese do not enter."

Our companions everywhere received the most hospitable welcome, lodging in the houses of the natives, who for the most part refused to accept the smallest present. The houses are built on a uniform model; they are set on the hillside, so that they are level with the slope on the inner side while the opposite end of the house is raised high above the ground. The cellar constitutes a stable; the house itself, whose principal entrance is in the outer wall, and is reached by a staircase, comprises a large common room in the centre, which contains the altar of the ancestors; on either side is a variable number of smaller rooms. These houses are very large; the roof is high and carefully constructed, and all is meticulously clean. The greatest good-nature reigns throughout.

Yet these peasants who welcome the traveller so affably are most jealous of their liberty, and extremely courageous. At the time of the last war, forty years ago, they were never conquered; after the Mussulmans and the Taiping were crushed they dispersed, and the Chinese did not pursue them into their inaccessible mountains. Their one source of weakness is the seigneurs; they, in order to squeeze them at their ease, seek and obtain support from the Chinese authorities. The situation is therefore absolutely the reverse of that we observed among the independent Lolos.

This bad understanding between peasants and seigneurs is the more remarkable in that the Tai are distinguished by their solidarity. A man of no matter what village is everywhere received and sheltered in the most cordial fashion, and in case of war all will hasten to the assistance of their fellow-countrymen. Yet their physical dissimilarities are so great that we cannot assign them to any definite type; they are truly "sons of all races." Their seigneurs are probably distinguished by a special origin.

It is at Wang-Mu that the great native chief of the region generally resides: Mu, who was unfortunately absent during Fleurelle's visit.[1]

Once more they entered unexplored territory, in order to reach Kwei-Hua, where they would find a Catholic mission. The fact that unknown territories exist near so many of the French missions proves how enterprising our missionaries are, and how exceedingly difficult of penetration those territories must be to have hitherto escaped their efforts. And indeed Captain Fleurelle's notes are a continual record of ever-recurring obstacles, of dangerous or exhausting experiences, and under the impassive style of the record it is easy for one who knows the country to divine the continual

[1] A section of the Lyons Mission has reached Wang-Mu by following the valley of the Hua-Kiang after leaving Tze-Heng, thus avoiding the impracticable mountains which my officers perseveringly explored. The activity and courage of the Mission Lyonnaise, various groups of which have covered the whole of Western China with their journeyings, have forced us, in our search for the truly unexplored, to tackle the most inaccessible territories. The excellent narratives of the Mission exempt me from giving any account of Chinese affairs, and enable me to devote myself solely to the natives.

and extraordinary efforts without which advance had been impossible.

Finally, when approaching Kwei-Hua, our comrades at last discovered what they had sought so long: the Miao-Tze.

They were not difficult to recognise! Nothing could be more typical than the costume of the women, which was exactly the same as we had observed it in Yunnan and Tonkin: a short petticoat, falling barely to the knee, leaving the calves and ankles bare, and a bodice with a sailor's collar, cut low in a triangle in front. From now onwards the Miao-Tze were encountered everywhere, mingled, but not confounded, with the Tai; the two peoples usually occupied separate villages and obeyed their own chiefs.

The name Miao-Tze has been applied to all these populations by the Chinese: for to any one travelling from Kwei-Yang, the capital of Kwei-Chu, which lay not far away, the Miao-Tze would be the first people encountered, and they would attract the greatest attention by their costume and bearing. But they do not deserve the title of "independent"; only the Tai deserve it, and only in a limited degree. The village chiefs of the Miao-Tze are in most places not hereditary, but appointed or at least approved by the Chinese authorities; and in time of revolt the Miao-Tze have held aloof while the Tai have risen.

The submission of the Miao-Tze to the Imperial authority must be attributed in the first place to their lack of cohesion: one tribe has no acquaintance with another, and there is no system of mutual aid or co-operation; in the second place they were formerly vanquished and dispossessed of the greater part of their territory by the Tai.

According to traditions, which we have every reason for believing, the country was formerly inhabited by other peoples, the Yao and the Keilao. The Miao-Tze, coming from Hu-Nan or Kiang-Si, took possession of it

MIAO-TZE DANCERS.

To face page 155.

at a period which we cannot precisely determine, and put the population to the sword, leaving but a few insignificant remnants. Numerous tumuli are found in this country, which are known as the tombs of the Keilao; it appears that after their extermination they were buried there fifty at a time. As for the Yao, for some unknown reason the Miao-Tze have conceived a very tardy fear of them, and every year they hold an expiatory ceremony over their tombs for the purpose of appeasing their *manes*.

These Yao, of whom I have also found traces in the north of Yunnan, are none other than the Man, whom we had observed in Tonkin. The important result of such ethnographical discoveries is obvious: certain tribes of French Indo-China are evidently representatives of a race which has occupied enormous tracts of territory, and which, according to certain Chinese historians, has played an important part in history, and to-day, in all probability, thanks to the alliance of the conquerors with the women of the conquered races, they still form the basis of numerous populations.

But the Miao-Tze conquerors were themselves conquered by the Tai, who followed them from the same regions of central China: and in the country which rumour calls their own they play only a secondary part. The Tai have retained the prestige of victory in such a degree that when one of them dies in a neighbourhood inhabited by Miao-Tze, his decease is announced to the population by firing a triple salute.[1]

The Miao-Tze are distinguishable wherever found by one absolute peculiarity: they love and practise the dance. Dancing is absolutely foreign to the Chinese; not that they despise the art, as has been stated; on

[1] The arrival and departure of important personages is thus signalled in China. It goes without saying that as there are no cannon anywhere in this region the three shots are really caused by the explosion of heavy petards.

the contrary, the rites of certain ceremonies comprise dances of a noble and dignified character; but as an amusement dancing is unknown. The Miao-Tze, on the contrary, are passionately fond of dancing as a recreation.

Their dance, which is highly original, is everywhere the same. The men play a curious instrument—a kind of tube like that of the hautboy ; the reed is usually of copper. The instrument is closed at the end, and six tubes of bamboo of varying lengths are attached to it ; it is by these tubes that the wind emerges, giving notes regulated by means of holes which the musician stops or leaves open with his ten fingers ; in short, the instrument is like a little organ with six pipes.[1] While playing the musician himself cuts capers ; very lively in Tonkin, less so in Yunnan and Kwei-Chu.

When the women take part in the dance they form a circle round the dancers, all holding hands and revolving in time to the music.

The market of the town of Chen-Ning-Chu is celebrated afar for the number of various native tribes and of costumes of many colours which are to be seen assembled there like a bed of flowers : Miao-Tze in red, blue, and white, and black (most remarkable of all, and very different from the rest) ; Miao-Tze ornamented with flowers, and Miao-Tze unadorned. The market is known as the Flowery Market. The sight is a charming one, and the ethnographer may reap an easy and abundant harvest.

One of the most curious customs of these people is that of profiting by all solemn occasions—marriages, feasts of whatever nature, or funerals—to relate the traditions referring to the earliest ages of the world, the Creation, the Deluge, and so forth. It is an interminable story, to which the crowd listens without

[1] Afterwards I found an almost identical instrument among the Mongols. In the regions in between it is absolutely unknown.

fatigue; they will interrupt it in order to eat or sleep, and once more it is resumed, often to last for several days; and able narrators have acquired a widespread fame by these performances. Their recitals vary slightly from one village to another. The most singular point about these traditions is the almost perfect identity, in spite of certain items of purely local colour, of their account of the Deluge with that of the Bible.

At Chen-Ning-Chu our comrades[1] rejoined the high-road from Hing-Yi-fu to Kwei-Yang, which runs round the "country where the Chinese do not go"; but their task was far from being completed.

They had first of all to visit an inscription famous throughout the south of China: that of the Red Rock. This is an inscription in unknown characters which give rise to all manner of hypotheses. Are they Chinese characters so ancient that their form is forgotten, or those of some non-Chinese race which has disappeared? The Chinese have published certain learned monographs on this inscription, and agree in attributing it to the Emperor Yiu-Kao-Tsong (1300 B.C.), who erected it in commemoration of his conquest of Kwei-Chu: this would make it by far the most ancient monument in China. Hitherto we had possessed two casts of it in France, which were bought from the Chinese; but as they did not agree, and as no European had ever seen the inscription itself, you may judge of the importance of studying it on the spot.

It is situated on the summit of a mountain, which is not easily climbed. What was the amazement of my companions on reaching it to find that it was not incised, but painted, which rendered the process of casting impossible, and that it did not in any way whatever resemble the reproductions published or in circulation!

From the inquiry they then undertook it appeared

[1] They could not sufficiently praise the good offices of Father Ménel at Kwei-Hua and Fathers Roux, Bazin, and Grimard at Chen-Ning-fu.

clearly that all the facsimiles current have been fabricated by people who had not even seen the Red Rock, but emitted their forgeries in perfect security, the difficulty of access to the inscription, hidden away in the heart of a remote province, having prevented any discovery of their trickery. The tracing which my colleagues took of this gigantic inscription—not without difficulty, for it is twenty feet long by ten feet in height—condemns all the known reproductions, as well as the ingenious studies based upon them. It is the same with the verification of all the Chinese monuments of high antiquity. As for the origin and sense of this mysterious inscription, the problem is still unsolved.

Returning to Hing-Yi-fu, our comrades set out in the direction of Yunnan by a new route. This enabled them to study other groups of Lolos, and to study a number of steles of great importance.[1] Leaving Kyu-Tsing, their route coincided with that which I was to follow with Boyve a little later on, so that we were able to compare our data.

Finally, on July 8th, our two comrades re-entered Yunnan-sen, anticipating my own arrival. They were worn out with fatigue, for they had dispensed with the most elementary comforts during their long circuit; but they had obtained the most valuable results.

In the first place, they had travelled 800 miles: 220 through country absolutely unknown, and 220 more through country already explored, but not charted; which enabled them to fill up extensive lacunæ in the maps and to correct considerable errors; they had collected thirty inscriptions relating to the history of the country; eleven vocabularies of native dialects; seven Lolo manuscripts; numerous photographs of characteristic types, costumes and landscapes; anthropometric measurements; detailed notes relating to the different tribes; and finally, observations of great interest on

[1] With the efficient assistance of Father Tapponnier and especially of Father Badie.

the economic possibilities of the country and its relations with French Indo-China.

Above all, they revealed the singular and unexpected fact that the " independent Miao-Tze " do not exist; that the country is inhabited by the Tai—an intelligent, hospitable people, with a historic past, and, like their brothers the Siamese, capable of great progress—a people that must hereafter be included in the category of civilised peoples, and within the range of our political and scientific preoccupations.

Captain de Fleurelle, by his spirit of initiative, his calm and unfailing tenacity in the face of obstacles, and the methodical manner in which he directed this exploration, and Captain Lepage, by his knowledge of Chinese and his zeal in gathering information, had succeeded in accomplishing in the happiest and completest manner the mission I had confided to them.

CHAPTER VII

ROUND THE LOLO TERRITORY

ON the 1st of September the whole Mission was once more united at Yunnan-sen. Each of the two groups brought many documents which had to be classified and compared so as to determine which points were settled and which should be further examined. Routes had to be plotted, photographs developed and printed.[1] It also required a considerable amount of labour to decipher the rubbings and impressions of inscriptions, even summarily.

During this time our archæological researches were continued. The details of these researches will find place in our scientific publications; but it will not perhaps be out of place to give the reader, now that a railway is running to Yunnan-sen, some idea of the curious monuments to be found there.

Three miles to the east of the town a grove of trees shelters a majestic stairway, which leads, under a series of triumphal arches, to the summit of a hill from which a most beautiful temple rises. The central monument is a pagoda, constructed entirely of chiselled and gilded bronze; this is situated on a lofty terrace

[1] During all the remainder of our journeys our negatives were developed at latest within three or four days of exposure, thanks to the development tank, which enabled us to operate in full daylight, and which I cannot praise too highly; but the reduction of our baggage made it impossible to take it with us while exploring the Lolo country.

MOUNTAINS OF KWEI-CHU.

MIAO-TZE WOMEN.

To face page 148.

BRONZE PAGODA.

THE PAGODA OF THE FIVE HUNDRED GENII.

To face page 160.

Sculpture in stone, which we usually find at the very dawn of all civilisations, and of which we discover magnificent specimens at later periods—though due, perhaps, to another race—seems to be only now in its infancy in the China we know to be already aged, although it often gives the impression of a young and promising people. In many places we have discovered bas-reliefs or statues of stone executed of late years by peasants, while the preceding centuries have left us nothing of the kind.

The "Mountain of the West" offers an example of this kind. It overhangs the lake of Yunnan-sen, a vertical wall many hundreds of feet in height. The Chinese, who "arrange" the most wonderful landscapes, have here done their best. The accessible terraces are covered with pagodas and pleasure-pavilions; higher still the thickness of the rocky wall is pierced by a gallery, which is lighted by bays, and finally, passing under a series of porticoes, ends in a slight projection of the rock. Here are grottoes excavated by the hand of man, peopled with divinities hewn out of the living rock, and covered with high and low reliefs. These sculptures are crude and clumsy; but there is really great art in the conception of this gallery, by means of which you taste the refined and paradoxical pleasure of burying yourself in the entrails of the rock in order to discover the sky, the azure reaches of the lake, and the middle spaces of air.

In the city itself the pagoda of Wen Tong Tze, which is built against a hill, conceals a quantity of steles and inscriptions, which are scattered over the rocks in the most picturesque fashion. The pagoda itself is remarkable for the paintings adorning the principal temple, and for two gigantic dragons which protect the high altar. It is approached by a characteristic avenue, passing under a triumphal arch.

Not far away is another pagoda, which should be

of marble, ornamented by graceful festoons. It is protected by a circular rampart, surmounted by towers, whence a magnificent view may be enjoyed. Dating from the thirteenth century, this temple was restored by the celebrated General Wu-San-Kwei, who placed the present Manchu dynasty on the throne, and received from it the government of Yunnan with the title of king; finally he revolted and proclaimed himself Emperor. At his death he was obeyed by half China.

This rebel, who so nearly overturned the dynasty he erected, is officially venerated at Yunnan, and we may see on each side of the bronze pagoda a gigantic sword and club, which are supposed to represent his arms, accompanied by laudatory inscriptions. There are many legends relating to Wu-San-Kwei; one, which is universally believed, is to the effect that his body has never been buried, but reposes in a silver coffin hanging from the ceiling of a secret chamber in the palace of the Viceroy; and on the day on which it touches the ground the Manchu dynasty will fall.

Another pagoda, far less artistic but extremely curious, stands among the mountains to the west; it is the Temple of the Five Hundred Genii. There is scarcely a large town in all China that has not a pagoda so named (unless it be the Temple of the Ten Thousand Genii). It contains an extraordinary collection of statues representing the saints of Buddhism, to which have been added the heroes of Taoïsm and Confucianism. These statues are usually of life size, made of a paste of loam, and painted. Some are life-like and expressive, others grimacing and grotesque. Sculpture is not an art in China, but a trade practised by poor devils who are wretchedly ill-paid; it would be expecting too much of them to demand that they should all be talented. Yet we cannot deny that there is imagination, a sense of the picturesque, and sometimes a wonderful truth in these productions of simple artisans.

THE "MOUNTAIN OF THE WEST."

To face page 162.

visited by those who believe that China despises war and soldiers. This temple is raised to the memory of the natives of Yunnan killed by the enemy. Vertical tablets, of a size in proportion to the rank or grade recorded, bear the names of each of the officers and soldiers, with the name of the campaign in which he perished; which is equivalent to saying that Tonkin and the French often figure in these funereal but glorious lists. Such temples exist in all the provincial capitals, and in many other cities also; but I have never seen them mentioned, nor any other of the many characteristics of the absolute worship which is accorded military valour. But perhaps people will prefer to go on denying the fact.[1]

Torrential and exceptionally late rains, occasioning dangerous inundations, delayed us at Yunnan-sen far longer than I had intended. It was not that we were afraid of getting wet; we had marched through the whole of the principal rainy season, which lasts from June 15th to September 15th, and I have not even mentioned the storms—much less severe, by the way, than we had expected—which we encountered during that period. But to resume our advance in this time of deluge would have been absurd, for we should have risked the total loss of our belongings, especially in crossing the flooded rivers, and a few days of waiting might bring us settled fair weather. Delaying thus from day to day, it was the 1st of November before we could leave Yunnan-sen, where the devoted assistance of the consul and the missionaries had greatly facilitated our researches.[2]

We were now going to complete the circle I had already begun to trace around the independent Lolo

[1] I should like to refer all these persons for whom an idea once admitted is not an impregnable dogma to my book, "La Chine novatrice et guerrière" ("Progressive and War-like China").

[2] We had particularly to thank Fathers Maire, Ducloux, Oster, and Liétard.

territory, which was so far complete only from Swei-Fu to Yunnan-sen ; studying on the way the various more or less subject populations—Lolo, Miao-Tze, Lissu, Si-Fan ; and seeking among them the ethnical characteristics which we had already observed among the pure remnants of the race. To attain these objects we should have to penetrate the heart of a mountain region impracticable to our convoy, so I adopted as the axis of our march the ordinary highway from Yunnan-sen to Sze-Chuan by way of the Kien-Chang. This road would be followed by our baggage, while we ourselves, taking a light equipment, should push forward to such points as appeared necessary.[1]

In this way Wu-Ting-Chu would serve as a centre for the study of the numerous varieties of Lolos, Miao-Tze, and Lissu—a race which hitherto had only been reported in a very distant region, in the direction of Tibet ; and our present route would form a continuation of the route which Boyve and I had already followed as far as Ning-Wen-fu, and would enable us to collect the curious traditions relating to the second Emperor of the Ming dynasty, Kien-Wen. The official history states that he was burned when the rebels fired his palace in 1402, while admitting that in 1440 an old bonze, who was then on the point of death, asserted that he was the Emperor. Now at Wu-Ting-Chu every one asserts that the Emperor, escaping in disguise, found refuge in the fine monastery which overlooks that city. His survival under a borrowed name gave rise to the most romantic episodes, the localities of which we were shown ; it was a Chinese version of the escape of Louis XVII. from the Temple. We recommend the elucidation of this fascinating point of history to the specialists.

At a distance of eighteen miles from Wu-Ting-Chu we

[1] Map II. This highway has been followed by several travellers: M. Bonvalot, Prince Henri d'Orléans, M. Madrolle, the French consul, &c.

IN THE PAGODA OF YUAN-TONG-TZE.

To face page 164.

went to visit the only two Lolo inscriptions that had previously been reported, and we had the good fortune to find that one of them, which had never been seen by any European, was duplicated by a Chinese text which had not been recorded and which furnished the sense of the inscription. All these inscriptions, dating from 1533 and 1534, celebrate a Lolo prince of that region.

A little further on we made Ma-Kai our centre. We finally discovered yet another Lolo inscription—the fifth—not far from the residence of the young prince of Fan-Chu and his mother, the regent, whose guests we were.

At Long-Kai we once more crossed the Blue River, but without immediately entering Sze-Chuan; a small slice of territory on the north bank belonging to Yunnan.

We discovered the reason of this anomaly while visiting the Lolo prince of Li-Tse-Chu; his grandfather, when marrying his daughter to the prince of Fan-Chu (the regent we had lately visited), gave her twenty-seven villages as dowry, and as Fan-Chu is a dependency of Yunnan these twenty-seven villages, although on the Sze-Chuan side of the river, were made over to Yunnan; notwithstanding the protests of the Viceroy of Sze-Chuan, who thus lost the only practicable passage across the Blue River, as well as an excellent point for gathering toll. What of the "perfect homogeneity" of the Chinese Empire, when the matrimonial dispositions of two "barbarian" chiefs can modify the frontiers of provinces!

The reader may perhaps recall the competition between two princes of which I spoke when narrating our passage across the independent Lolo country, and which I promised to elucidate. The dispossessed pretender, Ngan, resides at Sa-Lien, to the west of Wei-Li-chu, at the house of one of his relatives, the seigneur of the place. He is a Christian, and hoped, with the help of Father de Guébriant—who was practically powerless in such a matter—to win his cause ; and he very willingly showed us the copy of a stele which constitutes his principal title, and which was to us of the greatest interest. But when we expressed a desire to see the original he became more reticent ; the stele was in a distant and inconvenient place. No matter, we would go there ; would he not show us the way? No, it was broken now ; it could not be read any longer. We then professed to take no further interest in his cause, and finally, at the very moment of our departure, as though he were making a desperate resolve, he led us into an empty room : and there was the precious monument ! This is a mysterious country, and at any moment one runs the risk of overlooking the most precious documents.

It was a stele of 1392, which recorded the conquest of the country by the Chinese, the defeat of the last princes of the Mongol dynasty, and the partition of the territory among the victorious generals, who became hereditary princes. For more than five hundred years these dynasties have survived, making war upon one another, some waxing fat at the expense of others, and continuing the feudal age down to the present time. In conclusion the pretender assured us that if right did not prove to be might he would have recourse to arms, with the aid of all the nzemos to whom he was related.

From this precious inscription we obtained the explanation of this disconcerting fact, that the most intractable of the Lolos are governed by princes of Chinese origin, for the ancestors of the latter conquered the country at a period when, as our previous inquiries had proved, the Lolos had not yet arrived. When the new-comers did install themselves, progressively and in small numbers, they recognised the suzerainty of the princes. Gradually our conceptions were taking final shape, and the whole history of the country was becoming clear.

CROSSING THE BLUE RIVER AT LONG-KAI.

To face page 166.

At Sa-Lien we divided our forces. With Captain Lepage I intended to rejoin my first itinerary at Kong-Mu-Ying, so as to survey the entire course of the Ngan-Ning-ho, and to complete the imperfect ideas of the half-submissive Lolos of that region which I had acquired during my first journey. To Fleurelle and Boyve I entrusted a much more arduous and dangerous task: that of gaining the Ya-long, the great affluent of the Blue River, and of rejoining us afterwards at Te-Chang; on the way they were to visit the nzemo of Pu-Tze-Chu.

To explain the interest of this undertaking I should inform the reader that the stream we call the Ya-long is regarded by the Chinese not as an affluent of the Blue River, but as the Blue River itself; and they regard the stream which we declare to be the river itself as an affluent. This river Ya-long—which does not really go by that name at all, the latter being only known to literature—runs at the bottom of a gorge with perpendicular sides. No road follows its course, and hitherto it had never been surveyed; it was therefore important to map out a portion of it, and to explore the terribly rugged and precipitous range which divides it from the Ngan-Ning-ho. I had warned Fleurelle of the dangerous obstacles he would probably encounter, but for him these were merely a further attraction, another difficulty to be vanquished.

Lepage and I found the country I had previously traversed with Boyve in a state of ebullition; the Lolos, nominally loyal, had been indulging in repeated incursions; troops had been sent against them, and were defeated; new attempts were being made, unsuccessfully so far, to obtain an honourable arrangement.

At Te-Chang, where I was delighted, as before, to meet Father Castanet, we saw large numbers of the Mosso. To judge them by what I have seen of them on my two journeys, they are a magnificent race, even taller than the Lolos: many of the men are six feet six in height ; their features are very strongly marked, and they are wonderfully like the gipsies. They wear hempen breeches and scarlet leggings, a short tunic bound at the waist with a scarlet belt, and a scarlet turban ; they are shod with sandals of straw. They resemble the Lolos, but must not be confounded with them.

It was lucky for us that we had found such novel and interesting material to study, for the snow was falling heavily, and Fleurelle and Boyve failed to arrive ; I knew they must be experiencing terrible difficulties in the mountains, and I deplored having exposed them to such dangers without having the means of helping them, for I did not even know what road they would take.

At last, at the end of ten days of real anxiety, our two comrades arrived. The going had been terrible, and a horse had been lost among the precipices, with many things of value. However, the reconnaissance of the Ya-long had been made from point to point, and a considerable section of its course surveyed. The reception accorded by the nzemo of Pu-Tze-Chu was at first distinctly chilly, on account of the presence of the two Chinese soldiers of the escort ; but matters were immediately improved by the sight of the letters of introduction from our friend the pretender of Sa-Lien. Fleurelle was able to gather valuable information relating to the Si-Fan, the true autochthonous population, now subjected by the Lolos ; the latter arrived less than a century ago, and are already beginning to cross the Ya-long in their conquering march towards the west.

The end of the journey had been terrible. Surprised by the snow high up on the mountains, they were lucky enough to reach a Lolo cabin, but the inmates, being invited to act as guides, and to help them to open up a passage, had preferred to disappear, and my companions were five days imprisoned in this hut,

IN THE MOUNTAINS OF YA-LONG.

VALLEY OF THE KIEN-CHANG, NEAR TE-CHANG.

To face page 168.

open to all the winds. Fortunately they had as fellow-lodgers some pigs, which saved them from dying of hunger. When the blizzard was over the going was exceedingly dangerous, along a track which the snow had completely concealed. Happily, the slopes were not so steep on this side of the mountain as on the other, or they could never have gone forward.

A series of visits to Lolo chiefs on the right bank of the Ngan-Ning-ho finally brought us to Ning-Yua-fu. We were delighted once more to see this picturesque city, and, above all, the first peaks of the independent territory, for we now seemed to have left something of ourselves among them. Father de Guébriant won us the warmest of welcomes ; all his Christians, who had trembled for his safety while he was travelling with us, but were now extremely proud of the important part he had played in the expedition, received us in triumph. We arrived, moreover, though involuntarily, at a most appropriate moment ; for we appeared just as the official news came that the prefect, our ancient adversary, who so nearly made our plans miscarry, and the enemy of the Christians, was recalled as a result of the inquiry ordered by the Viceroy, and this coincidence gave us a triumphant appearance.

It must not be supposed that the disgrace of this prefect was a small matter for the country ; far from having been exaggerated, the dangers run by converted Chinese are extremely serious if the magistrate is at all corrupt. It is not that the people have, as has been said, the least aversion to Christianity as such ; quite the contrary ; but as the Christians are never very numerous there are always a few scoundrels who try to profit by their weakness in order to possess themselves of their goods, upon any imaginable pretext ; if the mandarin can be corrupted the Christians will find themselves condemned if they appeal to his judgment, and if they defend themselves they will be massacred or executed as rebels. It is in no way a question of religion, but merely a matter of cupidity, and of the strong crushing the weak.

Now since our previous visit the open partiality of the prefect had let loose the passion of covetousness, and the Christians had been through a most perilous time. An ex-officer of the army—the same who had made himself famous by saving, at Soso-leang-tze, the expeditionary force which had been defeated by the Lolos—had just declared for Christianity, and, having by his reputation reinforced the Catholic camp, he was attacked by assassins, receiving twenty-eight wounds. However, having plenty of vitality, he had survived, and began to recover. But he dared no longer leave the mission, being certain that he would be again attacked ; so at Father de Guébriant's request we took him into our service, in order to take him out of the country, and he was thenceforth our chief of convoy.

At Father de Guébriant's I found several pimos, for whom at my request he had sent to the independent territory, in order that I might, with their help, succeed in deciphering their writing. One of them was particularly intelligent and well informed ; he became my professor-in-chief.

For a fortnight we laboured together without intermission. The Lolo began by writing several pages of characters ; then he began to explain them to me, one by one. It was no easy matter, for he knew not a word of Chinese ; but he had brought with him a loyal Lolo who spoke Chinese, who translated his words, which my interpreter had then to put into French.

The reader may ask what accuracy there could be in this series of transpositions. Certainly the method did not make for absolute accuracy, but it was, I think, sufficiently exact. It is always possible to come to a precise understanding if one takes sufficient time ; one must take care to verify every definition by examples, and to repeat the process after an interval, when the error, if there is one, cannot fail to appear. Moreover, such work contains intrinsic proofs of its degree of accuracy. But it does, I admit, require a certain amount of patience !

My professor gave me, as a reward for my zeal, five volumes which summarised the knowledge of the Lolos : they treated, he told me, of religion, geography, history, mathematics, and the various sciences. I own I am curious to learn the contents of these books, but I have not yet had the leisure to apply to their translation the resources of the dictionary which I compiled.

We received a visit from the famous nzemo Len, of whom I have spoken so often in the course of my narrative ; the most powerful of all the Lolo princes, and the usurper of the crown of the unfortunate Ngan of Sa-Lien. Despite the historic rights of the latter, his successful rival inspired us with a lively sympathy. Although he was magnificently dressed as a Chinese mandarin in honour of his visit, and was carried in a palanquin, he is a Lolo of pure blood, and full of a remarkably intelligent nationalism ; he understood that the Lolos, if they would not disappear, must rely both on tradition and on progress. Not only has he become one of the most learned men of his race, of which he was pleased to furnish us immediate proofs, but he has founded a school where eighteen pupils are instructed at his expense, and where they learn to write Lolo, not Chinese. Better still, he has had blocks of Lolo characters engraved for printing—undoubtedly the first ever to be prepared—so that now this race, which has been regarded as one of barbarians, is publishing a book in its own characters and language !

And what do you think this book contains? Firstly a summary of Lolo knowledge ; then a *résumé* of European science, with explanations of our discoveries : railways, telegraphs, balloons, &c. The great majority of the Chinese are completely ignorant of such matters ! We shall see later on how the nzemo was able to acquire this knowledge.

The prince, delighted with the interest we manifested in everything relating to his race, presented us with one of his sabres, the scabbard of which is ornamented with work of extreme originality, and a copy of his valuable printed book.

I had barely completed the arduous compilation of the Lolo dictionary, while my companions were collecting a host of facts relating to the history of the region, when we said goodbye, this time finally and with genuine sorrow, to Father de Guébriant, who had assisted the Mission in such an extraordinary degree, and to whom we all of us owe an eternal gratitude. For that matter, he was still to help us ; wherever we went the Christians of the town would come out to meet us in procession, exploding innumerable petards, and placing themselves entirely at our disposal as intermediaries in our dealings with the Lolos [1] or as sources of information regarding that people.

The route we were about to follow was a sector of the great fortified road which encircles the Lolo country. Every kilometre—or if possible more frequently, so that each is in view of its neighbours—a small fort is built, containing a garrison of a few soldiers, while stronger points of support are arranged in convenient places. This route is directly commanded by the independent Lolos between Ning-Yuan-fu and Hi-Tang, and in the neighbourhood of the Sia-Sang-Ling (10,000 feet) their attacks are continual.

To enter into relations with the Lolos more easily, I took my professor with me. On the way he exerted himself to complete my instruction ; for he, strange to say, like Prince Len, liked to prove that although poor

[1] Just as this work is going through the press we have had the pleasure of learning that Kien-Chang is created into a diocese, and that Father de Guébriant is appointed Bishop. With a larger district his influence will be even greater. I hope this narrative may help to show that the services this admirable evangelist has rendered his country are as great as those he has rendered his religion.

LOLO ENVOYS AWAITING THE MISSION.

A CHINESE FORT.

To face page 172.

and rude mountaineers, the Lolos are not entirely savages.

What should prove this better than their ideas of religion, which are not only elevated, but closely akin to the Christian conceptions? [1] If I have not spoken of them before it is because the occasion did not arise. They are, as a matter of fact, pure theists. They have no religious worship properly so called: neither temples, nor priests, nor ceremonies in which the people can participate. But they believe in one God, perfect and omnipotent, and in a maleficent Spirit.

After their death the good are called to God and the wicked are tormented by the Demon. But as a rule the dead man has been neither wholly good nor wholly bad; he therefore spends three years in roaming the earth around his home, intervening in events, and the celestial judgment is deferred until the end of that period. This is why the Lolos keep for three years in their houses, either in a box or under the roof, a kind of effigy of the deceased, made of wood, or hemp, or the root of an orchid, in which magical formulæ have fixed the soul of the deceased. On certain anniversaries this figure is brought out and prayers are recited. At the third *year's end* the figure is thrown away; the soul is judged. At the same date also, or at all events among some of the tribes, the body is exhumed and burned, and the ashes, collected in an urn, are buried in another place.

The Demon has under his orders evil spirits who play all sorts of objectionable tricks; the most notable are those that cause illness in men and animals. The Lolos therefore use no remedies; the pimo, by various procedures, consults destiny, discovers what evil spirit is incarnated, and chases it out of the body of the

[1] There is no Christian influence perceptible in these ideas, or at least no recent influence; we found them everywhere, with very insignificant variations, even where the missionaries had never been heard of.

sufferer by ritual formulæ, accompanied by the sacrifice of an animal.

But the pimo has no sacerdotal character; his power consists only of his knowledge of books, and like all his race he is chiefly proud of his prowess in war.

Many times during this journey Lolos came out to meet us and to invite us to their houses; our journey through the independent territory was already famous, and every one wanted to have the friends of the Lolos as his guests. Our visit to Matu, "chief of a thousand families," in the valley of Kang-Siang-Ying, resulted in a discovery which, alas! came rather late, and a precious acquisition.

The discovery was that the Lolos understand the art of a succulent cookery. Upon our arrival at the eagle's nest which commands the whole valley in which this seigneur dwells—with villages of serfs hidden away in all the surrounding corners of the mountains, although one never suspects their presence from below—we were offered a pig which was immediately killed, singed, and quartered. Half an hour later we were invited to take our places, of course on the ground, and we were served with two of the best dishes I have ever eaten in my life; I do not know what ingredients were used in making the sauces, but they were enough to make one lick one's fingers—which, however, no one must fail to do, as the Lolos are as ignorant of the Chinese chop-sticks as of our forks.[1]

If we had known earlier of the culinary talent of the Lolos, how greatly our passage across their country would have been facilitated, and how joyfully we should have dispensed with the detestable food prepared for us by our Chinese servants!

But our visit to Matu had one magnificent result.

[1] On the other hand they employ wooden spoons, unknown to the Chinese, and cups of all sizes in carved wood, which is painted and varnished. These are by no means devoid of beauty. We brought a series home with us.

We knew that the Lolos possessed veritable suits of armour, but had never seen them, as they are only worn in time of war, and in the midst of our incessant negotiations we never had time to ask that we might see them. Now Matu was renowned for the possession of an especially fine suit, and we were extremely anxious to acquire it.

In order to induce him to exhibit it, we displayed our own improved weapons, which excited his emulation. This step was successful; as soon as he had seen our rifles and revolvers fired, Matu rushed into the house and presently returned armed from head to foot. On his head was a casque composed of three pieces, to cover the skull and the cheeks, which was surmounted and reinforced by the turban; on his body a cuirass of dressed hide, covering the chest and back, and prolonged by a kind of skirt of mail composed of small overlapping strips of leather; on the left arm an armlet of hardened leather, which every Lolo of an age to bear arms wears permanently; thigh-pieces of red embroidered cloth, leggings or footless boots of felt, and slippers of straw. Over the shoulder was a baldric supporting the sabre, and on the hip a quiver full of poisoned arrows. A squire held his bow, and another brandished his lance, full sixteen feet in length, while Matu rushed towards us with uplifted sabre, shouting his war-cry.

Scarcely had he received our congratulations upon his fine appearance in his knightly armour than he removed it, and said to me, with a graceful gesture, "It is yours!" Great was my joy, for the existence of such armour was something quite unknown in Europe, and the cuirass especially, lacquered in red with yellow and black designs, was a truly remarkable piece of work.

But this lordly present must meet with a seemly return. I discreetly inquired if Matu would like a revolver; we had several intended as presents. He would accept with gratitude anything we liked to offer him, but the only thing that would really give him pleasure was one of our automatic carbines. We had only four, for our personal use. I explained that I had not offered him that weapon because he would never be able to get cartridges for it. "Oh, that is nothing!" he replied; "I should never require to use it; no one would ever dare to oppose me if it were known I had such a rifle!" What could we reply to this argument? After he had stripped himself of his one suit of armour, which he inherited from his ancestors, and which he could only with difficulty replace, for artisans capable of such a masterpiece are rare, how could we hesitate to make a sacrifice which was really not so great: moreover, was it not the classic custom of heroes to exchange arms?

Filled with delight, Matu offered us a further present of a saddle, with its curious sabot-like stirrups; then, in company with all his vassals, he escorted us as far as the bounds of his territory. Fully sharing the joy of their master, the warriors wished to show us that they knew how to behave themselves correctly; so for a distance of nine miles they disported themselves upon our flanks in a series of furious charges, accompanied by the most frightful shouts and leaps worthy of panthers.

In these mountains you breathe an odour of battle which accords well with the tragic scenery. At every step we met a group of Lolos under arms. All along this great highway we heard nothing but tales of the aggressions of these intractable mountaineers; each post had had some portion of its effective killed or wounded. We ourselves had nothing to fear, for the Lolos have never been known to attack any of the Europeans, missionaries or travellers, who have passed along this road, even at the most turbulent periods; it is only against the Imperials that they bear a grudge. However, the Chinese outposts, being responsible for

MATU (LOLO NOBLE IN ARMOUR).

To face page 179.

our safety, made a great parade of their zeal; the whole garrison would turn out at our approach, forming a hedge of majestic banners; and half the force would escort us to the neighbouring post.

We were almost sorry, I must confess, that the immunity enjoyed by our persons prevented us from ever witnessing one of the actions which occurred almost daily before or behind us. But this supreme favour, which our perseverance in studying the Lolos had really merited, was at last reserved for us; four miles from the stronghold of We-He the village of Chong-So-Pa, where we were lying for the night, was taken by the Lolos.

Towards midnight we heard shots, more and more numerous, closer and closer, and the terrible cry, "Man-tsu lei-lo!" ("Here are the Barbarians!") resounded. The whole terrified population ran tumultuously into the road, rushing for the other exit from the village, although the shots came from all around us.

Resolved not to meddle in an affair which did not concern us, we remained in the barricaded inn, determining to make use of our arms only if an attempt were made to force an entrance. The Lolos, masters of the village, advanced as far as our door, as we could tell by their shouting, but by nothing else, for the whole scene of violence occurred in the midst of the profoundest darkness, lit only by the shots fired at random. Already we thought the moment had come to defend ourselves when the Lolos—we shall never know why—beat a retreat. At daybreak we found that all the houses as far as ours had been sacked; in the next house a woman who had not fled, and who doubtless had attempted to defend her property, had her head split open; and two soldiers were found dead.

But I must abridge my remarks, although a number of instructive incidents deserve to be reported. To observe such, even on a known high-road, it is enough to go slowly; to stop as often as some detail attracts one's attention; not to sleep or eat at the customary places when everything is prepared; in short, to mix as far as possible in the local life, instead of going ahead like a hurried traveller, as isolated from the country he is crossing on his horse or in his native cart or palanquin as he would be in a railway compartment.

I will record here only our visit to Father Martin, who for eighteen years has devoted himself to the evangelisation of the Lolos. Perhaps—he recognises it now himself, but at the outset he could not even guess at the organisation of native society—perhaps he was wrong to believe that his teaching, delivered first on the periphery, would act as the thin end of the wedge, and eventually open a way for him to the centre. He settled at Ghieiluka, the first Lolo village across the Chinese border, and dependent upon our friend Prince Len. The inhabitants of the village received his teaching very kindly, and became Christians; but recently the prince sent one of his officers to conduct a ceremony of celebration in honour of his ancestors, and on that day the unhappy priest saw all his flock return, without the least trace of hesitation, to the religion of their masters: for they are all merely serfs and slaves of the nzemo. He should have converted the prince or some powerful noble, not the slaves who are Lolo only in name.

We therefore found Father Martin completely forsaken, although M. and Mme. Berthelot, M. Bons d'Anty, and M. Legendre, coming from Cheng-Tu, had seen him surrounded by a flourishing Christianity; now for six months no one had dared to re-enter the poor house which he had built himself at the bottom of a wild ravine. Our advent was a happy pretext for re-establishing relations, and the whole population quickly collected.

This afforded us occasion to admire the astonishing result of his efforts. He was not content to trade his religion to the natives; he wished at the same time to

A CHINESE GARRISON SALUTING THE MISSION.

AT THE FOOT OF THE LOLO MOUNTAINS.

To face page 178.

raise their minds ; and he worked out a system by which the Lolo language was written in Latin characters, and wrote books for them in which he expounded some general ideas of the world and of science. The Father thought his pupils would have forgotten everything since their disappearance ; but no, they had not, and we were amazed to see these young people writing in our own alphabet, and doing sums on the blackboard, and to hear them speak to us of the telephone and the dirigible balloon. We thought we knew now whence Prince Len, whom Father Martin regarded as the author of his misfortune and his cruellest enemy, had derived the ideas which he had taught in his own school : from Father Martin's own books, which he had read to him by one of the Father's own pupils, and which he translated into Lolo characters. Well, even if the missionary has not succeeded in converting the Lolos, nor even in entering their territory, he has none the less succeeded unawares in giving them the rudiments of knowledge which will lift them far above the mass of the Chinese, and will make it easier for Europeans to open up relations with them. And who knows but the Christian ideas which he has taught will not also make their way ; who knows but this apostle whose defeat appears so absolute has not in reality laboured for the future?

The visit to Ghieiluka was the conclusion of our researches among our friends the Lolos. A new phase of our journey was to begin.

CHAPTER VIII

THE GATE OF TIBET. ROCK SCULPTURES

WE were now about to devote ourselves to the study of the Si-Fan, or Western Barbarians. Under this very vague appellation the Chinese confound all the populations which we call Tibetan. This latter designation is also somewhat loose, for Tibet—a name fabricated by the Arabs, who have transmitted it to us, but as unknown to the Tibetans as to the Chinese—is not a definite entity; it is impossible to determine its limits, whether geographical or political, and it is, as we shall see, by no means certain that its populations are homogeneous.

The populations of Tibet, however, are connected by one common trait which at once distinguishes them from all their neighbours: they practise the religion of Lamaism. The bitter cold, consequent on the altitude of the country, has imposed upon them certain similar fashions of clothing and of building; and as their poverty-stricken mountains are unfit for agriculture they have not excited the cupidity of the Chinese peasant, so that they have been able without difficulty to preserve their autonomy and individuality.

We should no longer be dealing with autochthonous populations hemmed in by the Chinese, or so submerged by the latter as to be barely distinguishable. On the frontier of the Si-Fan China comes clearly and definitely to a stop, and even where the Imperial authority is recognised it is known only as a foreign suzerainty

TEA-PACKERS ON THE ROAD TO TA-TSIEN-LU.

TIBETAN CARRYING A BALE OF TEA.

To face page 180.

These peoples obey either the Dalai-Lama or, on the borders of China, princes who are subject to Pekin. Except in Lhassa itself travellers have succeeded in travelling all over the country without meeting other obstacles than those created by nature, which are certainly sufficiently formidable ; and since Lhassa, already visited by Father Huc, has been entered by an English military mission there remain, of unknown Tibet, only the two vast regions to the north-east and the south-west, the latter of which, a desert and impracticable mass of mountains, was at this very time (1908) being explored by Sven Hedin.

The north-eastern region, on the other hand, is the most thickly populated part of Tibet. But the fact that should be the best known has been avoided by travellers, as it is inhabited by confederations of nomadic tribes which decline all obedience and live by the pillage of their neighbours. What was related of them agreed not at all with the descriptions of the ordinary Tibetans. This was the region we wished to explore.

To reach it we should have to cross the whole of Sze-Chuan ; but before doing that one task was still before us. Certain of the Tibetan populations are contiguous to the Lolos ; already we had found representatives of them in the regions we had already explored—regions formerly occupied by them, until the Lolos drove them back. We wished to determine the limits of the expansion and influence of the Lolos ; at the same time, in order that our observations of the nomads of the north should be more fruitful it was necessary that we should first of all see something of the Tibetans as already known. For this reason, on leaving Kien-Chang we made for Ta-Tsien-Lu, the great gate of Tibet.

All travellers have followed this route, and I need only refer the reader to the descriptions of Father Huc and Gill of the Mission Lyonnaise. However, we discovered a certain number of interesting descriptions referring to the conquest of these regions and the history of their populations. Moreover, every one has not travelled by this route in January, and this monopoly procured us the enviable privilege of encountering serious difficulties when at another season of the year we should have met with none; but was it not better to face such obstacles in a peaceful country, utilising the more agreeable seasons for the more difficult part of our work?

Descending the pass of Fei-We-Ling (10,000 feet) we found the trail covered with a layer of ice that shone like a mirror. We requisitioned some porters who were laden with tea for Tibet, and who were provided with climbing-irons for the ice, and made them carry the packs of our pack-train; but how were the animals themselves to descend?

Who has not read in Father Huc of that terrible avalanche of yaks, thrown down the frozen mountain-side? It has been taken for an amiable traveller's yarn. Well, our horses discovered this method for themselves, though without intention. The first horse which we tried to lead down the road, after covering his shoes with rags and seizing him by the head and the tail, slipped, slid, and fell, with his attendants, who let go in time to save themselves from falling with him; and in the wink of an eye he was flying on his side towards the bottom of the slope. We thought him as good as dead; but no, there were thickets and abundant snow-drifts; he came slowly to a halt, snorted—and ate a little snow to refresh himself. A second animal had precisely the same fate. Would it not have been better to throw them down than to let them fall involuntarily?

Well, such things are more amusing to read about than to do. Happily there was a moon, which enabled us to reach the inn by ten o'clock at night, having left nearly all our baggage on the road. Yet in ordinary

TEMPLE OF THE RED LAMAS AT TA-TSIEN-LU.

THE BRIDGE OF LU-TING-KIAO.

To face page 182.

weather there is nothing difficult about this pass ; we ourselves ascended it with perfect ease three weeks later.

The bridge of Lu-Ting-Kiao, by which one crosses the Ta-Tu-ho, a deep, wide river, and an affluent of the Min, has already been celebrated by many travellers ; but it has lately made fresh progress—towards ruin. It consists of chains, suspended across a hundred yards of river ; and on these chains there ought to be a wooden platform, but most of the planks are gone ; there is not very much left of the beams intended to support them, which lie here and there across the chains. So light a bridge oscillates considerably ; and the chains which ought to serve as a railing are missing from one side ; yet this bridge is practically the only road from China to Tibet !

The photograph gives a totally false idea of this bridge ; it shows a platform, or at least something vaguely resembling one. This platform, however, was placed there in our honour ; our horses were to cross by it ! I need not repeat that a Chinese horse will travel where no European horse would take a step ; and it is as well, for otherwise the whole species would have disappeared long ago, and its bones would litter the depths of the abysses. Scarcely had we crossed (having had only one horse fall into the water sixty feet below—and he swam ashore) when the keepers of the bridge rushed forward and removed the planks ; which would enable them to claim a reward from such as might ask to have them replaced. A kindly country !

The Ta-Tsien-Lu road, this bridge excepted, was by far one of the best roads we had seen in China. It was almost everywhere six or seven feet wide, and there was no very good reason why we should fall over precipices. This road is traversed by an extraordinary number of porters carrying bales of tea ; for tea, as every one knows, forms the greater part of the Tibetans' dietary, and it comes exclusively by this route. The loads carried by not very robust-looking porters are prodigious ; we saw and weighed some that turned the scale at over 300 lbs. ! Add to this that the road consists entirely of a series of ascents and equally fatiguing descents, and that it finally reaches a level of 10,000 feet above the sea ! The city of Ta-Tsien-Lu, which has both a Tibetan king and a Chinese prefect, is really the door of Tibet. The Tibetan houses are infinitely more handsome, more comfortable, cleaner, and more like our own—while retaining a quite individual style—than are those of the Chinese ; I do not think travellers have done them sufficient justice.

But I must not linger to describe this well-known city ; not even the convents of the red and yellow Lamas in the suburbs, nor the Tibetans of the town, nor those who come in from a distance, with their caravans of yaks, for the bales of tea which arrive on the backs of porters. Tibet is a world in itself, and the task of writing of it should legitimately be left to those who have made a special study of it. We had gone thither in search of terms of comparison, and it was well that we did, for this brief visit was to guide us in our future researches and enable us to verify some remarkable ethnical differences.

I will confine myself to mentioning the uneasiness which prevailed throughout the country. The rumour ran that the Lamas, vanquished the year before by the terrible Chao-Yul-Fong, the Imperial commissary, were profiting by the fact that he had been recalled as interim viceroy of Sze-Chuan to prepare their revenge. Chao was aware of this, and preparing to return ; already numerous troops had arrived. Two years later these troops were to take Lhassa.

Having returned to Sze-Chuan, we thought we should find nothing there but epigraphic documents. This province has been and is incessantly crossed by a large number of Catholic and Protestant missionaries, diplomatists, business men, explorers and tourists. If any

ROCK-SCULPTURES NEAR YONG-KING-HIEN]

To face page 184.

curious work of art remained to be discovered in China it surely would not be there.

Our astonishment was therefore great when, to the south of Yong-King-yen, at a distance of only fifteen yards from the high-road, protected by a shed, we found two rocks which had formerly fallen from the mountain, and which were covered with wonderful bas-reliefs representing Buddhistic figures. We had as yet seen nothing of the kind in China; indeed, we were constantly regretting that we had found no sculpture in stone in a country whose earthen or composition statues are numbered in millions.

The most apparent qualities of the works of art now before us were profusion and fantasy, allied to a certain symmetry. Not a finger's-breadth of stone was without ornament; and in order to utilise the form of the blocks while respecting the subjects represented, the latter had been given the most varied dimensions; a multitude of figures of all sizes stood out from the stone, although in correct alignment and regularly superimposed. The majority of the faces had nothing Chinese about them; neither had the poses. We recognised several characteristics of Hindoo art, and we noted them with astonishment, not knowing that at that very moment M. Chavannes, the eminent member of the Institute of France, was making similar discoveries in the subterranean temples of Long-Men and Yun-Kang—which we were to see later on—and was establishing their direct affiliation with the Græco-Buddhist art of Gandara.[1]

Three days later, near Ya-Chu, we discovered a monument no less remarkable; a great pillar of limestone blocks, ten feet wide by six feet deep and sixteen feet in height, which was prolonged by a buttress of almost equal dimensions. Two friezes ornamented the

[1] By this name is denoted the art that developed in Gandara (the north of the Punjaub) under the influence of the Greek artisans introduced by the Seleucides, the successors of Alexander.

upper portion, one in low and one in high relief. The bas-relief represented a magnificent procession of horsemen and chariots drawn by fiery horses not unlike those seen on Egyptian bas-reliefs. Among the high-reliefs was a series of atlantes, one being distinguished by his Semitic type and Assyrian beard. At a distance of fifty yards, and facing this pillar, were two winged lions or tigers in stone, of a type hitherto entirely unknown in China, and obviously related to the winged beasts of Assyria. An inscription of the year 209 A.D. dated the monument, which is one of the most ancient in China as well as one of the most interesting.[1]

The descent from Ya-Chu to Kia-Ting by the River Ya is one of the most delightful stretches of country in the world. The landscape is continually enchanting: mountains, forests, rocks, waterfalls, pagodas—everything is delightful.

And above all the mode of locomotion is picturesque. The river is continually barred by rapids: it is simply a succession of wide, shallow steps, over which flows only a thread-like stream of water. No boat, however flat-bottomed, could float there. The Chinese have therefore constructed rafts of bamboo, about fifty feet long, extremely light and drawing practically nothing; they certainly collide a good deal with the rocks, but owing to their length and their permeability to water, which flows freely between the bamboos, they cannot come to harm in the rapids. At each fall the raft disappears bodily under the water, but the passengers, who are installed on a little platform, have only to

[1] A spell of horrible weather, which lasted several days, prevented us from completing the moulds of these bas-reliefs, nor could we take satisfactory photographs. Father Gire, missionary at Ya-Chu, had the kindness to complete the moulding for us after our departure, and as he had no camera another missionary, Father Mansuy, made an eight-days' journey on horseback to obtain the desired photographs, which he afterwards sent us.

THE ROCKS OF THE THOUSAND BUDDHAS, NEAR THE RIVER YA.

To face page 186.

raise their legs. With a roar as of thunder, the boiling waters hem them in on every side, while they rush forward at full speed, sitting, so it seems, on the foam itself, until insensibly the raft regains the surface and glides peacefully down to the next rapid.

"Exciting, but safe," you may read in Japan above the rapids of Lake Biwa, which take twenty minutes to shoot. The descent of the River Ya takes three hours, particularly enchanting to travellers who are used to other "excitements" far more fatiguing and not nearly so safe. With the exception of Fleurelle, always absorbed in plotting the course of the river—and well that he did so, for nothing could be more erroneous than the course of this much-frequented river as marked on the maps—we were all conscious, during this enchanting journey, of the illusion that we were simple tourists with nothing to do but enjoy life, while depriving of theirs the innumerable ducks and other waterfowl that rose as we went by. And another surprise was in store for us: the Rock of the Thousand Buddhas.

This is a cliff entirely covered with niches containing Buddhistic figures, several of them being sculptured in one of the poses peculiar to the art of Gandara. In the centre of the cliff a chapel hollowed out of the rock contains a fine Buddha, with two Apsara at his side, the type of the latter being distinctly Greek.

We now entered the most astonishing stretch of country. The mountains fell away, and the river ran between low hills. Hills—or were they rather mysterious palaces? Innumerable doors opened in the rock, leading into the bowels of the earth. Their shape was Egyptian, wider at the bottom than at the top; above them the rock was often ornamented by sculptural foliage and an overhanging vaulted arch. These were caverns, the work of men's hands, but long deserted. Their architectural character was striking; we hoped to find marvels of sculpture, but we visited them with no result but that of tiring ourselves. We searched hundreds of them, but discovered nothing save signs that they had been utilised in very various ways. Some had served as dwellings; we saw the hearth, the manger, the water-tank, the shelves for holding different utensils; others had been stables or byres, and there were always stone coffins, but they had been plundered, as the disturbed covers indicated.

A people once lived in these caverns, which they had excavated according to exact designs. In vain we dug and rummaged about; we found only shards of characterless pottery, and once some fragments of figures of baked clay: curious, but there was nothing to prove their antiquity. Local tradition pretends that the Tibetans of Ta-Tsien-Lu lived here until the time of the Ming dynasty; and from time to time one of them would come to dig in this or that cavern, and remove the treasures of his ancestors, who had left their secrets in safe keeping.

The problem is all the more curious in that the Chinese books scarcely mention these caves.[1] There are few races that prefer to live underground, and with very rare exceptions the modern inhabitants do not use these caves, even as granaries or stables. Yet in Kan-Su and Shen-Si precisely similar caverns are excavated in the hill-side, and even to-day they are the favourite dwellings of the people.

Kia-Ting, where our voyage ended, possesses one of the most astonishing, though not the most admirable works of art ever produced by human hands. In a cliff overhanging the confluence of the Ya, the Ta-Tu-ho, and the Min, there is a Buddha, cut out of the solid rock, no less than 180 feet in height. It is by far the largest

[1] All the European travellers who have seen these caves have spoken of them with astonishment, and have suggested the most diverse theories as to their origin; but it is probable that they had not the patience to enter very many, for they did not observe the objects I have mentioned, which were visible in a number of caverns, nor even the magnificent sculptures of which I shall speak further on.

ROCK-TEMPLES OF PAI-YEN-TING.

To face page 188.

statue in the world. It occupies a recess some sixty feet in width and depth, the sides of which contain a number of smaller niches which must once have contained statues, but are now empty. The god is represented sitting in European fashion.

It must be confessed, however, that this great statue is no longer effective. Under the action of the weather the contours are worn and crumbling; great blocks have fallen away, and the vegetation—mosses, bushes, and even trees—has attacked and is disfiguring what remains. Without being able to understand how Colborne Baber "failed to discover, except in the face, any trace of the sculptor's hand," we must admit no traces of actual art are now visible. It looks as though the hewers of stone had roughed out of the rock a rudimentary statue, like a snow man, which the artist never completed.

As a crowning misfortune, the idea was conceived at some recent period of restoring Buddha's head of curls, of the characteristic kind known as "breadfruit." This was an easy matter, requiring no scaffolding, as the top of the head touches the plateau which crowns the hill; and a number of round flagstone were let into the skull with a most miserable result.

I do not know what would be the result of a complete scouring of the statue; the beauty of many of the niches seems to justify some hope; but at present the vastness of the labour which has resulted only in this unshapely figure merely produces an impression of absurdity and impotence.

However, a fine statue of Poussa, cut in the rock at a short distance from the Buddha, and a few bas-reliefs further upstream, make the locality an interesting one, and a number of sumptuous pagodas are the object of frequent pilgrimages.

Continuing our visits to the grottoes surrounding the city, we at last had the good fortune to discover a group some nine miles to the north which had served as Buddhist sanctuaries. A number of statues lay on the ground, broken; but one could still realise the imposing effect that must have been produced by these ranks of gods and saints which seemed to be issuing from the bowels of the earth in order to hold council.

From Kia-Ting, retracing our steps a little, we made the ascent of Mount O-mei, the sacred mountain of Sze-Chuan.

Of this journey I will not speak: an eight or ten days' excursion which has been made and recorded by so many others that it belongs to the domain of the tourist. I will merely note that from this pyramid, 11,400 feet in height, one of the most beautiful views in the world is to be obtained—a profusion of temples and convents, crouching on the smallest hills, surrounded by a rampart of wooded mountain buttresses, these also covered with sumptuous pagodas.

What I wish to emphasise once more, in speaking of this region, and in again referring the reader to my previous book for the astonishing history of religion in China, is the fundamental error of those who maintain that the Chinese are devoid of the spirit of religion. The number of pagodas encountered everywhere is prodigious; not a hamlet but has its temple, and in even the smaller towns they are to be counted by dozens. They are built, moreover, not by the State, but by private individuals who subscribe for the purpose. It is difficult to understand that the practical and money-loving Chinaman so often depicted should delight in expending considerable sums of money in erecting temples in honour of gods who inspire him only with sceptism and indifference.

But, it will be said, these temples are always deserted; no one goes there to pray. Another mistake, which a more methodical observation would have obviated. In France every day is a saint's day; so it is in China, and the pagoda consecrated to the saint or genius whose anniversary it is is invaded by a host of pilgrims who have come from all directions to bring their offerings and their prayers. Next morning the pagoda has resumed, perhaps for a year, the deserted silence which has impressed the passing European; but the worshippers have only gone elsewhere, and elsewhere the pious crowd will again be concentrated in prayer.

But there are also places so sacred that people visit them in pilgrimage all the year round. The Tai-Shan at Shan-Tong, the Won-Tai-Shan at Shan-sei, the Heng-Shan at Hu-Nan, and the O-Mei-Shan at Sze-Chuan are four centres of ardent devotion. People travel thither from every part, enduring the greatest fatigue. We made the ascent of Mount O-mei in February, in the coldest month of the year, during the most bitter cold; and hundreds of pilgrims, barefooted in the snow and shivering under their thin cotton garments, were descending, or ascending behind us, having come from all the provinces of China. Among them all there was not a single woman; the weather was too severe. It is obvious, then, that the men do not abandon piety to the weaker sex.

In a place so long sacred—for it was sanctified by one of the first apostles of Buddhism, Pu-Hien, at the beginning of the Christian era—we had hoped to find some marvels of religious art. Alas! except for the celebrated Pagoda of the Thousand Years, known for its elephant in "white copper," a life-size work with an astonishing look of reality, the image of the legendary animal on which Pu-Hien arrived from India, and various other monuments, which were of interest but have been already reported—although with regrettable carelessness of attribution—there was scarcely anything artistic nor even ancient in these numerous monasteries. In the course of so many wars and revolts the tide of pillage has carried them away.

We were returning, considerably disappointed, from

this magnificent excursion when we were consoled by two discoveries in two pagodas near the town which is built at the foot of the mountain. One was a ravishing stupa (Buddhistic pyramid) in copper, bearing nearly 4,700 little figures, all delicately chiselled: Fleurelle, who made a sketch of it, photography being impossible, counted them. The other find was a colossal statue of Avalokiteshvara,[1] nearly forty feet in height, in gilt bronze, dating from three centuries back; surrounded by a number of other statues in bronze and wood, it is sheltered by a pagoda especially built to its measure. Its archaic style, its multitudinous arms, like tentacles waving in the shadows, the light coming through the high windows which nevertheless light it from below, and above all the mystic expression of the face, looking out from such a height, all result in producing a most vivid impression. This was truly the art, a little crude and awkward, but strange, powerful, prodigious, which we had hoped to find at every step in China, but, alas! such examples are rare.

Having returned to Kia-Ting, we set out in a northerly direction to gain Cheng-Tu, the capital of Sze-Chuan. The country is charming, broken by hills covered with pine-woods. Who is it says the Chinese detest trees? On the contrary, no people loves them more; every house has one or several in its courtyard or garden, so that you may expect a village in the distance when you see a wood; and the pagodas, which are the only places of public assembly, all possess groves which are usually ancient. In short, you see trees everywhere in the neighbourhood of houses: a sufficient proof that they are not unpleasing.

Why, then, do the Chinese, who loves to have trees about his house, so pitilessly destroy those at a distance, thus grievously denuding the mountains? A simple question which I ought not to ask the reader, for he will have formulated the answer before I can give it:

[1] One of the principal Boddhisatvas, or future Buddhas.

BAS-RELIEFS AT KANG-KYU.

To face page 192.

because wood, the only material used in building, is very expensive, and when it belongs to no one it is naturally taken. All the great mountain ranges were no-man's lands ; every one took what he could for fear lest his neighbour should be before him. On his own property, however, the Chinaman carefully preserves his woodland or his trees, and makes many plantations; this is why Sze-Chuan, where there is scarcely any vacant land, is particularly well wooded. If only the State would adopt a policy of afforestation, and apply it to the immense tracts of land now without owners, the forests would soon spring up again to the great satisfaction of the people.

Our unexpected discovery, that of rock-sculptures of great antiquity, and pertaining to a vanished art, filled us with delight: for it revealed a past that was practically unknown. The reader may imagine that we were always on the alert for anything that might put us on the track of fresh discoveries, but I must own the results were consistently negative. One missionary only, at Kia-Ting, told me that in traversing a valley near the village of Kiang-Kyu he had noticed some rocks carved into figures of Buddha, so we marched in that direction. I was by no means confident, however; none of the Chinese on the way knew of these sculptures.

The moment we arrived at Kiang-Kyu we began to ask for information; but no one understood what we wanted to discover. We went to see the mayor, the commandant of the river police of the Min, an important official who resides at Kiang-Kyu ; he overwhelmed us with amiability, but knew nothing of the sculptures. We questioned all the inhabitants, with the same success. Finally, however, some one seemed to remember something. " Sculptured rocks? A statue of Buddha? Why, yes, you will find it at Hoang-Long-Ke, twelve miles from here! " Good: Hoang-Long-Ke for to-morrow, but Kiang-Kyu for to-day!

Since no one could tell us anything, we must look for ourselves. And feeling decidedly mournful at seeing our hopes take wings and fly, not knowing whether to believe the brief statement, perhaps misunderstood, of a travelling missionary or the categorical affirmations of the inhabitants, we set out with the obstinacy of despair and entered a little valley at hazard.

It was already five in the afternoon, and the night was falling. We walked a mile or more without encountering anything, except more inhabitants who knew nothing. Discouragement was overtaking us when we noticed, through the darkness, for it was now night, a vertical mountain wall such as rock-sculptors affect. Quickly we knocked at a peasant's hut: "A light, good man, and take us to see the Buddha." The man obediently came out with a torch, and without hesitation led us by a goat-track about half-way up the mountain. "There! " he said, and we saw nothing at all but shapeless rocks in the pitchy darkness. But he, lowering his torch, showed us what we were holding on by—two enormous feet, sculptured in the rock, which belonged surely to some giant; but the flickering light failed to evoke him from the darkness.

This was enough; we had found our colossus, and would return on the morrow; we could return to enjoy a well-earned repose, and to dream of the now assured discovery.

On the morrow, in fact, we found two enormous statues of Buddha, sixty feet or more in height, side by side, one standing and the other seated in the Eastern fashion on a lotus-flower. The strata of the mountain constituted their throne; their heads reached almost to the summit, and the mountain seemed as though made only to serve as a frame and background. Under a sky like that of Egypt these colossi would have taken rank beside those of Abou-Simbel! Here, alas! the rainy skies of Sze-Chuan had weathered the friable limestone; many fragments had fallen, many contours

COLOSSI OF KANG-KYU.

To face page 194.

were worn and degraded; but at least no attempt at restoration had dishonoured these vestiges of a colossal art which was fit to be the glory of a race.

Nor was this all: the alveoli of the lotus-flower contained a most delightful surprise. Each was a chapel, peopled with life-sized figures! Better protected from the rain, they had retained a certain sharpness of contour, and the Buddhas, seated European-wise, the folds of drapery, the supple and sometimes even undulating poses, all showed the evident influence of Greek and of Hindoo art; very different from Chinese art as we know it.

Here was yet another proof of the fact that China, which people like to think of as isolated from the rest of the world until it was discovered by Europeans, has in reality had a history like our own. The same barbarians hemmed her in and isolated us from the yellow world; periodically, just as in Europe, she fell under their yoke, when the barrier naturally disappeared.

It was thanks to the advance of the Mongols, checked only on Hungarian soil, that we first had knowledge of China; similarly, seven centuries earlier the conquest of the north of China by the Tongons, the ancestors of the Mongols, opened up relations with India. To the Tongon emperors, the Wei, who were fervent Buddhists, or their successors, the Tang, are due the admirable monuments of Sze-Chuan, as well as those I shall have occasion to speak of later. No doubt the Buddhist apostles were accompanied from India by the first sculptors, who carved out of the rock, in the Hindoo manner, these extraordinary monuments: unprecedented in China, and containing characteristic details of the Græco-Buddhist type.

Greece in Sze-Chuan! Art introduced by the Barbarians, to disappear after their fall! How contrary to the conventional ideas of the subject!

But this was not all. The same people who had

denied that there were statues here asserted that there were some at Hoang-Long-Ke. We hastened thither. The comedy recommenced; no Buddhas there, but there was a very fine one at Yong-Hien, some fifty miles to the south-east.

Of course we ended by discovering the Buddha. He was only thirty feet high, and unhappily his head, long ago broken, was coarsely repaired with stucco; but the body was well preserved, as well as two statues of adorers, and the whole was impressive.

Yong-Hien was too far from our route, and we had no intention of going in search of its colossus. No doubt, had we gone, we should have been directed to another!

But now the desired result was achieved; it appeared that this part of Sze-Chuan was the centre of a flourishing and prodigious art; one of the strangest and most grandiose ever known. For those desirous of studying it, the harvest should be as easily gathered as rich. It is enough for us to have pointed the way. Our duty lay elsewhere: in the desolate countries which no traveller visits.

SCULPTURES IN HIGH RELIEF.

BUDDHA SEATED IN EUROPEAN FASHION.

To face page 196.

CHAPTER IX

THE TIBETAN BORDER

At Cheng-Tu, a city of 800,000 inhabitants, we spent a month in giving all the members of our expedition a well-deserved rest, in repairing our equipment, in refreshing our worn-out horses, and in clearing up and arranging our survey notes and our collection of documents, while our search for archæological and historical monuments continued as usual. Those relating to the Chinese Mahommedans, hitherto very little known, yielded most interesting results, which promised yet more if the inquiry was persevered with. For this reason I added to the two scholars entrusted with the deciphering of the steles a learned Mussulman, whose task would be to gather all information relating to his religion along the line of march; he would be especially useful to us at Kansu.

We received, at Cheng-Tu, a particularly warm welcome from our consul-general, M. Bons d'Anty, and the vice-consul, M. Bodard. M. Bons d'Anty is one of the best-informed men living in respect of China; he had then just returned to his post from a most interesting journey in Kwei-Chu, on which he was accompanied by Lieutenant Noiret, who undertook the duties of surveyor. Our routes had crossed each other at a few days' interval eight months earlier, at Yong-Ning, which enabled us to compare our journeys.[1]

The reader will not expect me to describe a city so well known; he will prefer the unknown. I will merely refer to the activity displayed by the interim Viceroy, Chao-Yul-Fong, in bringing his army to the degree of efficiency he desired. He was about to return to Ta-Tsien-Lu, and had doubtless for some time been meditating the attack upon Lhassa. In order that he need have no fear of being ill-supported, the Chinese Government, which is so lightly accused of lack of foresight, had taken an exceedingly sensible measure; it had appointed, as viceroy of Sze-Chuan, Chao's brother, thus assuring the general of all the resources of the province as support in his audacious campaign.

On the 23rd of March we took the road for Song-Pan-ting, at the northern extremity of Sze-Chuan, and on the very brink of the parts of Tibet which we wished to explore. Two routes led thither; one by Long-Ngan-fu, the other by the River Min; both were followed by Gill, by the Lyons Mission, and various travellers. We intended to take a third, between the two, which would have the advantage of offering us a new route to survey; and directly we had crossed the plain we intended to plunge into the mountainous districts inhabited by non-Chinese populations.

Sze-Chuan has the reputation of being the richest and most cultured province of China, and it is deserved. But it would be a mistake to suppose that this wealth and refinement correspond to what we understand by

[1] We had also the pleasure of finding at Cheng-Tu the members of the Franco-Chinese School of Medicine; in particular, Dr. Mouillac, who is to-day its chief. The then director, Dr. Legendre, was absent; as had been his custom for several years, he had profited by a term of leave in journeying to the confines of the territory of the independent Lolos, there to study the inhabitants. It will be seen that France is very well represented in Sze-Chuan. It was also here that I met the unfortunate Mr. Brooke.

TRIUMPHAL ARCHES.

A STREET IN HAN-CHU.

To face page 198.

COLOSSAL STATUE OF AVALOKITESHVARA.
(Note the soldier at the foot of the statue).

To face page 190.

these words. A European suddenly transported to Sze-Chuan would see nothing but poverty, dirt, and absence of the most elementary conditions of art, welfare, or comfort.

Along the river many hundreds of thousands of boatmen work in absolute nudity and without any other shelter than the boat which they tow like beasts of burden. Millions of porters also live the lives of pack-animals, and the suburbs of each city conceal a population which wakes each morning without knowing where the day's food is to come from. As everywhere in China, the majority of the monuments are falling into ruins; even when new they seem very wretched when compared to our palaces and cathedrals. And as for the inns, the worst hovel of the poorest hamlet in France is less filthy than the most renowned of these hostelries.

Yet when one is accustomed to China the superiority of Sze-Chuan appears incontestable. If the monuments are falling into ruins it is because the Chinese, for various reasons, some of which are a mystery, do not care either to restore or maintain them; but they construct large numbers of new ones. For instance, one encounters numbers of those triumphal arches raised at the public expense to commemorate some worthy citizen, or more frequently some widow who has remained a widow; covered with very fine sculpture, or rather fretwork, in stone, they prove what magnificent works, worthy of those whose forgotten vestiges we had found, the Chinese artisans would be capable of producing; whereas they are unhappily seldom commissioned to make anything better than crude images of painted loam.

But even so their art is sometimes brilliant. Thus in the north of Sin-Tu-Nyu, the pagoda of the Thousand Genii contains a collection of extremely expressive figures, which are arranged with much more than the usual taste. The central motive is a Kwan-yn

(Kwannon), the goddess of pity, holding in her arms a child symbolical of humanity ; the faces—for the statue has nine—are really charming, and the thirty-six arms outstretched with an understanding of effect.

The whole of this pagoda, by the way, is really remarkable. We found there one of the three steles in Mongol of which we brought back impressions, and which are the only examples of the kind yet found in China. We were shown with veneration, in a sort of cupboard, in which it is commonly kept, the statue of a monk, crouching in the ritual position, and clothed in the authentic costume of a bonze ; the face was an astonishingly true piece of work. But no, not astonishingly : it was not a statue, but the actual body of a saint who died in the act of prayer, two centuries ago, which had been embalmed and gilded in the pose he had assumed when his soul took flight. It is the object of much devotion, and works many miracles, so the bonzes assured us. We had several times come across these mummified statues, or statuefied mummies.

In this same prefecture of Sin-Ton is the only public garden which we know in China, with the exception of that of Nankin ; each was really an ancient private garden, which was offered by its owner to the city. This shows how utterly lacking in China are the accessories which seem to us indispensable to a tolerable life, and are found in our smallest towns.

The architecture of Sze-Chuan affects walls of grey brick, in which are sunken panels with motives worked out in plaster or enamel. Although in themselves they may be but indifferently artistic, very often the total result of these decorated walls, with the stone lions that guard the porches of the houses, produces a very characteristic effect, quite in conformity with the conventional picturesque which we attribute to China, but so rarely find there.

One of the greatest surprises of the traveller arriving in Sze-Chuan by the mountains, where he has met

KWANNON.

To face page [illegible].

caravans of horses travelling paths fit for goats, is to see none at all on the plain, which would seem the place for them. The explanation is simple; the soil in these alluvial valleys is excessively fertile, and is cultivated with absolute devotion; not a finger's-breadth can be wasted to produce fodder for horses. The latter can only find food in the poor mountain countries, where nearly all the soil is of necessity uncultivated. This is why caravans of pack-horses stop when in sight of the plains. Moreover, they have not the right to advance. The reader may know that in China all trades and vocations constitute guilds or unions, which use and abuse their power; well, the guild of porters simply forbids all horses to enter the country in which porterage, being not too greatly fatiguing, constitutes a convenient trade for all those, and they are legion, who have no other. Only the horses of private persons may enter, and these are rare and very costly to feed.

Since there are no draught animals there are no carriages, although the roads are level. They are replaced by the wheelbarrow. These are of two sorts, based on two different principles. One is exactly like ours—I have not seen it elsewhere in China—but an original use is made of it: a seat is placed on it, and well-to-do people take their carriage exercise by this means. The other device, peculiar to China, and found all over the plains, consists of a large wheel, on either side of which two platforms rest in equilibrium; the whole has only to be pushed; the person pushing, not having to sustain any of the weight, has only to overcome friction and the grip of the road. By this ingenious system, which only demands a perfect equilibrium—a condition *sine qua non*—a man can transport astonishing loads; I have seen wheelbarrows carrying eight women seated back to back, four on each platform, and the coolie had by no means the appearance of finding his task an arduous one.

To facilitate it yet further, the Chinese invented the railway; in the flagstones which form the pavement two little channels are cut, which all wheelbarrows follow, coming or going.

Nothing is more curious than to see, of a morning, the long, uninterrupted files of wheelbarrows bearing to market the peasants, holding their children in their arms, and pushed by their servants. Wheelbarrow stands or stations are everywhere, at the disposition of the public.

The plains of Sze-Chuan are delightful. There are hardly any villages properly so called, except those that serve as markets; nearly all the country-folk live in isolated farm-houses, although the distance between them is not great. Each of these houses is surrounded by a little wood of pines and tall bamboos, which form a rather astonishing combination, but the foliage harmonises wonderfully. These little scattered groves, and the rice-fields, now covered with stems of a lovely green, now flooded, like so many lakes, would really give one the impression of a park, if the houses and people were cleaner and not so poverty-stricken.

For these plains, which after all are not so large, have to nourish an enormous population; for in the Sze-Chuan alone, according to the official census, there are eighty millions of inhabitants. Only rice, by its enormous yield, could accomplish such a miracle; but rice requires water. The system of canals which distributes throughout the plain the waters of the Min, diverted as they leave the mountain, is deservedly famous; but the ingenuity of the peasants in utilising the water of these canals is not sufficiently appreciated.

To bring it up to the level of their fields—for these are almost always higher than the canals—they employ the chain-pump or "water-carriage." This is an inclined trough, one end of which dips into the canal; the other end is at the edge of the rice-field. A series of palettes are fixed on an endless chain, actuated by

THE "WATER-CARRIAGE," SZE-CHUAN.

To face page 202.

a hardwood wheel which is rotated by foot, by two men; the palettes drag the water up the trough and spill it into the field. Various mechanisms may be combined with the "water-carriage"; the most usual is a windlass worked by a horse, ox, or ass, which by means of a simple gear fulfils the office of the two men aforesaid.

On every side one sees these devices in movement, producing the illusion of one of those country fairs at which wooden horses go circling round, or bicyclists pedal frantically on machines fixed to the ground. Their rotation seems to be the natural movement of this unfamiliar world, and to replace the "august gesture of the sower."

When the water is running, and has to be raised to a greater height, the Chinese employ the irrigating-wheel. This carries paddles which the current pushes, thus turning the wheel; and bamboo buckets, fixed to the paddles at an angle of 45°, fill themselves as they dip in the water, and then, on reaching the uppermost portion of the periphery, empty their contents into a trough, whence a flume supported on props leads the water to the fields. We saw wheels sixty feet in height, made of bamboo by simple peasants with an admirable precision and ingenuity. Nor is this all. The surplus water returning from the field forms a fall or a current, which may be utilised again to work another smaller wheel; so that once these devices are in position a stream will raise part of its own waters to quite a considerable height, without any need of further human intervention.

The large wheels complete the impression of a fair; but in China all these inventions are applied to labour.

The famous plain of Cheng-Tu, the largest in Sze-Chuan, but which even so is broken up by low hills, is scarcely more than sixty miles wide; a circle of mountains, very high to the north and west, but lower to the south and east, completely encloses it. It was toward the former that we were marching. They were preceded by hills covered with rolling stones, which the evil spirits had brought thither ; the view from their summits swept a vast horizon, cheerful and majestic at the same time. Look well, I thought, for we shall see nothing more like this !

The high wall that seemed to bar our way had not to be climbed : it opened for us. We entered by the narrow breach worn by a river ; for a long while henceforth we should be passing through the depths of such gorges. They too are beautiful, although the absence of forests deprives one of the sense of mystery and hidden life. There as everywhere the artistic sense of the Chinese and their love of nature—which so many European residents deny out of sheer prejudice—are plainly manifest. We often came to a pagoda springing from the mountain-side, or a tower perched upon a point of rock ; evidently they served the purposes of religion—despite the irreligion of the Chinese, proclaimed by the same observers ; but an inscription took pains to tell the passing traveller that such or such a rich man had constructed this monument because it seemed to him that it would harmonise with the site and complete the beauty of the place. Thus the Chinese Carnegies, instead of founding schools, offer their fellow-citizens a landscape ; their money is employed not in purchasing for a few a knowledge for which they will probably be no happier, but in pointing out to all, rich or poor, the beauty of nature, that they may enjoy it more truly.

Among the monuments constructed in the way of æsthetic altruism the most numerous are towers for the purpose of burning paper. We know that for the Chinese the written character, which in a sense is the incarnation of the idea, has something divine and sacred about it ; it is therefore a reprehensible action to use old written or printed paper for base purposes : it must therefore be burned. The towers contain a

IRRIGATION WHEEL.

BAGGAGE PORTERS.

To face page 204.

grate for this purpose ; they are consecrated to some god, towards whom the fumes ascend as a holocaust. Is there not something truly noble in this simultaneous worship of Beauty and the Idea, addressed to the Divinity whose gift they are?

One of the motives which had guided us in our choice of this route was the desire to visit, at Che-Tsiuan-hien, the pretended birthplace of the great Yu, the legendary emperor who would have reigned from about 2223 to 2216 B.C., and is supposed, by his strenuous civilising efforts, to have irrigated China and made it a healthier country to live in.[1]

This mythical personage had the good sense to choose, for one of his imaginary birthplaces—for other sites have claimed him—a particularly picturesque locality. A fine bridge of hempen cords—a speciality of the region, of which we had seen a number of instances—connects the city and the suburbs. It was some nine miles from here, in an extremely wild gorge, in which his mother had sought for refuge at a time when the Imperial anger had fallen on her husband, that the great Yu first saw the light. Or, at least, so says an inscription of the eleventh century A.D. ; and if that is not enough to prove the authenticity of an event which took place 3,000 years ago, at least it is in itself a very interesting document, which we were glad to copy.

But it was not precisely an easy task to take an impression of an inscription no less than thirty feet in height. Fortunately we found a scaffolding all ready ; it had been prepared by the local prefect for the same purpose. We had merely to cover, with sheets of damp paper,

[1] I must remind the reader that Chinese history anterior to the ninth century is based on no monuments, no contemporary documents. The antiquity of China is a legend, and the works of the great Yu merit about as much belief as the labours of Hercules. None the less it would be useful to search on the spot for the foundations of the legends on which China bases her national pride.

which the wind tore as we held it in our fingers, this enormous wall; then to get rid of air-bubbles with a brush, so that the paper should adhere perfectly; and then to dab it with powdered ink, so that the characters, where the paper could not be reached by the tamping-brush, would be white on a black ground. If the operation is successful—that is, if the paper does not tear, and if it does not dry and fall off before the whole surface is blackened—it will only occupy some four or five hours; and one must take at least two copies of documents one has come so far to obtain; so really one may call it at least a two-days' job. The collection of epigraphic documents is full of charm.

* * *

Our route rejoined the valley of the Min, which we did not leave again until we had discovered its source. This deep valley is usually wide enough to make room, sometimes on one side of the stream, sometimes on the other, for a few fields, and from time to time a village. The eastern bank, which we were following, is Chinese, and the western bank Tibetan—or rather it is not Chinese, for neither its inhabitants nor its administration are Chinese, but neither does it obey the Dalai-Lama. Between China properly so called and the territory governed by the pontiff-king of Lhassa lies a vast tract of land occupied by principalities or confederations for which it would be useless to find a name. One might perhaps reserve the title of Tibetans for subjects of the Dalai-Lama, calling the rest Si-Fan, a name applied by the Chinese to all the Barbarians of the west of the Empire; but this would be only a rough provisional nomenclature, for all these populations are most certainly of diverse races, which we intended as far as possible to distinguish.

The Tibetan villages may be distinguished at a glance by their method of construction. The houses are of one

TOWER FOR BURNING PAPER.

CAPTAIN LEPAGE TAKING A MOULD.

To face page 206.

floor only, and are covered not with a roof, but with a flat terrace; they have scarcely any openings in the outer wall, so that their resemblance to the Arab villages is very striking. It should be noted, by the way, that these flat roofs, which are not Chinese, are found in various places, at considerable intervals, from Tibet as far as the borders of Tonkin: a fact of some interest.

The Chinese hardly ever cross to the opposite bank, where they would not be safe, but the Tibetans cross to the Chinese bank to sell their produce, which enabled us to compile vocabularies and investigate their division into populations. Communication is effected sometimes by a bridge of ropes, sometimes by a simple cable across which a seat or saddle runs on a pulley, so that one only has to sit in the contrivance in order to be transported across the valley: once more one of the amusements of the country fair!—only at the fair there is no river flowing beneath the cable, and a river is a great improvement.

Sometimes the valley closes in until the river occupies the entire floor; then the road rises by means of passably dizzy cornices. It is, however, with the Ta-Tsien-Lu road, the best mountain road of those we had travelled. An intelligent prefect had lately improved it, and we admired a number of tunnels; one of them was actually helical in form, like the famous tunnel of Saint-Gothard!

As a rule the valley walls are too close to allow one to realise the true height of the mountains; one must wait for an affluent, the valley of which allows of an open view. At such times we could see the magnificent range of 16,000 feet, towards which we were gradually rising, and which finally we should have to cross.

All this country has been the scene of incessant fighting. The Chinese wanted possession of this long valley, ending as it does in the heart of Sze-Chuan; and on both banks one sees nothing but ruined fortresses beside the new forts. Past the picturesque district of Tie-Hi, where we found some rock-sculptures of the eighth century, the Tibetan buildings assumed a truly remarkable aspect. They were fortified houses or castles, of formidable appearance, which transported us into the midst of the Middle Ages ; the square mass of the main building reminded us of the solid Florentine palaces, but the obliquity of lines that should have been vertical evoked a more ancient architecture, and sometimes we could have believed ourselves before the pylon of some Egyptian temple. Seen close at hand these buildings certainly lost something of their majesty. They should have been of hewn stone, like the castles of Europe : they are only of earth, supported by frameworks of wood.

Nevertheless, they surprised us by an arrangement very like that of our own dwelling-houses. The various stories contained numerous rooms, served by corridors and interior staircases, of which the Chinese have no conception. A common hall united the family and the servants around the hearth, which is the seat of the tutelary divinity of the house ; it would be a sacrilege to stride over the buttress of cement which binds it to the wall.

Tall dressers are covered with services of red and yellow copper with ornaments inlaid with silver ; tea-urns, milk- or beer-cans, soup-tureens, cups and plates of all sizes and shapes, and all true works of art.

The smoke ascends freely towards a kind of cupola, where it is captured and escapes into the air ; prayer-mills, just like the little windmills sold to our children by itinerant hawkers, are placed above the hearth so that the hot air ascending therefrom turns them and carries the invocations to heaven.

Every guest is at once given a bowl of tea with butter or cream, and a pint of a drink very like a somewhat sourish beer, which is made from soured milk ; the same, no doubt, as that which Herodotus mentions as

IN TIBET—FORTIFIED HOUSES.

To face page 208.

CASTLES IN TIBET.

To face page 208.

being prepared by the Scythians, and the *koumiss* of the Mongols.

The most curious room is the chapel. Not only are the statuettes of copper representing Buddha, and the numerous divinities known as "Protectors of Religion," gracious both in pose and expression ; not only is there a host of curious accessories surrounding them—tom-toms, trumpets, sea-shells bound in silver, cymbals, clarionets, lanterns, and banners—but the walls are covered with lacquered woodwork, on which are painted religious or decorative motives, with a delicate and finished art, which would not be out of place in a Louis XV. boudoir. The wood flooring is waxed, and all the objects are of a perfect cleanliness and shine like mirrors. One asks oneself into what country one has suddenly been transported?

*

* *

At last, on the 8th of April, we arrived at Song-Pan-ting (Sung-pan). This city, which is exceedingly picturesque with its bridge covered with shops, like the Rialto or the Ponte Vecchio, and its ramparts climbing up the mountain-side—that part of the town is unfortunately not in the photograph—is a place of great importance ; situated where Sze-Chuan meets Kan-Su, it maintains communications by checking the incursions of the intractable nomads whose territory commences at a distance of eighteen miles. It has withstood numerous sieges, and has been taken three times, the last occasion being forty years ago.

Here we were at the very gate of the country we wished to explore : that of the independent Si-Fan—or Tibetans. From here to the sources of the Yellow River lie the tribes whom all the travellers who have skirted this region—Huc, Prjevalski, Rockhill, Grenard—depict as the most formidable of brigands. No one had hitherto attempted to go among them. It was to avoid them, as his companion relates, that Dutreuil de Rhins, whose courage was never in question, chose as less dangerous the route on which he met his death. The country was absolutely unknown ; the immense loop of the Yellow River had been plotted from Chinese information. For the Chinese have gone thither ; they have even made numerous expeditions into those regions ; but, just as in the Lolo country, they had finally to evacuate the country and content themselves with guarding the borders.[1]

To explore this virgin but difficult region had even before we left France been one of the objects assigned to our Mission. Great was our disappointment on arriving at Song-Pan-ting to learn that two Germans, Lieutenant Filchner and Dr. Tafel, had crossed this country while we ourselves were among Lolos and the Miao-Tze. True, they had been attacked, wounded, made prisoners, and were despoiled of all their baggage ; but they had finally contrived to get through. Dr. Tafel, encouraged by this somewhat mitigated success, had tried to begin over again ; deprived of his baggage a second time he had only with difficulty escaped, when he fitted out yet again and crossed the country a second time, although he lost his third caravan in doing so.

We were therefore anticipated. We learned this very annoying piece of news from Father Dury—for even in this remote outpost there is a French missionary —who had on each occasion received the explorers on their return, and had heard from their own lips the tale of their perilous adventures. This was a fortunate

[1] These independent tribes are called *Kolo*, *Ngolo*, or *Ngolog* by all travellers. Kolo, I may mention, is also the name given in ancient Chinese volumes to the tribes we now call Lolo. The Ngolo constitute only one of the confederations of nomads which cover the country ; if travellers have heard their name only it is because they are nearest to the northern roads hitherto followed ; the other tribes are no whit inferior in importance and in their warlike temper.

BRIDGE OF ROPES AT TZUAN-HIEN.

THE ROAD TO SONG-PAN-TING.

To face page 210.

chance, as I was able to learn that a great part of this immense region was still after all unknown, and that while we must leave to our predecessors the honour of having succeeded, by their heroic efforts, in making the first explorations, we could still pass through unknown country.

This new expedition required serious preparations. First of all we needed guides, for unless we knew where to get fuel we should risk death by cold and hunger; then Tibetan interpreters; a gang of coolies to strike the tents, and seek for water, wood, or argol; and finally, a caravan of yaks. In the altitudes in which we were going to live only the yak or the long-haired buffalo—the "grumbling buffalo" of the ancient naturalists and Father Huc—can be used as a beast of burden. Now there were no yaks at Song-Pan-ting; we had to send for them.

It was useless to hope that we could conceal such preparations from the authorities. Their opposition was certain beforehand, from the same motives as actuated them where we were starting for Lolo territory, and it was impossible to engage a single yak without their consent. We should have to employ diplomacy.

From the very first day I kept the prefect acquainted with our plans. We had the good fortune to chance on an intelligent and amiable man, although perfectly determined not to let us start. Thereupon interminable negotiations commenced. We had, on both sides, a peremptory argument. "The German officers went on, so you cannot possibly prevent us from doing the same," we said. "I am responsible for your safety," replied the prefect. "Now they were wounded and robbed. The same thing will happen to you, and the blame will fall on me."

The two points of view were irreconcilable; the only hope of either party was to tire out the other. Letters followed letters and visits succeeded to visits, without the least progress effected.

Happily this delay was not waste of time. Every day the city was filling with Tibetans coming in from the neighbouring mountains, from whom we obtained copious information. Their clothing, with its blaze of colour, enchanted us, and the women, with their parti-coloured petticoats and the great pieces of jewellery stuck in their huge knots of hair, were fair prey for our cameras.

In the surroundings of the city there are monasteries of red and yellow lamas: the Pon-bo also—or Pönbo, to follow the local pronunciation—are very numerous. It is impossible for any one who is not a specialist in these matters to distinguish precisely how their divinities differ from those of Buddhism; we brought back statuettes appertaining to both the cults, and they are identical. The Buddhist and Pon-bo religions are regarded by European scholars as rival and antagonistic systems; the Pon-bo, the national religion, would have been dethroned by Hindoo Buddhism; but the better to defend itself borrowed the greater part of its myths and rites. I can say nothing as to the theological merits of the case, but wherever we encountered it, together with Buddhism—and these regions are one of their principal centres—the followers of the Pon-bo cult were rather considered, and considered themselves, as forming a particular sect of Buddhism.

Their most obvious peculiarity is that they perform from left to right what the Buddhists do from right to left; this is the case, for instance, when they turn a prayer-mill, tell their beads, or make the circuit of a monument. Another obvious difference is that the Pon-bo monks let their hair grow long, while the lamas are almost shaven. The accompanying photograph shows a Pon-bo monk whose hair falls to his knees.

The Pon-bo, like all Buddhists, boast of reincarnated saints. It is perhaps not generally known how numerous these reincarnations are among the Buddhist saints; every self-respecting monastery has a saint of

SONG-PAN-TING.

To face page 212.

its own. A child is born ; the family proclaims everywhere that the child declared, on coming into the world, that it was a celebrated saint, and that they intend to offer it, for a consideration, to such convents as do not yet possess a saint. If the market is good the child is declared a reincarnated saint, and makes the fortune of the monastery by becoming the object of pilgrimages. During our stay at Song-Pan-ting there was such a young incarnation to sell, but the parents were asking too high a price, and no convent would purchase a patron so dearly.

Our negotiations never flagged. They became further complicated by the fact that the general intervened, whose advice the prefect was bound to respect; for in China, where it is an understood thing that the military mandarins are decidedly looked down upon, they really have precedence over civil mandarins, and an ordinary colonel comes before the prefect in his own prefecture. One really might think there was some unheard-of conspiracy to teach Europeans precisely the opposite of the truth in respect of China!

However, a certain amount of progress was evident. The prefect did not fail to grasp the fact that he would cause France to complain if he prevented us from doing what he had allowed the Germans to do. Then our success with the Lolos, the news of which had reached him, was a precedent of a kind to inspire confidence; while the disgrace of the prefect who had opposed us was another reason for going slowly. Of course all these considerations were not urged in the first person; but the confidential servants of the prefect and our own were continually exchanging visits, and were instructed to make matters understood that could not be openly discussed.

The prefect finally consented to our following the same route as Dr. Tafel, who regained Chinese territory at Tao-Chu ; an expedition had chastised the thieving tribes of the district the year before and inspired some temporary respect for the Chinese colours. But this was precisely the way we did not wish to go, as we wanted to trace a new itinerary, and one much longer, past the unknown confluence of the Great and Little Yellow Rivers and the famous lamasery of Lhabrang. The prefect refused to hear of this: we should come to harm and he would be removed.

Well, we would free him of his responsibility! I wrote him an official letter, referring to the facts that he had warned us of the dangers of the journey, that he had declared himself unable to protect us, and that he had most strongly advised us to abandon our plans; that in consequence he would be in nowise responsible for such accidents as might befall us, if he would take the three following measures: (1) furnish us with an escort of eight men—quite incapable of defending us in case of attack, but sufficient to mount guard at night and reconnoitre by day; (2) advise the first tribe which we should encounter, which although independent had considerable commercial relations with Song-Panting, that we were friends; (3) and advise the viceroy of Kan-Su that we should on leaving Tibet cross into his territory, so that he might make similar arrangements from the Lhabrang end.

I knew that nothing could be more dangerous than such an engagement if contracted with a knave: he could cause us to be massacred by a single promise of immunity given secretly to the tribes, and then triumphantly prove by my letter that he had done everything to avert the catastrophe. But we had no other resource, and we had fortunately an honest man to deal with. Far from taking no interest in our fate now that he was relieved of his responsibility, he assisted me in taking all measures and arranging all details likely to ensure our success.

One of the soldiers of the escort was appointed by request of Father Dury, being the best of his flock; and it was partly to the devotion and intrepid courage

TIBETAN WOMEN—DISTRICT OF SONG-PAN-TING.

To face page 214.

of this man that we owed our lives. The rest were chosen among those who spoke Tibetan fluently; three of them were actually Tibetans, and two others had already been to Tibet either to trade or to fight. The general thought to please us and to crown this excellent selection by placing over the escort a Christian non-commissioned officer. In this he was unhappily mistaken, for the man was surely the most indifferent Christian in all Christendom, and he was not much better as a soldier.

A troop of twenty-six yaks, conducted by three Tibetans who knew the country, was loaded with our baggage; they were to take us to Lhabrang, and there only they would be paid, which would guarantee their fidelity. These yaks carried our tents, our personal baggage reduced to a minimum, a month's provisions for the whole expedition, and two months' grain for our mounts. The majority of the latter were replaced by Tibetan horses.

The rest of the baggage, notably our silver and all the documents collected, which we did not care to expose to the risk of pillage, would follow the Chinese road, making a vast circuit to the east in order to avoid the dangerous country, and would await us at Ho-Chu; so that if we met with misfortune at least our discoveries would not perish with us. Our chief scholar, being useless in Tibet, was to conduct this caravan.

All was ready, and the yaks were being loaded, when the most wretched contretemps occurred. The prospect of this expedition caused our men no pleasure; the reputation of the nomads in no way encouraged them, and the snow, which had frequently fallen since our arrival in Song-Pan-ting, was not calculated to help them to enjoy the charms of camp-life. The majority had declared themselves too exhausted to follow us, and were replaced by natives of the country, accustomed to the climate and the Tibetans. Our Chinese interpreter had vainly tried to dissuade us from our project;

when he found himself in this dilemma, that he must either follow us or lose his lucrative situation, he did not hesitate: he fell ill. What can one do with a man whose temperature is 106°? We had perforce to send him by palanquin with our baggage to Ho-Chu.

Then only Captain Lepage was left as interpreter. This would never do; he could not be both at the front and the rear of the caravan; moreover, circumstances might arise which would result in our being temporarily separated; and what would happen were he too to fall ill?

Must we abandon plans so long in ripening, at the very moment when all obstacles were apparently overcome? Could we let it be believed that we had shrunk from dangers which had not checked our rivals of the German army? Without hesitation I went to knock on Father Dury's door, to ask him to take the place of the sick interpreter, and, very simply, he accepted. He would only gain suffering and peril by following us, with neither glory nor profit, even for the task of evangelisation to which he was vowed; but it was enough for him to render a service to a French Mission. "But see, you must get Monseigneur to forgive me!" he said in some alarm; for he was going to quit his post and disappear without authorisation. But the Bishop bore him no ill-feeling for that!

Finally, on April 24th, our troop took the road. It comprised, besides the five of us, eight mounted Chinese and Tibetan soldiers, our four Annamites, two scholars, three Tibetan transport drivers, and ten servants and coolies to care for the horses and do the work of the camp. In all we were twenty-four on horseback and eight on foot.

Our departure from Song-Pan-ting was magnificent. Decidedly the general and the prefect did things well; more than fifty soldiers and satellites preceded us, bearing flags and parasols, and petards exploded as we went. It was a triumphant progress.

PON-BO MONK, TIBETAN MUSSULMAN, AND LAMAISTIC NOVICE.

A TIBETAN VILLAGE.

To face page 216

A day's march through Tibetan villages of a type new to us—the houses all of wood, provided with balconies, like Swiss chalets, with an astonishing profusion of piety in the shape of masts with banners—and we came to a lofty rampart, guarded by an outpost of soldiers, which barred the valley of the Min. This was a prolongation of the Great Wall of China which protects the frontier against the Barbarians: the "Barrier of the Empire."

We crossed it joyfully, and proceeded to pitch our camp in the "Country of Grass."

CHAPTER X

ENTERING TIBET[1]

We pitched our camp three miles from the frontier, at the confluence of two of the branches of the River Min. Dr. Tafel had followed up the western source; we were going to ascend the northern branch. For eight days we never met a soul. To leave a void next to a powerful neighbour is always the tactics of a nation fond of its independence.

We halted early, for with new hands the installation of a camp is no easy matter. It was always arranged in a square: our three tents forming one face, those of our men forming the two adjacent faces, while the fourth was closed by the yaks, attached by means of a ring in the nose to a cord lying along the ground. In front of them our Tibetan transport drivers pitched their tent, and their enormous dog—the famous molossus—added to the safety of that side, and, we hoped, of the whole camp. Our horses were hobbled and picketed in the centre of the square.

This typical form of camp had of course to allow for inequalities of the soil; to take the wind into account, so that the doors of the tents should be to windward; and the fires, so that no one should be smoked out. A thousand details have to be considered, all unsuspected by beginners; practice, and practice only, will produce the necessary craft.

[1] Chapters X. and XI. appeared in the *Revue des Deux-Mondes*, February 14, 1911.

CAMPING IN TIBET.

OUR ESCORT.

To face page 218.

The landscape delighted us; we had seen nothing like it since leaving the Lolo country. It was a smiling valley, with rounded, turf-covered slopes; in the background rose a high, snowy range, the Tama Mountains, which for several days served us as a landmark toward which to travel; and—what was lacking among the Lolos—the clumps of woodland were numerous. What a contrast with the wild, barren valleys which had led us thither! Truly no "Barrier of the Empire" was needed to show us where the new country began!

Men and beasts were both affected by the change. All their habits were deranged; they all showed themselves singularly at sea, our horses especially. According to the custom of the "Country of Grass," we had left them to graze at will, contenting ourselves with hobbling them. Our Chinese horses, used neither to the liberty nor the impediment, threw themselves at one another, bit and broke their hobbles, and fled into the distance. We had to organise a party to recapture them. But then a singular scene occurred: one of our horses, very tall and powerful for a Chinese horse, and always very difficult, so that we had unanimously offered it to Boyve, had become absolutely furious, and pounced upon all who approached it. Two of our men in succession were laid out by this ferocious beast, who, holding them down with his feet, began to tear at them with his teeth; and without the help of the rest they would infallibly have been torn to pieces. The poor fellows could do no work of any kind for several days, so badly did they suffer from those bites. We had to use all the paraphernalia of the desert—lasso, slip-knot, and so forth—before we could recapture this indomitable brute.

Then, suddenly, a terrible blast of wind went by, the lightning flashed, the thunder crashed, and whirling eddies of snow enveloped us. All night the storm continued. Several badly pitched tents were overturned by the gale, and the poor devils whom they had sheltered were half-buried by the dense masses of snow-flakes; another time they would fix their tent-pegs more firmly! The thunder rolled without interruption. Truly all things had combined to give us a high idea of the charms of Tibet! But I remembered that an equally wild welcome—curious coincidence!—had met us at the gate of the Lolo country, where, none the less, success awaited us. Are not all the seekers of the Golden Fleece subjected to trial?—and would any country remain virgin to the adventurer, were it not, like the Valkyrie, protected by a circle of fire or of ice? Come! this tempest was of good omen!

Alas, it seemed otherwise in the morning! Three of our horses were gone—the best; their tethers were cut with a knife; their tracks, in company with those of two strange animals, led over the mountains; they had been raided.

For a beginning this was too much! To be raided three miles from the frontier, in our own camp, ten feet from the soldiers' tent! Yet we had posted a sentinel; during the lulls in the storm we had heard his watchman's cry. During the squalls he had doubtless taken refuge in his tent, leaving the terrible weather to be our protection. And our Tibetan molossus had not so much as bayed.[1] Ah! why had we not those Annamite sharpshooters? If matters were to continue thus the catastrophe would not be long deferred.

However, this theft was so extraordinary, its competence and audacity so amazing, it was so peculiar that there should be ambushed thieves in our near neighbourhood in a deserted zone, through which the rumour of our coming could not have spread already, that we asked ourselves whether the mandarins had

[1] This animal had decided to guard only his own masters, so that we could never approach their tent without running the risk of being devoured. What happened in the rest of the camp was to him a matter of the supremest indifference. He was absolutely useless to us.

not arranged the matter to frighten us and make us return.

We should have to put a bold face on the matter. I wrote to the prefect and the general, saying that by the negligence of their soldiers our three best horses had been carried off, and that they were consequently themselves responsible for the loss, since it did not come under the heading of *force majeure*, in which case they had my discharge. We should continue our journey, but if he did not take the necessary measures to restore our horses I should address a complaint to the Viceroy.

Then, to prove that we should not allow ourselves to be intimidated, and that we considered the soldiers at fault, I gave orders to strike camp, and requisitioned three of the escort's horses for our dismounted horsemen; but after a short march we halted again to await the reply of the authorities.

It arrived on the following day, taking the extremely satisfactory form of three excellent horses, which the mandarins offered us with their apologies. They pressed us to profit by this annoying experience, and to return; but they could not more fairly have enabled us to act as we chose. It is an admirable conception of the duties of authority that requires every functionary to repair, out of his own pocket, all the thefts that a better supervision might have prevented.

We resumed our march. The many incidents of the previous night were a lesson to us. In future the tents would be more firmly pitched, the horses tethered in groups by chains and padlocks, the military guard would be doubled by one of our own men on the opposite side of the camp, and rounds would be made regularly. Every one began to understand that every fault would be paid for.

The march was delightful. There was no need to follow the trail; the turf made easy going everywhere, although we had to look out for frequent bogs; and if we had not been afraid to tire our horses, which would have many trials before them, what splendid gallops we could have had! We frequently put up hares or pheasants, which made an agreeable change in our diet of rice, bacon, and ham.

Only those who have travelled in the desert realise how much life this solitude conceals. Once man has disappeared Nature assumes a singular personality : the least accident of the soil takes on a new importance. Such a hollow is a good site for a camp, for it gives a shelter from the wind; here the water is bad, coming as it does from bogs; there you will find wood; this valley is the road by which the raiders of caravans travel, and there is the rock you must climb to search the surroundings for signs of men in ambush; in case of attack there is the bog behind which to take refuge from their charge; if yonder peak has put on its cap of clouds there will be a fall of snow; but if the snow has disappeared in yonder valley the winter is at an end. Thus everything lives, everything speaks, everything plays its part, and man, dropping his pose as master, asks respectfully for information and conforms to the conditions imposed.

This change was soon apparent. In China it is only man that counts : beyond the villages he inhabits and the fields he cultivates there are no place-names ; even the great rivers and important mountain ranges have only vague and uncertain designations ; as for the streams and peaks, if by any chance they boast of a name it is purely local, and unknown elsewhere. In Tibet, on the contrary, the smallest heap of earth has its place in the world, and when we used each day to discuss with our guides the next day's march, in order to determine where we had best make the midday halt and where pitch the camp, one might well have thought, on hearing such a host of names, that we were travelling through a particularly populous country. The abundant indications on our maps should deceive no one ; they

THE CARAVAN EN ROUTE.

THE LAST FORESTS.

To face page 222.

represent only absolutely desolate spots ; but these places are more important to those who are travelling through the country than the largest city in a densely peopled land.

The absence of flocks and herds in this deserted region is favourable to the growth and survival of medicinal plants ; so men come from a great distance to gather such plants, for the herbs of Tibet are of great repute all over China. They are gathered by parties whose deserted encampments are often encountered. Another medicinal though not vegetable substance is found here in abundance : the antlers of the deer, which at the moment of their fall contain a marrow which enters into the composition of a host of medicaments. The Chinese pharmacopœia, like that of the Middle Ages, makes extensive use of animal substances.

These solitudes are more frequented than appears. Our men often pulled up to examine footprints on the soil ; so many horsemen passed this way yesterday, or on such a day. By their number, their direction, and the weight upon their horses they appear to be a hunting party, in which case there is nothing to fear from them. We often heard the sounds of horsemen in the night, and a conversation would be held between our sentinels and invisible riders, for the darkness does not hinder these children of the desert, whose senses are prodigiously developed, and who know the least molehill.

The pleasant nature of the march, so long as the weather was passable, made us forget the slowness of the yaks. These animals have their necks so conveniently disposed that they can graze as they march—a habit which does nothing to accelerate their pace. At the same time, however, they give practically no further trouble ; the horses, which cannot graze as they go, arrive in camp with empty stomachs, so that one has to pitch the camp early in order to give them sufficient time to graze.

That is, if the snow permits. It fell every evening and often during the night; sometimes from four or five in the afternoon; and in the morning the ground would be covered to a depth of six inches. Here is a remarkable phenomenon: by ten o'clock or so it would have completely disappeared, yet it did not melt, nor was the ground moist on which it had lain: it had evaporated, so dry is the air, and so swift the wind, which passes before it can be saturated.

Nevertheless, it had prevented the animals from grazing before the start, and it often prevents their feeding on pitching the camp at night, so that while the yaks have fed on the uncovered pasture through which they have marched, the horses arrive fasting. For this reason, to prevent their dying of hunger, we had to bring a large store of dried peas, an eminently sustaining diet.

Woods were plentiful; deciduous trees in the valleys, pines on the hill-sides. No one fells them; even before the "Barrier of the Empire" was reached the river was no longer navigable, and the transport of timber was impossible; and since the country is not frequented by shepherds or herdsmen it is in no one's interest to destroy the forests. We wondered why they did not cover more ground, and why they were not continuous, as they must have been at one time, for it is the nature of the forest to gain ground wherever man does not oppose it.

The explanation was quickly furnished. We found whole forests laid low; a fire lit by some hunter or herbalist, and imperfectly extinguished on breaking camp, had resulted in a forest fire, and the wind had uprooted the calcined trunks. A spectacle as tragic as a battle-field heaped with rifled bodies! Thus, through the negligence of man, the secular forests are disappearing; and at many points in these smiling valleys the waters ravage the slopes where nothing is left to bind the earth and check the rains. In a few

FATHER DURY.

THE PASS OF LANG-KIA-LING (13,500 FEET).

To face page 224.

Alas! the welcome of Tibet, as we penetrated the country further, was no more hospitable than at first: on the contrary, the cold redoubled. The snow fell now almost without a break. Lashed by an incessant wind, which by some evil fate blew always directly in our faces, we were blinded and blistered. In a few days our skin, blackened as though by the rays of a burning sun, was stripping off in great flakes, which exposed a new and still tender skin; and the contrast of these brown and rosy stripes which barred our faces was by no means becoming. Our lips were cracked and swollen; each of us regarded his companions with horror, and, without daring to consult a mirror, asked himself uneasily if he too were as hideous. Should we ever dare to face civilised folks again?

I must own that we were to some extent the victims of our own carelessness. All these woes had been described by our predecessors, but we had not believed they would effect us so soon or so suddenly. We ought, from the very first day—if we did not completely imitate our Tibetans and our Chinese escort, who entirely abandoned the practice of washing themselves—at least to have annointed our faces with grease. And why had we not recollected the joy of Father Huc, on receiving from a benevolent lama a "pair of spectacles" made of yak's hair? Our Tibetans possessed them, and we envied them. Stout motor-goggles and masks would have saved us a great deal of suffering.

As for the Chinese, and above all our Annamites, you may imagine whether they found the climate agreeable. We had taken all necessary precautions for their benefit, buying them padded cloaks, hoods of waterproof felt, and long-haired dogs' pelts on which to lie. But he who suffered most of all, although he did not complain, was certainly Father Dury. We had not thought of him—I confess it to my shame—and as we had asked him to accompany us at the last moment he had had no time to procure furs. Even when wearing all the coats he possessed he shivered with cold, but he never admitted it until we heard him cough.

Our animals had the greatest difficulty in finding food, rooting in the snow to get at the grass, and even swallowing the snow itself ; for yaks and even horses will eat a great deal of snow.

Yet all went fairly well so long as we found means to make a fire. Since there was no more timber the only fuel was argol ; which poetical title signifies the dried droppings of animals. Father Huc has treated of this matter in a masterly fashion, and we were perfectly aware of the different kinds of argol, and their virtues : the only difficulty was—to find any.

How, it may be asked, can you find it in the desert? Well, the matter is less complicated than it looks. All the nomads camp in the same places, which present favourable conditions, such as shelter from the wind, the proximity of unfrozen springs, &c. It results that each party, on leaving, leaves a deposit of fresh argol, which is dry by the time the next visitors camp on the spot.

There was, therefore, little trouble so long as the snow fell only by night, and the earth lay bare by day ; but when it snowed both by night and by day the precious combustible was buried from sight. Under such conditions we were forced, as soon as we halted, to scatter our men over the whole area in which its presence was probable, and each man feverishly raked in the frozen snow until he discovered the precious manna. Sometimes we saw the darkness falling, and nothing was found ; a gloomy outlook, that of a night without fire, in that bitter cold and freezing wind, with no cooked food, without even a drink of tea ! Finally a cry of triumph would rise from some corner of the camping ground, and every one would rush to collect the precious deposit.

All these trials, which told cruelly on our staff, were lightened by the thought of our mission ; and if they

THE FRENCH FLAG.

SEARCHING FOR ARGOL.

To face page 228.

centuries they will be as scarred and bare as those we had traversed in China.

But here was the end of trees and forests. By dint of continued ascents we had reached the source of the River Min, at a height of 13,800 feet, in the Lang-Kia-Ling Pass. We then descended the course of the Paotso, which runs in the opposite direction ; this was the source, hitherto undiscovered, of the river with the white waters—Pei-Chuei-ho—the great tributary, which after a course of five hundred miles flows into the Blue River at Chong-King. Yet another pass, the Tangoma, of 14,000 feet, and we should enter the basin of the Yellow River. We had left the belt of vegetation —above 12,300 feet we never found so much as a thicket—and had reached the region of snowfields. Are they eternal? I do not think so : their scanty depth, due to evaporation, could hardly resist the suns of August. But now, although we were entering on the merry month of May, the layer of snow was daily renewed.

Here we stood on the crest of the great border chain of Tibet, and we gazed far into the interior. The reader might expect, in accordance with the reports of all the travellers who have explored this mysterious country, a description of the most terrific mountains. On the contrary, the multitude of ranges which encompassed us, although as high as or higher than Mont Blanc, appeared only as insignificant hills with rounded outlines. We might have forgotten the height at which we stood, only that behind us, in the direction of China, a few pointed summits, rising from the void, betrayed the fact that their roots were established in the stupendous depths which surrounded us.

In the pass of Lang-Kia-Ling our Tibetans, and even our Chinese, did not fail to throw a stone on the *latsi*. This is the local name for what the Mongols call *obo*, a heap of stones, rising in a pyramidal cairn, composed of the stones which pious people have placed there in passing. Poles were thrust into the cairn, from which floated pennons bearing pious invocations. In spite of what has been written on the subject, these *latsi* are not found on every pass; on the contrary, they are quite as commonly found in valleys, and indeed on all sorts of sites. In whose honour are they raised? In the minds of the simple, in honour of the *genius loci*, for Buddhists and Pon-bo are really preeminently Pantheists, and see spirits everywhere. Our people also gave the divinity of this famous pass, whence one sees for the last time the mountains of China, offerings of gold or silver money—represented by paper, which they had brought for the purpose.

We were now about to descend once more—but the descent was insignificant. We were leaving the territory of the Paotso tribe, a people we had not seen, who lived in a valley some distance from the trail, and entering the domain of the great confederation of the Dzorgei, which occupies the apex of the loop of the Yellow River, in the midst of the Ngolo, the Ngapa, the Paotso, the Samsa, and the Tatze.

All these people were to be feared, as they live by pillage as much as by their stock: only the Paotso and the first tribe of the Dzorgei, the Pan-Yu or Pain-Yu, were for the moment on friendly terms with the Chinese authority, and the prefect, in accordance with our request, had asked them to receive us well. It was a good sign that we had already crossed the territory of the Paotso without incident, but we should have to keep a particularly watchful eye on our men, since it was from that direction that the Ngapa were wont to raid the caravans bound for the Pan-Yu. The nomads do not raid their next-door neighbours except in times of open war, but they do not scruple in the least to invade their territory in order to pillage any strangers who may be passing, or to cross it in order to lift the cattle of a remoter tribe.

sometimes seemed a little too painful we had only to raise our eyes to the French flag which floated in the gusty wind of these inviolate solitudes.

Continually descending the gradual slope of the little streams which slowly increased in volume, we came at length to the brink of a considerable river: the principal affluent of the Yellow River in its upper course, and regarded by all as the second source, as is proved by the name by which the Chinese know it—the Second Yellow River—Yul-tao Hoang-ho. The Tibetans call it Maichu, and call the main river Machu or Machi.

Now we had only to descend its course. A few thickets, full of hares and pheasants, reappeared along its banks; the weather grew milder; the grass showed once more; antelopes, always out of range, gracefully defied us; the valley widened; and an indefinite, inexpressible softening of the landscape made us anticipate the neighbourhood of man. At last we saw cattle. It was time. Those eight days of marching through almost unbroken snow, the insufficient food, and the terrible cold of the nights, had exhausted our horses; already one of them had fallen never to rise again, and others were ready to do the same.

The chief of the Pan-Yu came to meet us, followed by a number of armed horsemen. He was a man of about thirty-five, with rather fine features. He wore a hooded mantle of sheepskin with the wool inside, edged with a collar of panther skin; this, with a pair of boots, was all.

Such is the costume of all these nomads. They are absolutely naked in this Arctic temperature except for this hooded cloak, which they raise as high as the knees by means of a girdle, without troubling about the cold which rises from the frozen ground. Yet they are often too hot; they throw off the right sleeve, sometimes even the left, and almost constantly go about with the body bare, at least on the right side. What a hardy race!

However, I am forgetting one item of clothing, a very essential one, which yields the indispensable protection ; never washing, they are covered with a dense coat of filth, accumulated since their birth. Their skin, which ought to be pink and white—as it shows, when they take their boots off, on their feet and calves, which from time to time are washed by the streams through which they wade—is an almost blackish brown. Certainly the sun, which is hot enough in summer, must count for something, and the icy wind for more, for nothing tans one more deeply ; but this negroid tint arises chiefly from a layer of solidly incrusted dirt.

Do not believe, however, on the faith of authors who have only seen—or smelt—the sedentary unwashed, that the perfume of these nomads is disagreeable ; above all, do not get the idea into your head that they are unclean ! By no means.

The keen air with which their bodies are continually bathed from head to foot carries off all trace of odour, and the dirt, sinking into the pores of the skin, incorporating itself in its substance, has not the appearance of a foreign matter whose incongruous presence calls for expulsion ; no, it is an integral part of the tissue, and seems no more than a deep and very effective *patina*.

What a blow to our hygienic theories of cleanliness ! For this impermeability of the skin seems a very logical measure, since the penetration of the icy air would be mortal, and the races which best resist the cold, Tibetans and Lolos, Siberians and Esquimaux, all have the same custom ! When travelling the nomads wear a curious headgear. It is a cone of sheepskin ; sometimes the outer side is covered with red or blue cloth, and the edges are always turned up, so that the white wool of the lining forms an elegant border. This cap undergoes an infinity of variations ; sometimes it is low and splayed out at the brim ; sometimes it is disproportionately high ; sometimes the point re-enters ; sometimes it falls to one side like the headgear of our

THE LESSER YELLOW RIVER.

To face page 230.

old Dragoons ; sometimes it points skyward ; sometimes the woolly border is perfectly symmetrical, and sometimes it is displayed more fully in front, and enlarged into a kind of visor. These hats had about them something at once comical and elegant which was a joy to us.

About their own homes, and often when travelling, the nomads go bareheaded, displaying their cropped but not shaven polls, which distinguish them from all other races of the Chinese Empire hitherto visited.[1] The Tibetans hitherto known wear two great twists of hair rolled round the head.

As throughout all Tibet, the horsemen wear a sword thrust horizontally into the girdle, across the waist, and a bandolier, and carry a musket equipped with an adjustable fork. This is an astonishingly useful contrivance ; the marksman thrusts his gun downwards so that the fork sticks upright in the soil, while the gun, being pivoted on the fork, is brought to the horizontal ; he can then, without the loss of a moment, take a steady aim. The Tibetans greatly appreciate this fork, and very justly ; so much so, indeed, that they fit it even to such modern fire-arms as fall into their hands. We have seen—and the contrast is striking—repeating rifles of the latest type equipped by their owners with this simple apparatus, which evokes the distant periods of the primitive musket.

But the chief weapon of the Tibetans is an enormous lance, from sixteen to twenty feet in length ; a lance exactly like that used by the Lolos, but which we never saw elsewhere than in Lolo territory and in Tibet.

The chief who met us announcing that he had found an excellent place for our camp, I expressed a desire that it should be in the village itself, so that we could make our observations the more readily. " Impossible,

[1] The young Lolos wear their hair in the same manner, except that in front there is usually a lock of hair which eventually becomes the famous " horn." The men, on the contrary, wear their hair fairly long.

on account of the dogs," replied our guides ; "they would kill you." "Well, you can tie them up," said I, rather taken aback by this arrangement, which seemed likely to keep us at more than arm's length. But my guides gazed at me with astonishment, and then began to laugh, and I am sure they mentally shrugged their shoulders.

We were accordingly led to a level meadow by the river-side, and with that we had to be content. A crowd of young people and children surrounded us in a moment. They were not in the least shy or sullen ; they were even obliging, and full of laughter.

But where was the great village of Pan-Yu, famous throughout the country? Were we camped so far away that we could not see it?—Where was it?—Why, right in front of us, at a hundred yards' distance. And we strained our eyes without seeing anything but some palisades that might enclose cattle-pens or corrals ; and yes ! in the centre of these rose little circular hillocks, on the top of which were perched groups of women who were watching us ; but never a sign of a house or tent !

By this time we were emphatically curious. We asked the chief if we might return his civilities by visiting him in his own house. "With pleasure," he said, "but be well on your guard ; take each of you a sword, or at least a staff ; and let those who are on the outside and at the rear protect the rest !" And he himself, drawing his sword, took the lead of our party. Whatever could this mean? What dangers threatened us?

The worthy chief did well to prepare us ! When we approached the palisade a dozen enormous molossi which had been lying on the ground made for us in a deliberate and resolute manner ; we had to whirl our sticks about like windmills in order to keep a yard or two between ourselves and these ferocious beasts, which would not even listen to their master's voice.

TIBETAN HORSEMEN.

TIBETAN HORSEMEN.

To face page 232.

These terrible watch-dogs are a characteristic of these agglomerations of nomads. When going from one village to another *even the inhabitants themselves* must be armed, and must go two at a time, or they would inevitably be torn to pieces. These dogs, happily, will not stray from the dwelling with whose care they are entrusted ; at a distance of fifty yards one is safe ; but woe to the foolhardy person who approaches more closely. Fleurelle, carried away by his photographic zeal, learned this by sad experience, and if we had not discovered his imprudence in time, so that we ran in a body to his rescue, he would have left more than his cloak between the fangs of the terrible hounds.

We crossed several palisaded enclosures, which were empty, the flocks and herds being abroad in the pastures, and arrived before the central hillock. Still there were no houses. "Be so good as to enter," said the chief, with a respectful bow. But enter what, and how? Were we to enter the ground?

Well, the door did turn out to be in the hillock itself ; through the darkness we dimly glimpsed a stable or byre, beyond which the cave grew lighter, and we came out into a great rotunda, from thirty to fifty feet in diameter, and from ten to twelve feet high.

The hillock which we had supposed to be natural was completely hollow ; thick beams and pillars supported the earth which rested on a framework of hurdles or bavins. Besides the door, which was masked by a wall dividing the byre from the great room, the only opening was at the very summit of the dome, through which the smoke escaped and a little light entered, with a great deal of rain and snow ; but when these latter became too plentiful some one would pick up a lance just as among the Lolos, and slide forwards a few planks which ran in grooves, thus closing the aperture ; the darkness was then complete.

It is of course always gloomy in these artificially subterranean dwellings. When the eye grows accustomed to the darkness it enjoys an interior which is magnificently barbaric and primitive.

The most prominent object is a long hearth of baked earth containing two braziers and two receptacles in which argol is kept ready for burning. On these braziers are great pots of water which is kept continually hot for making tea. This hearth divides the floor of the dwelling into two compartments: that on the right is reserved for the master and his guests, that on the left for the women and the servants.

At the back of the men's compartment is an altar with a few Buddhist statuettes, and a multitude of little saucers full of butter, one of which is always burning like a night-light; and a continuation of the hearth contains banners on which are imprinted the image of the divine horse, a symbol which plays a great part in this land of horsemen. All about the floor is scattered the wealth of the family: saddles, weapons, and above all numbers of bales, some containing tea, salt, barley-flour, or rice, all of which are goods coming from a distance, while the others contain the pelts and furs which will form the currency for fresh purchases.

On the left-hand side are the cooking utensils and great vessels in which milk is kept or butter churned. There the women are kept busy attending on the men who are seated on the skins at the opposite side of the fire. To the right is the reception-room, to the left the kitchen.

The hearth does not completely separate the two divisions; there is an ample passage between it and the wall of the byre, against which a number of beds are usually arranged—couches of skins surrounded with curtains.

As soon as we entered the women's side grew busy: fuel was thrown into the braziers, fresh butter taken from the churn, and a vase was filled with a delicious cream slightly tart and pleasantly thick. Tea was served across the hearth as convention required, by the majestic mistress of the house.

A CROWD AT PAN-YU.

To face page 234.

The polyandry of Tibet has resulted in the spilling of a great deal of ink. Sociologists incline to regard it as one of the manifestations of the perfect communism of the family : all the brothers being as one with the eldest brother possess the same wife as they possess the same goods. But we encountered neither communism nor polyandry : on the death of the father his children divide his goods into equal parts, and each sets up for himself. Naturally each has his wife, or even several, though not very commonly. I was not able to discover whether polygamy was optional or confined to cases of sterility.

The male type is variable ; all are tall and many have long and refined features. The women, with somewhat rare exceptions, are of a very different type : they are short, sturdy, solid, fleshy ; their faces are wide and roughly hewn. The hair is divided by a parting in the middle of the forehead and twisted into a multitude of narrow tails, from which hangs at the back a band of cloth loaded with enormous jewels in silver, turquoise, and coral. Two similar bands, starting from the back of the neck, hang down in front to the feet, and are very often the only covering—and a very scanty one—of the breasts ; for these ladies, like their husbands, wear the sheepskin cloak as their only garment, and as it is very heavy, and cumbersome to any one occupied in household tasks, it is nearly always thrown aside as far as the waist.

What a vision of remote humanity is presented by these robust creatures, who, almost naked but always loaded with jewels like queens, solemnly devote themselves to the labours of a beast of burden, bending under the weight of hods of argol, or the great water-vessels which they fill at the river. One feels that they are as proud of the proper accomplishment of these heavy tasks, which necessity renders sacred to all such primitive beings, as of spreading over their bodies the tangible signs of the wealth and power of their spouses.

When, on the summit of each of those giant mole-hills, their houses, you see their massive silhouettes, as they stand in groups, their wide, astonished faces gleaming under locks that hang to the ground, their massive shoulders, their muscular arms, and their glittering jewels, you seem to behold, perched upon their chariots, the indomitable women of the Cimbri or the Teutons.

For two days we were never tired of visiting, one after another, these strange dwellings, the like of which resembled nothing that had to our knowledge been reported on the face of the globe. There were thirty, which might shelter some twenty to thirty persons apiece, counting masters and servants. Each dwelling, with its surrounding palisades, constituted an isolated fortress.

No one ever leaves his house without arming himself with a sword, and, if he goes into the country, with his lance and rifle or musket. Pastoral life, which we picture to ourselves under its bucolic aspect, is in reality a life of warfare and adventure. The wealth of the nomad, his flocks and herds, are not, like the wealth of the sedentary worker, contained in the soil, from which he must extract them by obstinate labour ; a surprise attack, and the herds of another are yours. Who would not be tempted? Each man's thought are always of attack and defence ; the pastoral neighbour is always a danger. Tibetans, Mongols, and Turks, Huns, Arabs, Touaregs—all the world over these insignificant tribes only await an Attila, a Genghis Khan, or a Mahomet to conquer the world ; and we must not forget that twice in the eighth century the Tibetans penetrated to the capital of the Chinese Empire, Si-Ngan-fu, and took the city.

But this love of sudden raids and profitable exploits by no means signifies that they are quarrelsome and overbearing. Like their African congeners, the Touaregs, whom they resemble at so many points, they are grave, reflective, and courteous.

NOMAD WOMEN.

To face page 234

We were hospitably received everywhere: everywhere also we responded to the offering of tea and cream by that of some rare and coveted article, such as a knife or a mirror.[1]

We were especially successful in winning the hearts of the women. Their favourite trinkets are gilt uniform buttons, and England has inaugurated in Tibet a new form of pacific penetration, by pouring into the country all the old buttons of the Indian army; so much so that in this northern extremity of Tibet we could easily have made an enumeration of her forces; we had only to look at the women, for the numbers of the Hindoo regiments were displayed upon their bosoms. Our patriotism could not suffer so crafty a form of annexation, and future explorers will see French uniform buttons shining beside the English on the ample bosoms of the Tibetan dames.

This long halt was extremely useful to us, as we were able to remount our horsemen and renew our provisions.

What provisions, the reader may ask? The nomads have absolutely *no* crops; they have no fowls even—it is the only country I know devoid of poultry—nor do they keep pigs. But their herds of yaks and goats and their flocks of sheep furnish them with meat—which they eat fairly often—with milk, cream, and especially butter, which they consume in considerable quantities, for it is the internal combustion of grease which enables them to resist the cold. They take it, as is the custom throughout Tibet, mixed into their tea: this is the famous buttered tea. To this they add, again as elsewhere, the *tsamba*, the parched barley-meal, which they procure in the high valleys of the border country, where agriculture is still possible, and where the populations do not disdain to practise it. We see that for two

[1] The famous *khata*, or *scarf of felicity*, so necessary to the ordinary Tibetans, was not employed here; we did not encounter its use until we reached Lhabrang, nor did any one put out his tongue at us.

necessary elements of their diet, the tea and the *tsamba*, they depend entirely on the exterior, which makes it the more surprising that they have been able to retain their perfect independence in the face of China, who might easily starve them out.

The reader will perhaps be astonished to learn of the existence of a village, even of so singular a type, among a people described as nomadic. They are nomadic ; but as it has been justly said, no one is more sedentary than the nomad. He follows in the rear of his herds, but only within the restricted circle of his own territory ; sooner or later he settles on a few particularly favoured camping grounds, and thenceforth goes from one to another according to the season. If, in the organisation of his camp, he hits on something that will last, like the rampart or the hearth, he leaves it and returns to it in the following year. Thus all tribes of nomads have two or three fixed places of residence, which always bear their name, so that if the traveller inquires whether such a village is to be found in such a valley, he will be told : "Yes, in winter, but in summer it is on the other side of the mountain." It must never be forgotten that all names of nomadic groups belong not to places, but to the inhabitants, and shift with them : and the maps ought to take this peculiarity into account.

For instance, Dr. Tafel, during his journey, passed by another Pan-Yu, the summer residence of the tribe, while we were at the winter Pan-Yu, and we believed ourselves to be the first Europeans to visit it. Great was our surprise at hearing the chief refer to the visit of two whites eight years ago. As no such exploration had ever been recorded, we remained in doubt ; however, one of our Chinese soldiers declared that he had been one of the escort of the two Europeans ; moreover, he described the route they followed, and gave us their Chinese names, Pei and Chu-li-se, which enabled us to identify them.

They were two English explorers, Mr. Birth (Pei) and Captain Watt Jones (Chu-li-se) ; they started in 1900 from Song-Pan-ting by the same route as Dr. Tafel followed ; they crossed our route at Pan-Yu, and then, passing further to the east, by way of Ashi and Zaru, they reached the Chinese city of Tao-Chao by way of Ya-Tang-Pa and Lamo-Se, as Tafel did later. Hardly had they left Tibet when one was drowned in the Yellow River and the other killed by the Boxers, at the Blue City, and their papers were destroyed. As a result nothing was known of this exploration, and the travelling diary of Mr. Birth, published after his death, contained merely the letters he had dispatched before leaving Sze-Chuan, and a later letter in which he stated that he had crossed a portion of Tibet, but gave no preciser details. We were glad to have discovered the traces of these two valiant and unfortunate precursors, and to render homage to their memory.

All that we saw—the physical aspect of the inhabitants, their dwellings, clothes, and customs—differed absolutely, except for a few details which the climate or the soil have necessarily rendered similar, from the descriptions which have been given by all the travellers in Tibet, and from what we ourselves had seen at Ta-Tsien-Lu. There was no resemblance between this tribe of warriors, who are always in the saddle, lance in hand, and the heavy agriculturalists, or the timid herdsmen hitherto described. The difference was completed and explained by the difference of language ; the vocabularies we compiled have nothing in common with Tibetan language nor the derivatives we had met with on the confines of the country. We were apparently dealing with a people absolutely unknown to Europe, although apparently ancient and illustrious : for to judge by their warlike virtues these nomads, and not the ordinary Tibetans, are the Tangoutians who have played so large a part in the history of China.

CHAPTER XI

CROSSING THE "LAND OF GRAS.

By way of the lamasery of Tartsa-Gomba—the reader must excuse the pleonasm, for *gomba* signifies "lamasery"—we were now about to visit the tribe of the Lai-Wa, the chief of the Pan-Yu having arranged that we should receive a warm welcome.

The confederation of the Dzorgei consists of twelve tribes. The authority of the chiefs is not great; they are scarcely more than more distinguished and influential notabilities. All the heads of families take part in the general decision, such as a change of residence, or a question of war or peace; but for the rest they act in perfect liberty, starting on their raids or pillaging expeditions without consulting others. Naturally the ties between the tribes are very lax; however, the result of blood ties and business intercourse is that good relations are maintained, and all the tribes would come to the aid of any one if attacked; but they were under no obligation to adopt the same attitude toward ourselves.

When we had left the prehistoric constructions of an-Yu, Tartsa-Gomba surprised us like a glimpse of a forgotten civilisation; its temple and its numerous cells had an orderly and architectural appearance. This was our first encounter with the lamas in their own country. Other travellers, excepting Father Huc, have had nothing good to say of them; and it is probable

STRIKING CAMP

LAMASERY OF TARTSA-GOMBA.

To face page 240.

that they do not witness the intrusion of strangers with a favourable eye. We might have passed the lamasery without visiting it, for the territory of the Dzorgei confederation does not belong to the lamas, and the nomads, although happy to receive them in their houses in order to ensure their own welfare by their prayers, do not concede them any authority. However, there are always a number of lamas travelling about the country, and if they had taken our abstention ill they might well have spread harmful rumours to our discredit.

We therefore had them informed of our desire to visit them. We were kept waiting a very long time for their reply; a violent hailstorm burst over us, and we remained exposed to it, although only five hundred yards from the monastery, from which we were plainly seen, without any one signing to us to go thither for shelter. It was only when the fine weather returned that we were invited to enter; and even then the welcome was cold, the superiors did not appear, and a crowd of little monks of the lower order, their feet naked in the freezing mud, surrounded us with a ring of somewhat scornful faces.

However, our curiosity and their own prolonged our visit, and the temple was opened for us. We admired above all the astonishing power of will that must have presided over the construction of so considerable a piece of timber-work in a country absolutely devoid of trees. The nearest forests are at Peshi, to the east of Pan-Yu, and two and a half days from the lamasery. The great tree-trunks which served as pillars must have been brought thence, although neither wagons nor water-courses were available.

But what surprised and confounded us no less were the frescoes which covered the walls. I will not say that they were worthy of Fra Angelico, but their naïvely mystical conception, and the slightly *gauche* grace of their execution could not fail to evoke the pre-Renaissance art of our French convents, while they had scarcely any relation whatever to Chinese art.

And who was it that painted or chiselled or moulded these numerous statues, these finely worked accessories of worship, these remarkable frescoes? Who traced the plans of this imposing architecture, which had been realised in spite of the scanty means of execution? We were among the very nomads who go half-naked in their sheepskins, and wholly naked under them; who live in underground lairs or indifferently sheltered in tents; who seem as yet never to have risen to the ordinary conceptions of clothing and dwelling-houses. Yet their fathers and brothers possess and practise all the arts, to say nothing of the sciences contained in their imposing books! Here is a particularly interesting problem in sociology!

During the night our camp was awakened by a party of horsemen. They were Tibetans of Song-Pan-ting: making sixty miles a day, thanks to relays of horses, they had overtaken us to bring us an urgent message from the Viceroy of Sze-Chuan. He sent us a letter written by Chao-Yul-Fong to the French consul-general at Cheng-Tu, explaining that the situation in Tibet had never been more precarious; that the lamas were in the most violent state of excitement and resentment against all that was Chinese or foreign, and that we were going to our death; consequently he begged the consul, knowing that his prefect had been unable to stop us, that he himself would intervene. And indeed this letter was accompanied by a pressing exhortation to return from M. Bons d'Anty, his information being in accordance with that of the Viceroy.

This advice was certainly significant. The future conqueror of Lhassa had already given proof in his previous expeditions against the Tibetans that he did not tremble at imaginary dangers; as for M. Bons d'Anty, who was always perfectly informed, he had on many occasions proved his valour as an explorer, and was not the man to advise French officers to retreat without the best of reasons. The very equivocal attitude of the lamas we had visited that day, although on the territory of a friendly tribe, confirmed the report of their hostility, and we foresaw a very poor welcome when we should reach their own territory.

But did we not know all this before we started? Were we travelling for amusement? I read these letters to my companions. "Good business," said Fleurelle simply; "with those papers no one will say, if we succeed, that our undertaking was too easy; if we don't get back they can't say it was through our own want of tact." We deliberated no further; I had only to thank the consul and the Viceroy for their solicitude, and inform them that we were going forward.

But it was comical to see the misery of our men when they received the order to resume the march: the couriers had spread the news that our Government ordered us to return, thus causing a general rejoicing. Now our undertaking would seem more insecure than ever.

The region through which we were advancing was a great plain encircled by high ranges, which were near on the north and east, but remoter on the south and west. The hills and valleys were insignificant; the slope was so gradual that the streams no longer knew which way to go, but kept on doubling back upon themselves in fantastic meanderings. And this phenomenon, which one might expect in a river near the end of its course, arrived too quickly at sea-level, was produced at a height of 13,000 feet!

It really seemed as though this girdle of mountains isolated this country from the rest of the world; both nature and man seemed ignorant of what surrounded them; nothing came to disturb them, and they only wished to continue living the same life. We, who, before coming hither, had impressed upon our eyes, our brains, and all our faculties the tragi. vision of an earth disembowelled by its rivers, the vertigo of so many abysses, the fatigue of so many ascents, were dumb with astonishment before this Eden—frozen, but so calm, so open, so pastoral, where life seemed so sweet to men who laughed at the frost. We felt that after long wandering through dark and subterranean passages we had at last reached the roof of the terrestrial edifice, where there was nothing left to do but to live, bathed in the heavens, without heed of the slaves who toiled in the depths. Happy masters of the roof of the world!

But their guests were less happy! We had in vain exhorted one another to adopt the fashions of the country, and to go with our shoulders naked. We were none too warm with goatskins over our cloaks, which covered coats of leather with the fur left on, which in turn covered woollen clothing, knitted spencers, and shirts of double flannel; for the snow raged worse than ever. At last we were unable to strike camp, and were forced to remain shut up in our tents, so violent was the blizzard. When at last we decided to start what a task it was to roll up the frozen canvas, and remove the tent-pegs and cords, covered as they were with an inch of ice! I pitied our poor men: without the example of the Tibetans, who seemed entirely at their ease, we should scarcely have been able to maintain discipline. Moreover, the horses were giving them a bad example; not a day passed but one of them fell dead under his rider. If we had not been able to buy others, I do not know what would have become of us.

One of the principal causes of their fatigue was the extraordinary nature of the soil thereabouts. We frequently encountered an impermeable ferruginous clay, which, under the action of rain and sun, was cracked and divided into squares like an irregular chess-board, the furrows between the squares being full of water or ice. The native animals crossed such places without difficulty, placing their feet on the squares of earth with the skill of circus-horses; but for those which came from China, which miscalculated their spring and risked falling with their riders at every step, it was a horribly arduous exercise, calling for abnormal and exhausting efforts.

The Lai-Wa tribe occupies a series of villages like that of Pan-Yu. However, from the lack of timber the mole-hill dwellings are less lofty, and the outer palisades are made of blocks of earth. Simultaneously with our arrival a family returned from the nearest forest: a journey of five days there and five days back, the object being to bring back a few beams of wood.

There we had the pleasure of finding that the season was evidently very mild, for the nomads had already decided to quit their winter villages for their summer encampments; already the tents were erected in the courtyards, so that their condition could be verified and repairs made. These preparations against the heat were very reassuring; but, alas! a Tibetan tent does not make a spring any more than a swallow.

But what of the cold? Were not our affairs going admirably? Not the least difficulty arose; the people were at first reserved, but simple, and, on the whole, hospitable. And these were the famous bandits whose reputation was so terrible! "Really," said one of us, "travelling here is too easy! Those who have been attacked by the Tibetans must have done it on purpose!" Imprudent fellow! Did he not know that the lucky player must never boast of his luck, lest it should turn? Like the avalanche, trembling in equilibrium, which a word will release, so a succession of unpleasant incidents was about to break upon us.

Next morning, just as we were about to leave Lai-Wa for the Mbulu tribe, the horsemen sent to arrange for our reception unexpectedly returned, and suddenly entered into an animated palaver with our escort. What was the matter? Simply that a strong party of Samsa horsemen was posted across our trail.

Samsa is a great confederation to the north of the Dzorgei, particularly feared by the people of Song-Pan-ting ; and this conflict was going to thrust a finger into the clockwork mechanism of the life of the desert.

The nomads are genuine raiders; they travel long distances to pillage caravans that pass outside their territory; but that does not suffice them for a living : for the Tibetan must have tea, which grows only in China. As it did not please these warriors and herdsmen to go thither and buy it, they have concluded a compact with the merchants of Song-Pan-ting. Twice a year a caravan loaded with tea starts from that city and crosses the country as far as the Lake Kukunur. On the way it gives everybody what tea he requires in exchange for the hides of his cattle, and notably of the precious Tibetan goat. At Kukunur what remains is bartered to the Mongols who live on the shores of the lake.

This caravan has nothing to fear from the tribes through which it travels, provided it pays a determined tribute, but nothing prevents other confederations from attacking it, and of all these that of Samsa is the most to be feared.

Was there no other route, so that we could avoid the ambuscade? Yes; close by was a ford across the Little Yellow River, which elsewhere had become impassable; if we crossed to the other bank the Samsa could not reach us.

An easy matter, the passage of a ford, but for our baggage! This contained our photographs, our notes, so many things that a drop of water would ruin. A false step on the part of the yak that bore them, and our labours would be lost!

However, we reached the other bank in safety. We were guided across the ford by the most cheerful

Tibetan we had ever met; a worthy old fellow of seventy years, with the face of an elderly Burgundian vine-grower—it even seemed that his nose was budding just a little—with whom we immediately got on terms of intimate friendship. He sat on our campstools, tasted our tea in our drinking-cups, rummaged in our canteens, and, delighted at the idea of pretending that he knew French, imitated us when we called our boys, shouting in a resounding voice, "Boy-Boy!"—which musical name we at once bestowed upon him.

The nomads were certainly right to pitch their tents, and we were obliged to conclude that the prediction of the weather is a more exact science in Tibet than in Europe. The temperature grew sensibly milder, the sun shone delightfully, and the marmots began to reappear. Their numbers were extraordinary; wherever the earth was dry and friable it was covered with the great mole-hills, usually with several entrances, which are the dwellings of these little animals. Hitherto, owing to the cold, we had scarcely seen the creatures themselves; but when the Tibetans leave their dwellings—which are imitations of the marmot's—they all come forth simultaneously.

Shooting them is an exciting sport; tremendously agile, having grown thin during the winter, they rush out of one hole and immediately pop into another. Only an extremely rapid shot will fire in time, and only a very good shot should fire, since even if wounded the creature will dive into a neighbouring burrow. None the less, we should have found this sport a real resource, for we knew the flesh of the marmot was good; but none of our men would touch it, and we had to abandon this agreeable sport, in order not to waste our ammunition. The ducks, which were very plentiful, happily provided us with compensations.

On the second day we found the tribe of the Ketei already installed in its summer encampments. The tents are usually arranged in a circle. The tent of the nomads, which is black, is made of a fabric of yak's wool. It is not hexagonal, as has been reported, but forms an irregular polygon; the method of pitching, which is highly ingenious, entails the use of poles *outside* the tent; the latter being attached to the poles in such a way that the whole interior space is free. The bales which contain the master's fortune are set in a circle in such a way that the wind cannot blow into the tent from below; the smoke escapes by a central opening, which is closed by a panel of cloth when desired. This tent, which is very wide, would be perfect if the stuff were not of so coarse a weave that both the sun and the cold enter at their ease.

Our plan was to continue along the bank of the river—where we were safe from Samsa—until its confluence with the Great Yellow River, which lies at no great distance; indeed, we had been marching parallel to its course for some days, at a distance of six to nine miles. There a ford would permit us to cross the lesser stream and to resume our interrupted itinerary, having passed the dangerous zone.

But on turning his head one of us saw behind us a column of fire. Had some imprudent smoker thrown a lighted match upon the grass, dried by this unseasonable sun? In a moment the flames had spread and were spreading all over the prairie. We had nothing to fear from it, for the wind drove it in an opposite direction; however, the danger was serious; even if the herds and tents were spared, and we hoped they would be, from the trend of the flames, a considerable stretch of pasture would be destroyed, which would be a disaster for the herd-owners, who would wish to avenge themselves on us.

Boy-boy, who did not wish to remain much longer in our compromising company, dragged us towards the river, made us cross it anew by a ford, where he quickly made his bow and disappeared with his men at a gallop.

Behold us now once more on the opposite bank, and close to the spot where the Samsa party had been signalled. By the worst of luck we could not, by hugging the bank, keep the mountains at a distance, for the ranges were much closer then; and all that bank was no better than a vast marsh. We should have to make for the foot-hills, precisely where our enemy lay hidden. Happily we found an ideal spot for a camp: a little peninsula in a swamp, with a narrow isthmus, easy to defend.

We had done well to take refuge across the river. During the night we heard the baying of hounds from all points of the plain; doubtless the warriors were concerting an attack upon us. We were safe against a surprise attack on our peninsula: but what of the morrow?

At daybreak we broke camp and hastened away. Between the base of the mountains and the marshes there was just room for the trail, and the enemy, who knew as much, had every facility for awaiting us at the right place. We therefore went forward with the utmost prudence, protected by skirmishers ahead, to the rear, and on our right flank; to the left the view swept across the marshes to the horizon. At each turn of the path, which was winding round a spur of the mountain, we waited until our skirmishers had crawled up the slope and signalled that the way was clear. Since fortune gave us the opportunity to watch the Chinese soldier under conditions of active service, I must admit that they manœuvred splendidly, making the very best use of the lie of the land without being seen. We could not have wished to see skirmishing better carried out, and we had no need to give them orders. Once more I marvelled at the strange blindness of those who refuse the Chinese every warlike virtue.

These precautions were by no means superfluous. Suddenly our vedettes made a sign to us to halt; one of them returned at a gallop to announce that two hundred Samsa horsemen were there, ambushed in a ravine before which we should have to pass.

A disagreeable situation! To force a passage with our fourteen rifles was scarcely to be thought of. Still less could we retreat, for we should fall back upon the burnt-out tribes; to the right lay the mountains, and the territory of our aggressors; to the left, the marshes. There was no room for hesitation: we must choose the marshes. We were not absolutely sure of remaining there, while anywhere else. . . .

So we waded through the inundated meadows, trying to avoid the deeper holes and, above all, the bogs. All those of our men who were on foot were sent ahead, dispersed over a wide front and testing the ground, in order to find the least dangerous passage for the horsemen and the yaks. None the less, at every moment some beast would founder, and in its efforts to free itself would fall sideways with its rider or its pack. What a labour it was then to extricate it from the mud! Streams running from the mountain, finding no further slope down which to run, made deep winding channels which always seemed in front of us, and we were constantly in danger of falling into them.

Interminable marshes! We had taken as our landmark a buttress of the mountain which, peninsula-wise, projected beyond the ambuscade, and which our enemies could not reach without showing themselves and exposing themselves to the fire of our long-range weapons. There was less than two miles of marsh to cross, and the passage took us five hours. What a sigh of relief went up when we set foot on solid ground!

And then what a joyful surprise awaited us! From the high ground on which we stood we at last perceived the Yellow River which was our goal, and which all the maps placed at least sixty miles farther on. Our information had been correct, and the discovery which it promised us was ours. There was that which paid us in a moment for all our hardships, and made us

WE HALT IN FRONT OF THE AMBUSCADE.

A GATHERING OF WARRIORS.

A CORNER OF THE CAMP.

To face page 250.

forget the danger which still threatened us. We would make a scientific record of the result at once, for who knew where we should be to-morrow! It was close upon noon; the sun was shining; the theodolite was installed and Fleurelle took the readings, taking multiple observations of the neighbouring heights.[1]

As soon as he had finished we proceeded, this time keeping to the solid ground. My uneasiness had not diminished, for our enemies could not have renounced the hope of seizing so easy and so tempting a prey. But now our advance-guard, who had breasted a low hill, were shouting and calling to us. We hurried up, and a striking spectacle lay before us.

In the plain at our feet an army was advancing—an innumerable army of sombre yaks and horsemen with long gleaming lances. The horsemen were riding in compact groups, which followed one another at short intervals. A column was descending from the opposite crest, and fresh masses of men appeared endlessly.

The exuberant joy of our men told us the truth: it was *the* caravan, the great caravan of Kukunur. Laden with hides and pelts, exchanged against the tea which it had carried into the country, it was returning by a providential chance a month sooner than it was expected, at precisely the right time to save our lives. For these were allies: Chinese or Tibetans of Song-Pan-ting, they ran in the desert the same risk as did we, and their goods would excite the cupidity of the same aggressors. Our men knew them all, and they met like brothers who have narrowly escaped shipwreck. Suddenly the head of the caravan halted, and our two camps were pitched together, while the file of yaks continued interminably to descend from the height.

[1] These observations were worked out upon our return by the Bureau des Longitudes. They prove that the Yellow River lies fifty-seven miles further east than was supposed. This entirely modifies the aspect of the region, since a great river runs through wide plains where it was believed that there were steep and lofty mountain ranges.

But there were serious matters to be remembered, we must not forget them in the charm of watching the endless procession. We informed the leaders how matters stood. They had barely spoken a few words to those surrounding them, when a horseman had left the camp; then two, then ten, then a hundred; silently, lance in hand, at the swiftest gallop of which their mounts were capable, they rushed on to a goal which we could not as yet divine. In the space of a few minutes two hundred warriors were assembled at a distance of a thousand yards from the camp, grouped in two squadrons, which immediately, preceded by vedettes, went to look for the enemy.

It was a pretty manœuvre, and executed how silently, easily, and suddenly! It revealed the habit of war, of sudden emergencies and sudden blows. No noisy orders; no explanations; a word quietly spoken, and the whole troop were in order of battle. Those whom the desert draws, be it only for purposes of trade, must all be amateurs of adventure—unless they are professionals. All those we had met, whether Chinese or Tibetans, might well have escaped from the pages of Gustav Aymard or Fenimore Cooper.

Meanwhile the camp was completely established. It was a town, with its streets and public squares. The caravan was divided into thirty groups, of which each always retained its respective position. Each formed a separate quarter of the camp, composed of a certain number of tents; at the angles a bastion was constructed of loads of pelts, piled together so as to form a rectangular rampart. A sentinel would mount guard there all night, supported by a pack of those terrible hounds which will not even allow the approach of neighbours. Several pickets were also posted at danger-points at a distance from the camp, and before dawn a squadron of horsemen would go out in readiness to receive the enemy, should the latter have succeeded in approaching under cover of the darkness.

All night long, seated on bales of pelts, in the acrid smoke of the fires which burned in every tent, we chatted with these sturdy adventurers. Their words were few, but how suggestive was every detail!

On account of their quarrel with the Samsa tribe, the majority of the rich merchants of Song-Pan-ting had drawn back at the idea of pillage, so that the caravan comprised only 250 horsemen and 1,500 yaks, instead of double that number, as was usual. On the way out, although it had merely skirted the territory of the Samsa, a party of horsemen had come to demand an exorbitant tribute, and a battle had ensued. The caravan had succeeded in forcing its way, killing a dozen of the enemy and losing as many; but on its way back it had made a considerable circuit in order to avoid the Samsa territory, to which fact we owed our meeting with them, for this was not their habitual route. The ambuscade into which we had nearly fallen was obviously intended for them, and we had, as a matter of fact, saved them from it by warning them.

The caravan resumed the march in the morning twilight. It was wonderful to see with what rapidity this town with its ramparts was demolished and loaded on yaks. But why did the column take a direction almost opposite to that which it should follow? For the reason that it was in nowise eager to risk a fight, especially under the unfavourable conditions which we had experienced the day before, helplessly cramped, in an immensely long file, between the marshes and the mountains, from which they could so easily be surprised. To risk battle in order to win treasure was good, but to retreat in order to save it was better! The caravan had therefore changed its route, and was about to perform the same manœuvre as we had done, namely, to place the river between itself and the bandits.

The ford for which it made was barely a third of a mile from the confluence. The Little Yellow River, checked by its windings across a level plain, has no longer the power to penetrate the Great Yellow River, which is rather more rapid, and which consequently repulses the slower stream, and holds it up, so that the alluvial matter in suspension in these sluggish waters is deposited in greater abundance along these lower reaches, until the channel is almost choked.

The crossing occupied three hours. All necessary military precautions were taken to repulse an attack on either bank. The groups crossed singly, each waiting until its predecessor had taken up a strong position on the farther bank.

The reader may imagine that the spectacle was in the highest degree picturesque; but how can I reproduce the effect of this scene of intense vitality in the midst of the immobile immensity that hemmed it in? In such contrasts the latent mystery that makes the strange charm of the desert is manifested in a striking degree.

Where there were neither houses, nor roads, nor fields, by what prodigy were all these men assembled? We perceived that insignificant communities which seem as though drowned in space and destitute of social life are actuated by secret forces; their apparent inertia hides combinations determined upon long beforehand; a mass of arrangements and understandings, very often of centuries' standing, which suddenly produce the explosion by which the silence and solitude are abruptly broken. To-day we witnessed the passage of this caravan; in six months, in a year, others would follow: and in view of such an event alliances are concluded and ambushes prepared; men reckon what profit they can obtain by exchange or by violence, and the herds increase, and lances are sharpened.

This caravan is the mainspring of the desert. Those who have not encountered it know nothing of the secret mechanism, having seen only the deceitful surface.

But the perception of this mystery was not sufficient

to explain the almost religious emotion which thrilled our hearts and will never be effaced from our memories. It was a vision of the first ages of humanity that lay before our eyes. Of these vast meadows of grass, these mountains, with their gleaming snows, this immense river, nothing has changed since the beginning of life; nothing bears the sign of man; Nature is still ignorant that she may find in him a master, and this people on the march, half-clad in the skins of animals, but armed with swords and spears, with their powerful but weirdly shaped yaks—animals that seem to belong to some long-vanished species—have all the appearance of a prehistoric horde. The majesty of the desert resides not only in the immensity of space, for its horizons are often near at hand, and its landscapes indifferent. Its infinity is in the category of time. The centuries pass over it, but they leave no imprint. The desert is always young, and by its aid man too remains young for ever, as in the earliest days. To the desert we owe the last Barbarians, who live the life our own forbears lived; in the desert we withdraw more profoundly into our own selves, and, under all the incrustations of civilisation, we seem to feel the ancestral soul awake in the depths.

But already the vision was fading: the mass of sombre yaks, the fighting-men with their long spears; all were trickling away in a receding line; they disappeared, the immensity absorbed them. A few remote bellowings, a few gleams of spear-heads on the summit of a low hill, and the desert had resumed its eternal, accustomed appearance.

CHAPTER XII

ATTACKED BY THE TIBETANS. ARRIVAL AT LHABRANG

NOW our object was attained; we had discovered the Yellow River at the only part of its capricious course which remained unexplored; so that it would now be possible, with the aid of the data obtained by our German rivals, to establish definitively the bases of the hydrographical and orographical systems of the country.

To our successors, however, we left an enviable task: that of studying the enormous range which rises on the farther bank, and which is one of the largest in the world. Celebrated afar, its name, according to the geographers, is *Amnei Machin* or *Matgyen*. I venture to propose a new form of this title: that employed by the nomads who surround the range and who doubtless first named it: *Anyei Machi*. In their language *anyei* signifies "ancestor," and *Machi* is their name for the Yellow River. This name signifies the "ancestor of Machi," and it is the universal belief that this range contains the principal springs of the river, which have hitherto been attributed to the lakes Nyoring-So and Doring-So.

Without guaranteeing the truth of this information, I give it as being both probable and emphatically asserted by the natives, and as worthy of being put to the proof. Anyei Machi is to them what Chonolevo is to the Lolos: the most important personality in the country. It is always present in thought and speech, and every one knows all that relates to it.

We were now going to make for the great lamasery of Lhabrang. I knew we should encounter some curious geographical and anthropological problems on the way; we should have to pass through wide tracts of land belonging to the lamasery, although inhabited by the nomads; we should thus be able to study the organisation of these great ecclesiastical domains, and see how their existence could accommodate itself with the presence of undisciplined clans of raiders.

We soon had the opportunity of coming into contact with the lamas. Near the confluent of the Yellow River, hidden in a hollow of the mountains, stood the convent of Chaga Weisyong, which maintained cordial relations with Lhabrang, although independent. We sent to inform the monks of our desire to visit them, but they flatly refused to receive us, and our envoy, the son of one of the principal notables of the region, even stated that he had been struck for daring to carry so audacious a message. This was an encouraging beginning!

We left the territory of the Dzorgei for that of the tribe of Lhardei. It contained four villages; the majority of the inhabitants were already living in their tents. A lamasery stood on the mountain-side.

All at once difficulties began to arise, all relating to petty details. The explanation was forthcoming next morning. The superior of the convent, to whom we had announced our visit, had urged the rule of his order as a reason for not receiving us; but at the same time he complained that we had sent him no presents. But why should we do so, since we were not his guests? Because he represented Lhabrang and the country was subject to Lhabrang.

The nomads are only tenants of the soil. In this quality they pay a revenue of cattle, butter, and milk;

otherwise they are perfectly free. But here it is that the spirit of organisation and responsibility triumphs : Lhabrang has a convent in the centre of each tribe, in which resides a lama entrusted with the temporal interests of the community; supported by all the power of their order, acquainted with the affairs of all the private persons whom the lamas visit in order to recite prayers, these lamas are indeed the real rulers of these apparently so independent tribes.

This we were not long in discovering. There were nearly always some monks in our camp; their air was friendly, and we did not expel them, for fear of provoking a violent rupture; but it was obvious that they were there to warn off such natives as might come to sell us their produce or offer us their services. Only our host held out; for he was the friend and frequent correspondent of the leader of our Tibetan convoy.

But at this very juncture the leader of our caravan, Renzei, sought us out ; his yaks were exhausted, our marches had been too long, and we should have made longer halts, giving them more leisure to find their food under the snow; in short, he could not proceed. We spoke to him severely, reminding him that he was bound, by the agreement made before the prefect, to conduct us as far as Lhabrang. This was true : so he would obtain us another caravan on the same conditions as to price; and our host would provide it.

This was not at all to our liking. The convoy-leaders of Song-Pan-ting were bound to be faithful to us, or they would be liable to receive a chastisement from the Chinese authorities, whom we had purposely brought into the affair. But what would prevent a fresh caravan from deserting us at the first opportunity? However, it was true that Renzei's yaks were scarcely able to stand up, and it was not impossible that if we relied on them we should be left helpless in the snow. We were accordingly obliged to agree to the arrangement,

LAMAS VISITING THE CAMP.

THE WINTER VILLAGE OF LHARDEI.

To face page 258.

but with the guarantee that Renzei would personally accompany us as far as Lhabrang, and that only there would we pay him the sum agreed upon. It was for him to see that those he furnished us with respected their engagements.

The villages of Lhardei presented the same appearance as all those we had previously encountered; but with one essential difference: there was an absolute lack of wood, so that it was impossible to construct the usual great mole-hill of earth, as there was no means of supporting it by an inner framework, so that in the centre of the ramparts one found not an earthen house, but a tent. A curious antithesis this tent, the symbol of the nomadic life surrounded by walls, the symbol of the sedentary existence!

All being settled, our usual harvest of information gathered, we resumed the march. With our old caravan we left one of our Chinese soldiers whose horse was dead, and who himself was too worn out to follow us. But the men-at-arms, relations or serfs of our host, accompanied us as escort; and these were powerful fellows of a savage, hardy appearance.

Our twenty new pack animals were a thousand times less docile than the old ones. The latter were *Pinyu,* crosses between the yak and the domestic cow, which are more easily broken in, and for that reason are preferred for use in caravans. Now we had real yaks, enormous ill-tempered creatures which are seldom reared except for their milk, their flesh, and their hair, and are exceedingly difficult to manage when it becomes a question of loading them. Matters went fairly well during the operation of loading, for the creatures were attached by the nose to the cords which served to "park" them at night; but hardly were they released when they shook their loads loose, turning them upside down, and rushed off across the plain, dragging behind them—for they were still attached to the creatures by the cords which had bound them—our unfortunate canteens, which bounced up and down with the most frightful clatter; it was a regular stampede. You may imagine whether our baggage thrived under this treatment. I should mention here that nowhere among the nomads is a pack-saddle employed as it is in the rest of Tibet. Only a thin mattress is placed on the back, and on this the various items are successively placed and brailed into position, so that equilibrium is finally obtained either by their weight or by the height of their point of attachment. The wide back of the yak lends itself to this system, at which the Tibetans are amazingly quick and skilful.

We were very soon out of the valley of the Yellow River, but we could still see it in the distance, continuing into the west the series of astonishing windings which had led it eastward. Truly this river is a "wanderer," to quote Dr. Tafel. How many times yet, before reaching Pekin, were we to re-encounter its capricious course!

We had now re-entered the mountains. We intended to follow, more or less closely, the line of the watershed between the basin of the Yellow River proper and that of a large affluent, the River Tao-Chu, which runs towards the east and does not flow into the Yellow River until it reaches a point beyond Ho-Chu. In so doing we cut across a multitude of streams near their sources, which were so astonishingly confused that it was no easy task to disentangle them.

We knew we should find the snow on the summits, for it scarcely ever leaves them; but we might reasonably hope to escape a fresh fall, for it was now the middle of May. Alas! it seemed as though the winter was beginning over again: the snow fell fast and furious, lashed by a violent wind, and in a little while advance became absolutely impossible. We were obliged to halt, just where we were, in a narrow, steeply sloping ravine, with never an inch of level ground. We took shelter hastily in our tents, which were erected Heaven [illegible]tion of the various kinds of argol, is hardly to be [illegible]orgiven for omitting the most essential detail. It is [illegible]ertainly useful to know that sheep's droppings burn better than yak-dung and the latter than horses' droppings: and we are grateful to him for telling us as much. But these notions are purely abstract, and only fit for scholars seated in their studies; for the best of these combustibles is useless when impregnated with snow. Only the bellows can induce it to burn—and after what efforts!

Nothing could be more original than these bellows. They consist of an iron tube fastened into an open bag of leather. The operator sits on the ground, the bellows between his legs, and opens the bag wide so that the air may enter; then, suddenly, by a peculiar twist of the hands which crosses the wrists, he closes the opening by pressing it upon his left calf, when the air, confined and compressed, escapes through the tube. I do not know whether this feat appears easy as I have described it: in reality it requires remarkable deftness; in the hands of a novice the aperture is imperfectly closed, allowing the air to escape, so that the bag remains flaccid and no blast is produced. Our clumsiness should have been one reason the more for supplying ourselves with a large number of these devices; yet for ourselves and our servants we had only one! May our successors profit by our cruel experience!

But the preparation of the tea leads me, without transition, to a nobler subject. As soon as the water is hot, before pouring it on the tea, a Tibetan takes a few drops three times over into his bowl, and throws it towards three points of the horizon, on each occasion reciting a rather long prayer. In whose honour are these libations? In honour of the Spirits of the Mountains which lie in these three directions, and especially in honour of the Genius of Anyei Machi.

The colossal range of Anyei Machi, which is the

knows how! Happily we had with us a store of a without which we might have perished of cold. rgol, blizzard lasted all the night. he

At early dawn there was a sudden lull in the stor and we hastened to leave our tents, for the crackin n, and slapping of the badly stretched canvas in the wind and the fear of seeing the tents carried away, had prevented our closing our eyes all night. We looked round for our Tibetans, meaning to order them to load the pack-train, but there were no Tibetans to be seen. Had they deserted? But no, their yaks were there, and even their enormous lances, thrust vertically into the soil. Where were they?

At the foot of the lances we saw the snow moving, and on looking closely we noticed swellings in the dense white carpet. These swellings represented our Tibetans, who were sleeping the sleep of the just. They had no need of tents: unloosing their girdles, which had kilted their sheepskins up to their knees, they allowed the former to fall over their feet, turned their collars up over their ears, turned down the woolly borders of their caps, and with their naked bodies thus protected they reclined peacefully in the snow, leaving it to cover them with a warm counterpane. Rather too warm, if anything! When, at our summons, they awoke, their first care was to throw back their cloaks and bathe their bodies in the freezing wind.

Happy Tibetans! For them the blizzard was a gentle zephyr, the snow a soft and comfortable bed. What adversity have they to fear? With such constitutions they are able to laugh at fate, and, like our fathers the Gauls, they are not even afraid that the sky may fall upon them: there are their spears to receive it!

For their diet a few pinches of tea, three handfuls of meal, and a little butter, and they are restored and refreshed. But they must have hot water, and therefore fire. Father Huc, the author of a masterly classifi-

EN ROUTE.

IN THE VALLEY OF THE YELLOW RIVER.

To face page 262.

more striking in that it is surrounded by the plains of the Yellow River, is a veritable Olympus. A formidable deity, Anyei-Machi-Ponra, holds his court there. He has under his orders 360 feudatories, 1,500 officers, and an incalculable number of soldiers. No one can stand against him. It is to him that men pray when going forth to battle; and in his honour the natives burn branches of pine, which are brought from a distance and anointed with butter.

But what of Buddha? How does he agree with Anyei-Machi-Ponra? No one knows, nor does any one greatly care: their kingdoms are not the same. People pray to Buddha in order to obtain happiness after death; that is the business of lamas or old men. But of the second they ask for success in this life: for abundant herds, good luck on their raiding expeditions, &c. Buddha will reward only virtuous people, but Anyei-Machi-Ponra cares nothing for morality: he helps those who pray to him and send up to him the fragrant smoke of resin and crackling butter. He is a warrior: he goes on horseback, bearing a lance, a sabre, and—a rifle!

A god armed with a rifle! Admirable touch! The gods of Homer carried the weapons of their times; those of to-day carry weapons of the latest model: humanity is always the same! But I truly believe this is the first appearance of the rifle in mythology.

*

* *

The snow had ceased to fall. We advanced across a series of valleys worn in the sandstone mountains, whose blood-red sides contrasted strangely with the immaculate snow.

Finally we emerged into the magnificent valley of Seirachong, inhabited by the Tatze tribe, and gazed with astonishment at the tents which covered the plain. They were no longer black and polygonal, but round and white. This form of tent was the Mongol *yourt*, and it was a horde of Mongolians that lay before us.

This was what we had been led by our information to expect ; however, in spite of the name of Tatze—Tartars—which might be a mere homophony, and in spite of the difference of language and of manners of which we had read, we could hardly believe that Mongols could be found here in the midst of Tibetan territory, and it was partly to verify this surprising fact that we had chosen this route.

The *yourt* has often been described. Its originality lies in the fact that the covers of white felt which compose it are fastened to two pliable frameworks of wood. That which supports the roof is like an umbrella-frame without the handle ; the radiating ribs which compose it fold up like an umbrella, their extremities resting on the cylindrical body of the tent. The latter, supported by a trellis of crossed laths, the apertures in the frame being lozenge-shaped, and the laths pivoted where they cross the frame, may be enlarged at will or closed into a very small volume. These ingenious devices allow of the tent being pitched, struck, and packed with great alacrity.

I must mention another peculiarity of these tents : besides the movable door or tent-flap of felt, each of these tents has a real door with two valves, either of wood or of felt stretched upon a framework, with wooden doorway and sill, as in a house.

Provided their stay is not likely to be a very short one, the Mongols immediately build an earthen furnace in the centre of the floor, not unlike that of the Tibetans, but with only one fireplace. As with the Tibetans, the long hearth divides the tent into two portions, one being reserved for the men and the other for the women ; but among the Mongols the left-hand side is appropriated by the men. The altar is just like that of the Tibetans, but there are also small chests and sideboards in many of the tents—furniture of a

A MONGOL YOURT.

To face page 264

kind hardly ever to be found among the other nomads.

The Mongols wear their heads completely shaven, except for a small lock of hair, the lock characteristic of their race, which is due to Chinese influence. As for their costume, it is by no means that of the Mongols of Mongolia, but rather that of the Tibetan nomads: a long sheepskin coat, furred boots, and a furred cap with a tassel. However, they have lately added a garment which all civilised people would regard as indispensable, although it is considered highly unnecessary by the Tibetans—namely, a short pair of trousers. Apart from this concession to tradition, they like to bare the body after the fashion of the Tibetan nomads, and both men and women frequently throw back their cloak as far as the girdle.

Their type, it must be admitted, is precisely the same as that of the Tibetan nomads; that is, not at all "Mongolian"; the eyes are neither oblique nor tight-lidded, the orbits are deep, the nose prominent, and the face oval, sometimes triangular. Have they been transformed by mixing with the Tibetans, or have they introduced the nomadic Tibetan type, which differs from the sedentary type? For, as we shall see later on, many of the Mongols of Mongolia are of the same fine and almost Caucasian type, so very far removed from that on which their name has unjustly been bestowed.

These Mongols welcomed us hospitably, but they spoke only their own language, which was known to none of our party, which made conversation difficult. As they had a king, who was then residing at Lhabrang, where we might find the necessary interpreters, we did not linger.

Through an astonishing breach, barely ten feet wide, through which ran a stream, we penetrated into the very heart of the mountains, and presently found ourselves in a steeply walled valley, which was bordered and scattered with blocks of porphyry, the effect of which was marvellous. As though the scene was not sufficient to itself, a magnificent cavalcade, issuing from the narrow defile behind us, presently passed us, and greatly heightened the effect of the landscape.

These were lamas, escorted by young monks and men-at-arms. They were wearing not the usual monastic clothing, but travelling costumes as varied as they were sumptuous; cassocks of yellow silk, waist-coats of cloth of gold, scarlet scarfs, great purple mantles; on their heads they wore cardinals' hats, lacquered with gold on the upper surface and red underneath; they jauntily carried lances, for these servants of God are not safe from the brigands: they might have formed part of the army of Pope Julius II.

In the rays of the declining sun, which lent a still greater brilliance to the reddish violet of the porphyry and the tender green of the turf, what a vision of fairyland was this of these princes of the Church, sumptuously clad and equipped for war, as they rode through the wild grandeur of the valley! It was one of those spectacles of an unreal, inconceivable beauty which one encounters only in Tibet; and the country in which they spontaneously occur seems to take, from that very fact, an august and supernatural character.

But our æsthetic enthusiasm was unpleasantly tempered by gloomy speculations. At the head of this splendid troop marched the lama who was the governor of Lhardei. Neither he nor his followers had saluted us, and we were anything but pleased to see people who were obviously hostile thus preceding us on the trail. It would not be a pleasant welcome that these magnificent precursors would prepare for us.

This miraculous valley had almost insensibly led us to the greatest altitude we had as yet attained: 14,140 feet above sea-level, on the plateau of Tartsong, which was overlooked by heights that rose yet 600 to 1,000 feet higher. Thence the sight was plunged into a maze

A LAMA TRAVELLING.

To face page 266.

of valleys belonging to different basins : first the artist was feasted, then the geographer.

But this ascent, which ended, of course, in the snow, was the occasion of our losing two more horses, and, worst of all, our men were failing too. To be precise, I ought to have mentioned on every page the suffering and inconvenience which the rarefaction of the air was always causing us ; an abrupt movement led to a feeling of suffocation, accompanied by a sort of momentary paralysis ; and with many of us the result of running a few yards was that we had to rest nearly half an hour in order to recover the use of our limbs. All climbing, however gradual, was utterly exhausting. Several of our men who were on foot fell down in the snow and were unable to pick themselves up : it demanded the greatest efforts to get them as far as the camp. It was doubtless due to this cause that we lost so many horses.[1]

We had expected to renew our supplies of food in the various summer encampments which we encountered on the farther slopes ; but the natives refused to sell, by order of the beautiful lama in red and gold.

Finally we came in sight of Kortzei, where a large population surrounded a lamasery. We were still approaching when a troop of horsemen under arms advanced, and halted facing us. Their attitude was not precisely hostile, but self-assured and haughty ; with their great lances grounded, these warriors seemed

[1] I think the surprisingly nervous condition of our men during our journey through Tibet was due to the altitude even more than to the sufferings we endured. Without a motive, with no better excuse than an idle contradiction or a futile discussion, they would fall into crises of absolute fury, seizing their weapons with the intention of assassinating their companions or killing themselves. "I dies only once, I does not die twice," yelled our cook, in despair, when he was fortunately disarmed in time. Practically none of our Chinese and Annamites escaped this singular derangement of the nervous system, which was the more remarkable because the Annamites were full of courage and devotion in the intervals of such attacks.

to constitute a barrier that we could not pass. We had perforce to halt ourselves, and the leader of our guides went forward to parley. A few words were enough ; the horsemen made a half-turn and departed ; but instead of resuming the march our convoy men began to unload the animals and place their burdens on the ground.

Having had this identical trouble in Africa, I knew at once what was wrong : the horsemen had given our convoy the order to desert us then and there. I hardly tried to retain them, and they did not even listen. Should we use force? In that case we were certain to be attacked by the tribes, and killed. So long as there was hope we must temporise ! I managed, with some difficulty, to arrange that our baggage should be unloaded on a little platform commanding the river ; on three sides it would be impossible for horsemen and difficult for pedestrians to surprise us ; and our convoy, pricking their beasts with their lances to escape more quickly, were in a very few minutes out of sight.

Perhaps the people of the village would prove accessible to persuasion. We sent thither the chief of our escort with our Tibetans. They were roughly repulsed.

Our position was far from encouraging. No yaks, no baggage ! Must we abandon our goods and depart on foot, loading our mounts with provisions? If necessary, we would ; but it would be a great and probably a useless sacrifice, for if the tribes had resolved to stop us they would use force.

There was, therefore, only one course to take. We knew whence the blow had fallen ; here, as in the preceding villages, the lama of Lhardei had announced that Lhabrang would not authorise our passage. At all costs we must warn the great lamasery. It should have been warned of our near arrival by the authorities of Kan-Su, informed by the Viceroy of Sze-Chuan. Certainly the monastery would issue orders as soon as

TIBETANS STOP THE MISSION.

To face page 268.

it knew where we were, and all obstacles would be removed.

Now we were only three stages from Lhabrang—about thirty-six to forty miles. A few riders, mounted on our best horses—and some, bought at Lhardei, were still fresh—might make the distance in a single day. Certainly they would run a risk, but scarcely more than in remaining where they were, since we were not in a state to resist open aggression, and if we were not attacked there was no reason why they should be. They might well be stopped, as we had been here, but the mountains were everywhere practicable to horsemen, and a detour would enable them to pass elsewhere.

I therefore entrusted Captain Lepage with this mission. He was to take with him two Chinese, one of them one of our Chinese scholars, who would be useful at Lhabrang, and two Tibetans, one of whom was Renzei, who knew the way. Boyve, always ready to run any risk, asked permission to accompany Lepage, and I gave it. They were to take food for thirty-six hours and double furs, for they would have to pass the night under the stars, and that, for one who is not a Tibetan, is by no means comfortable. I gave them a fairly large sum in silver ingots, so that they might purchase the necessary assistance.

Very wisely, Lepage waited for the approach of night, so that his departure should attract less attention, and so that there should be no time to take measures to pursue him before his trail was lost in the darkness. He would travel all night, and judge, when the day came, whether to proceed or hide until the following night.

When the time had come our comrades rapidly left the camp. Although we concealed our emotion, each of us felt a deep anxiety. In vain I told myself that our companions, all six well armed and well mounted, could hardly be running greater risks than were we, who were stuck fast and had only eight rifles to defend ourselves with. But this reasoning, which was correct in theory, and was indeed my justification for exposing them to danger, could not exclude accidents and unfortunate encounters.

Returning to my tent I was disagreeably surprised to find Lepage's revolver there ; he had taken it from his pocket in order to stow away the silver I had given him, and had forgotten to return it. It was impossible to send it after him then ; he was already out of sight. However, he had a repeating rifle taking ten cartridges and a Browning pistol taking five, which I hoped would be more than sufficient.

In the middle of the night a fusillade of shots rang out. First our sentinels and then all our soldiers vigorously discharged their rifles ; I do not know at what they shot, nor did any one else, although every one stated that he had seen shadows moving. The absence of dogs—for of course those of the convoy had departed with their masters—was greatly to be regretted.

Next day it struck me that the great Chinese standard confided to me by the general, which at the outset was day by day planted beside the French flag, and which I had not seen for some time, ought to obtain for us a certain amount of consideration ; it would show these brigands whom they had to deal with. "On the contrary," replied the Chinese non-com., "I concealed it as a measure of prudence ; the sight of it could only excite them further." This was why, since the occasion of the first ambush, he had carefully hidden it. Yet, according to the maps, this country forms part of China ! Well, if there was danger to encounter we would meet it under the French flag !

A few inhabitants of the village approached, not without suspicion. Hoping perhaps to bring about a change of front, and in any case to renew our store of provisions, we made them welcome, and they lost their shyness. They consented to sell us a little butter, milk, and some deliciously sour cream. This did not seem to argue any very great hostility—unless it were merely a pretext to observe the arrangement of our camp, with a view to a surprise attack ; so at nightfall, when we were alone, I altered the arrangement of the tents, and set them closer together.

All night the wind, rain, and thunder were raging. Father Dury, Fleurelle, and I doubled our rounds during our watches ; but each time we found the sentinels crouching on their heels, their heads under their sheepskins, thinking only of sheltering themselves from the terrible storm. In vain did we exhort them—using the most striking arguments, the boot and the stick—to fulfil their duties more conscientiously : at the next round we found them in exactly the same position !

In the morning, general stupefaction ! From the tent in which Father Dury and Fleurelle slept various objects were stolen, including two cameras, and from mine a small box containing various articles intended as presents, and a reserve of cartridges, and even my own repeating rifle, which lay beside me within reach of my hand ! The cords holding the bottom of the tent had in each case been cut, and the articles had thus been stolen from without, the terrific and continuous uproar of the wind in the tent-cloths and of the thunder having drowned all other sounds.

We were greatly taken aback. Either our sentinels were acting in concert with the brigands, or the latter were of an inconceivable audacity and address ; in either case we were at their mercy. Henceforward we should ourselves take our turn at mounting guard ; but this success would doubtless yet further increase the audacity of our enemies.

The next day passed without bringing the least change ; there were the same visits on the part of the natives in the morning—the same, perhaps, as our thieves of the night before, and coming only to prepare for some fresh act of brigandage. However, a diversion offered which charmed away our boredom ; more than fifty lamas on horseback, several of whom were of very high rank, as was shown by the umbrellas of yellow silk which were borne behind them, defiling from the opposite side of the valley with a multitude of men-at-arms and laden yaks. They were going on pilgrimage to Lhassa.

Towards the evening some horsemen entered the camp with a friendly air which seemed to announce news. They seated themselves among our men, drank tea, chatted of the snow and the fine weather, and at the end of an hour, considering that they had sufficiently proved that they were not excitable, undignified people, folk without any self-control, who did not know how to contain themselves when entrusted with a message, they produced a paper. It was a note from Lepage!

"Despite some annoying encounters which caused us a great deal of delay, we are half-way to Lhabrang. I have met with a caravan which is taking loads to Kortsei and would then return empty; I have engaged it for you, and the man who will give you this note is the leader." What! we have a caravan? Where is it? Close by; the yaks are grazing: to-morrow, at daybreak, our baggage will be loaded. Imagine our delight! We could only hope that the people of Kortsei would not modify the intentions of our new friends during the night.

But no: at dawn they arrived, the baggage was loaded, and we resumed the road. Our trail passed the village of Kortsei, which stood on a little plateau at the confluence of two valleys: the astonished lamas came out to see us go. Good winners and losers both, we exchanged a few amiable remarks. Among them was a splendid cavalier, chief of the tribe of Song-kourt; it was he who had escorted the lamas we had seen the day before. He was no longer dressed—or undressed—in the fashion of the nomads, but wore breeches, cassock, and cloak of felted silk, most brilliantly coloured. We felt that he came from more comfortable regions, and that we were no longer so far from safety.

We had been marching for about three hours; needless to say, with our eyes wide open. Suddenly, looking behind me, I saw a strong force of horsemen approaching at a quick gallop. They disappeared behind some rising ground. I quickly got all our men together in front of the yaks—since the danger came from behind—and every man took his rifle in his hands.

The horsemen reappeared on the top of the slope, and, uttering piercing cries, charged at full gallop, with pointed lances, in two lines of battle, one following the other at fifty paces.

"Should we open fire?" some one asked me. No; I forbade my men to fire. With our eight repeating rifles we might exterminate the eighty or a hundred horsemen before us, but what then? Our convoy, anxious on their own behalf, would find some means of leaving us in the lurch, and we should be at the mercy of the exasperated tribes. As for this charge, it was easy to see that it was going to miscarry ridiculously, and perhaps would have no sequel.

For the nomads, in a tumult of strident shouts, had reached the living rampart of our yaks, when their speed was checked; while we, from the other side, beyond the reach of their lances, and with our fingers on the trigger, quietly faced them. They looked extremely foolish and embarrassed. It was obvious that they wished themselves elsewhere—or that they had introduced themselves with greater civility.

But how were we to escape from the situation? To commence a conversation through the channel of two successive interpreters when rifles are ready to explode is scarcely convenient or useful, and I awaited, with some uneasiness, an outcome which, so far, I was hardly able to foresee; when suddenly a jocular voice rang out from beside me: "Hullo! Good morning, my friends! And where are you going in such a hurry?"

It was one of our Chinese soldiers, the Christian, an old converted Mussulman ; a little scatter-brained, but indefatigable, a fine rough-rider, a marvel at wriggling out of difficulties, with a laughable retort always on the tip of his tongue : a regular Parisian *gamin!*

The nomads caught the ball on the rebound : " Oh, we're going home, to Song-kourt, two days' ride from here." And indeed I could see in their midst, trying to hide himself, the handsome chief we had seen at Kortsei, who had evidently been instructed by the lamas, immediately after our departure, to punish us for our temerity. " Well, off you go ! The road's wide enough—a lucky journey ! "

Obeying the suggestion, just as though nothing had happened, the nomads rode off past the left of our caravan, while we prudently edged to the right, so as to keep the yaks still between us. Then they put their horses to the trot and were soon receding in the distance.[1] Presently, however, at a turn of the trail, we saw them halted in a narrow ravine, where they completely barred the way. We could not run into the wolf's jaws in that way ; so as naturally as possible I ordered a halt for breakfast. The nomads would either have to proceed, or—we should see.

However, four horsemen slowly approached us, spoke a few words to our caravan-leader, and returned to their troop. And thereupon our convoy precipitately unloaded our baggage ! It was the Kortsei trick over again : they had been given the order to make off !

But Lepage must have reached Lhabrang ; our difficulties were undoubtedly nearly at an end. Patience, then ! We pitched the camp on the least unfavourable ground, and the horsemen disappeared.

Now Lepage would expect us to arrive with the caravan he had sent for us, so would content himself with awaiting our arrival, and here we should remain

[1] The photograph was taken just as they were passing some of our men who were on foot, leading some lame horses.

THE LAMA HORTSEI IN FIGHTING TRIM.

THE TIBETAN HORSEMEN PASS US.

To face page 274.

indefinitely! We must warn him that we were once more stuck. We had only one decent horse left; our plucky Chinaman, the wag of the party, offered to risk the ride if we would mount him. At nightfall he started, leaving the trail and scaling the mountain directly, to avoid the Tibetans who would probably be posted along the road.

Although the valley we were in must have been a frequented route, no one else passed us. From time to time heads were visible on the crests of the mountains: we were being watched.

While we were thus checked and spied upon, what had become of our comrades?

At the outset the little party had found all the passes occupied by groups of Tibetans, and in order to avoid them they were forced to go a considerable distance out of their way, and often had to hide themselves. Thus it took them not one day but two and a half to reach Lhabrang; and when they arrived they had had nothing to eat for eighteen hours, having finished their provisions.

On approaching the convent some young lamas had assailed them with volleys of stones. Meeting with such a welcome it seemed imprudent to enter without being announced. A petty Chinese functionary, a kind of consular agent, resided at Lhabrang in order to negotiate business and other matters with the lamasery. The two Tibetans and one of the Chinese went to find him, so that they might warn the lamasery. During this time our comrades and the Chinese scholar remained in a solitary ravine.

It was four o'clock when the three men set out; at half-past six they had not returned. The Chinaman offered to go and see what was happening, and our comrades were left alone, seated beside their horses.

An hour went by. A Tibetan approached; then others. They did not look hostile. They gazed at the two strangers curiously; finally a man made a sign to the captain that he should show him his rifle. Perhaps it was imprudent to give it to him, but it might be just as imprudent to refuse: that would be a sign of distrust which would be misunderstood. Lepage handed the man the rifle.

Immediately he leapt away, calling for help. A hundred men, doubtless hidden behind the slopes of fallen rocks, rushed towards him. The two Frenchmen made for their horses, to which their carbines were attached; but those who had arrived at the outset had foreseen the movement, and prevented them from approaching by striking at them.

From every side they were assailed with stones. In vain did Captain Lepage attempt to protest in Chinese; no one understood him, and the stones redoubled.

Why did the Tibetans, many of whom were armed with guns, and the majority with sabres, use stones as their only weapon? It is very probable that they had received orders to that effect, so that the affair should have the appearance of an unforeseen quarrel with peasants and shepherds, as an official letter afterwards insinuated, and not a deliberate massacre. However that may be, the stones answered very well. In a moment Lepage was losing blood from four wounds, his head being protected only by a soft, light hat; he was stunned; he felt his strength giving out. He attempted to defend himself, and felt for his pistol—the pistol he had forgotten and left in my tent.

"Boyve, hand me your revolver," he said to his companion, who had not cared to make use of it himself without his superior's order. Lepage fired, and a man fell.[1] He tried to fire again, but the cartridge jammed, and this improved weapon, with an automatic ejection actuated by the recoil, was useless. The two Frenchmen were unarmed.

Happily the shot fired by one of two men whom

[1] His knee was broken; the ball having previously pierced the arm of another man. We were asked to examine the two wounded.

they had thought defenceless made the Tibetans draw back. An idea came to our companions that was truly a stroke of genius : they threw at their assailants all the ingots of silver—nearly 200 taels (£28)—which I had given them. The Tibetans, seeing this marvellous rain of silver falling instead of bullets, rushed forward to quarrel over the spoil.

Our comrades profited by the confusion to get away as quickly as they could. But the suffocation due to the altitude—Lhabrang stands at a height of 10,550 feet—stopped Lepage almost immediately. "I'm done for," he told Boyve ; "leave me, and try to get back to the commandant to warn him of this ambuscade." But Boyve, better protected against the stones by his helmet, and less sensible to suffocation, took his chief in his arms and carried him. A few yards away a ravine opened ; they hid themselves behind a rock.

The Tibetans had finished fighting over the picking up of the ingots, and remembered their two victims. No longer seeing them, they rushed off in pursuit. But it was almost dark—it was nearly eight o'clock—and they passed them without discovering them. Their savage yells died away in the distance, dispersed, and were silent.

But Lepage had no strength left, and again wished Boyve to leave him for the safety of the others. Boyve carried him almost to the summit of the mountain ; it took them several hours to reach it. The cold was glacial, and their mantles were strapped to their saddles. Lepage, weakened by loss of blood, exhausted by the effort of escape, was suffering from a kind of paralysis brought on by suffocation, and was attacked by a violent fever ; Boyve had to warm him with the heat of his own body.

When the day came they saw parties of men spreading over the country and shouting. These were doubtless looking for them in order to finish them off. Boyve and Lepage collected some masses of rock to throw down upon their assailants. The cold was followed by heat, and the sun burned them on their shadowless rock. Lepage's fever returned. Neither had eaten for forty-eight hours nor drunk anything for twenty-four.

Towards evening one of the bands of searchers appeared to have found their tracks, for they were climbing towards them. Our comrades made ready to hurl their rocks and sell their lives dearly, when they heard their Chinese names shouted aloud: these were friends, their own men. They were carried down the mountain and hoisted into the saddle, a horseman mounting the crupper of each horse to support them. They were then taken to the Mongol king of whom we had heard in the desert, who had a meal served them, upon which they flung themselves. Thence they were taken to the little Chinese city, the Chinatown of Lhabrang, to the house of the syndic, Ma-Lao-Yei.

He it was who had saved them. The petty mandarin to whom the soldiers had applied in the first instance had received no orders, so, fearing to be precipitate, he took a very prudent resolution: to leave Lhabrang! Thereupon Ma-Lao-Yei decided to intervene, and hurried with our men in search of the officers. But they arrived just after the fight, and our men were themselves nearly cut to pieces. Ma, to induce the mob to spare them, had to swear that they were his servants and had come from Kan-Su.

On the following day Ma went to visit the Mongol king, and succeeded in making him understand the serious nature of such a massacre. The king, now frightened, sent several squadrons of horsemen to search for the fugitives. Finally the print of nailed shoes was discovered, and they were found.

On the day after that our courier, the jolly Chinaman, arrived exhausted, his horse foundered, having, in spite of numerous detours, necessary to avoid the Tibetans, covered the distance in twenty-four hours. He brought the news that we were again blocked whereat the Mongol king, upon Lepage's energetic representations, intervened at the lamasery, and the lamas, pretending that they had known nothing until that moment, decided to send to our rescue the high lama charged with the supervision of the nomads. Ma-Lao-Yei voluntarily accompanied him with a body of his own men.

So, after four long days of waiting and watching, we saw a body of men approaching at a full gallop. At their head was a Chinaman of energetic appearance and an elegant Tibetan who was treated with great respect. These were Ma-Lao-Yei and the lama Hortsei.

It was time! All the neighbouring tribes, regarding us already as their prey, had assembled their fighting-men and were only waiting for the approbation—verbal or at least tacit—of Lhabrang in order to fall upon us. In spite of the couriers who had just been sent out to order them to leave us unmolested, they did not seem to have abandoned their intentions; the rescue party had encountered several unusual assemblages, and had been forced to fire on them.

We should accordingly have to continue all possible precautions. Scouts protected us on all sides, and climbed every ridge to examine the farther slopes. Several times parties of horsemen were signalled, and the lama, who knew very well with whom he had to deal, did not hesitate to give the command to fire. It was his way of requesting them to give us room.

We crossed a succession of ridges 13,000 feet high, and of valleys but little lower, in which numbers of tents were pitched. Should we never escape from these altitudes? At last, on the morning of the second day, we really began to descend: we had at last entered the vale of Lhabrang, which would lead us into China. Once more we pitched our camp, mounted guard, and tasted the after-joys of life in the desert—that life in which a man must every day conquer the elements or his fellow-man.

On the following day we crossed the vast circular plain occupied by the tribe of Song-kourt ; we recognised, with a friendly smile, the horsemen who had charged us so cheerfully. Brave fellows, we were grateful to you for the thrill you gave us !

In this plain ended a number of trails which converged upon Lhabrang from all points of the desert, for there is an incessant movement of pilgrims and caravans going to the great monastery or returning therefrom. At this moment the animation was greater than ever ; the Living Buddha of Lhabrang, who was sick, had just arrived, having come to breathe the air of the heights.

To those accustomed to the coarse black tents of the nomads his camp offered a splendid appearance. All was white and blue. Scattered across the prairie were the great tents of the lamas, of white cloth decorated with large blue characters, the initials of the divinity. In the centre rose the tent of the Man-God, protected from sight-seers by an enclosure of white cloth ornamented with scallops of blue ; a great awning adorned the entrance. Among these bright tints the lamas, in red or golden robes, were walking to and fro on the bright green turf ; and the whole scene was framed by the silver snows which still covered the mountain-tops.

This splendour, set in so wild a frame, and the peace, exempt from all material care, which seemed to emanate from all these magnificent personages ; the absence of anything revealing effort, suffering, or violence ; all seemed to shed over the picture a divine serenity, transforming it into one of those scenes of Paradise which the Tibetan artists love to paint.

Since the Living Buddha had sent to rescue us we had to pretend that we did not very well know that all our trials were really due to him or his representatives. Now we were his guests ; so we asked that we might see him in order to thank him for his intervention and lay our complaints before him.

We could not see him ; he was ill, as we had been told ; but one of the superiors of Lhabrang gave us a courteous welcome in his name, and expressed his sorrow at our annoying adventures. Nothing of the kind would have happened had the Viceroy of Kan-Su warned the convent. All that had been stolen from us should be restored, and the guilty should be punished. What more could we ask?

The tent of this lama was a little palace in itself ; bed, table, and arm-chairs in wood lacquered red or black, an altar loaded with statuettes, lamps, flowers, censers of smoking incense, caskets of lacquer, and a thousand curious and valuable *bibelots* ; and everywhere carpets and hangings of silk. The lama offered us a number of sweetmeats, which doubtless grew of themselves in that Eden, and finally gave each of us a handsome scarf, which we were urged to wear over the shoulder, as a sign of the protection of the Living Buddha.

Two hours later we entered Lhabrang.

CHAPTER XIII

FROM TIBET INTO MONGOLIA. THE DALAI-LAMA. ARRIVAL AT PEKIN

YOU may imagine with what joy we met our comrades. They were still suffering—Lepage especially—from the wounds and bruises which they had received, and the fever which resulted from their efforts and privations.

The Mongol king had caused a search to be made for the authors of the attack, and ten of them were arrested; as for the objects they had stolen—horses, carbines, cloaks, rifle, &c.—all were recovered and restored. Only the ingots of silver had escaped the king's police, but the king, on the simple declaration of Lepage, repaid him their full value.

This prince therefore deserved our sincere gratitude, and I am glad to express it. At the same time I felt that he ought to obtain and restore the articles stolen from us near Kortsei, and also that we ought to receive apologies for such attempts as were made upon us, assuredly by order of the lamasery. For the honour of our country and the whole white race we must eradicate the impression that Europeans could be attacked with impunity.

Those we saw about the king and at the house of the procurer-general of the lamasery, who administered it in the absence of the Living Buddha, were lost in protestations of friendship; the stolen objects should be restored to us without exception. But these

WE ENTER LHABRANG.

THE CITY OF LHABRANG.

To face page 282.

assurances were not enough; for we discovered that the majority of the lamas were violently hostile towards us. Our courtyard was constantly invaded by a crowd of young monks, who insulted our men and loaded with abuse the Chinese who had come to our rescue. I was afraid that the moment we had gone our aggressors would be released and the thieves left in peace, and that the moral of the adventure, so far as the mob was concerned, would be that anything may be done against the whites.

I therefore demanded recognition, *in writing*, of recent events as they had occurred, together with an expression of regret and a promise of complete reparation. As may be imagined, such a document was not obtained without trouble, and over and over again I had to employ the argument of a threatened complaint to the French Minister in Pekin.

A lively exchange of diplomatic notes, in which all sorts of formulæ were offered which we could not accept, ensued between the lamasery, the King, and ourselves.

This correspondence reveals a surprising fact. The Mongol prince signed his letters with the title of "King of Ho-Nan." Now Ho-Nan, as every one knows, is the most central province of China, in which are two of its ancient capitals, and the title of King of Ho-Nan was bestowed, as a reward for having conquered the country, on the most illustrious of the Mongolian generals of the heroic period, namely, that Subatai who conquered Russia and Hungary and bathed his horses in the Adriatic.

Well, it was actually his descendant that we were dealing with. When the Mongols were expelled from China the dynasty of the kings of Ho-Nan—kings without a kingdom—retired to the steppes; and when in their turn the Manchus seized the Empire they utilised the Mongols for the purpose of holding the Tibetans in check, for which reason a horde was sent to establish itself in this region. Was it not touching to find in this petty prince now commanding it, whom we were endeavouring to impress with our quality as Europeans, the descendant of the scourge who once made Europe tremble?

All these negotiations called for numerous interviews, of which we were far from complaining, for they obtained for us so many opportunities of penetrating the sacred city, which is forbidden ground to the profane.

Lhabrang consists of two cities: the lay city and the city of the monks, which are separated by a space of some 500 yards. The lay city contains 2,000 inhabitants, of whom half are Tibetans and half Mahommedan Chinese. Penned in a gorge up whose sides the houses climb, it offers a very unaccustomed appearance; all the buildings are of two stories with flat terraced roofs which meet over narrow alleys. The traveller could swear to being in some village of Egypt or Algeria.

But this picturesque little town is as nothing compared to the lama's city. The latter is the most important city in all Tibet after Lhassa and Tachilumpo. Five thousand monks dwell there in little white cells, all alike, forming clearly defined quarters. They are divided into twenty convents, each having its own rule, its own superior, its temple, its libraries, its reading- and assembly-rooms; and these buildings are the most magnificent we had ever seen in the whole Chinese Empire.

There is nothing in common between Chinese and Tibetan architecture. The Chinese, excepting their towns and city gates, build only houses of no great height, of light materials, such as brick, wood, cob or loam, and paper, without corridors or internal staircases; and the various parts of the house are inevitably built in a square round an inner courtyard. The Tibetan temples, even more than the private houses

A STREET IN THE LAMAS' QUARTER.

To face page 284.

which we had seen at Song-Pan-ting and Ta-Tsien-Lu, were buildings of notable height and solidity, some of those at Lhabrang being of seven stories.

These great buildings present many analogies with certain churches of the Italian Renaissance : for example, Santa Maria Maggiore. The sanctuary itself occupies the centre of the building; sacristies, galleries, and various halls, lighted by great windows not unlike our own, almost completely surround it. It is longer than it is wide; the central nave is extremely lofty, but the two lateral naves are lower, and are surmounted by galleries supported by pillars, which open on the central nave. Above the entrance, where the organ would be in a French church, is a large pulpit.

This is precisely the arrangement of our churches. Moreover, the altars are covered with images. With the fumes of incense rising before them, the artificial flowers, the lights, the benches for the assistants, the throne for the superior, the chair, the banners which hang from the vault and between the pillars—all is similar ; the walls are covered with frescoes representing a Paradise and a Hell such as the mediæval painters used to depict. Very often the façade is decorated with black hangings with decorative motives in white, just like those to be seen at a public funeral in France. Gilded cartouches containing the characters representing the name of Buddha exactly resemble the hatchment of the deceased. But here these were symbolic of a festival.

All these buildings, according to the fundamental rules of Tibetan architecture, have a certain " batter " or " camber "; that is, they are wider at the base than at the summit; the vertical lines are not plumb, but " tumble home." This is not merely a question of solidity; it is also a matter of artistic effect, for the windows follow the same rule, as also the wide borders, painted in dark green, which enclose them. It is a skilful artifice to give the illusion of greater height.

The roofs are flat terraces. Imediately below the roof is a frieze, from six to nine feet in depth, of a dull vermilion obtained by mixing red earth with chopped straw. This runs completely round the building, and is decorated with architectural details designed in black or yellow ochre, which simulate methods or details of construction—beam-ends, rafters, scantlings, &c.—which were doubtless employed of old. At the corners there are often gargoyles of green bronze, representing monsters, some of which have women's breasts, like the sphinx.

Chinese roofs, but *entirely in gilt copper*, rise above the roofs of the three most important temples ; they are those frequented by the Living Buddha, and it was impossible for us to visit their famous sanctuaries, as the Buddha had taken their keys away into the mountains.

Before the most important of these temples we happened upon a ceremony which was entirely unfamiliar to us, and which I believe has not been recorded in any book on Tibet.

Before the principal entrance was installed an orchestra, comprising trumpets of all sizes—some over a yard long—hautboys, conchs, tom-toms, and cymbals. All around the open terrace in front of the temple, which formed a wide half-circular space, were thirty young priests executing sacred dances. These consisted of rhythmical paces, accompanied by a balancing movement of the bust ; the naked arms, outstretched horizontally from the shoulders, sustaining the surplus folds of the plain red drapery which forms the monastic robe, producing the illusion of bats' wings. So that they might dance more lightly the dancers were all barefooted, their boots being set on one side. The steps were now slow and harmonious, now rapid, accompanied by twists and leaps; but the rhythm and organic unity were always perfect. Finally, after a lively, violent, almost frantic passage, both music and dance suddenly ceased.

THE INNER COURT OF THE MONASTERY.

To face page 286.

It was quite by chance that we witnessed this unexpected sight from a neighbouring housetop. Unfortunately the sun was facing us, so that we could not procure a decent photograph. These dances have nothing in common with the scenes, so often described, in which the lamas present the defeat of the demons; they are genuinely graceful and majestic. The ancient religions—Hebrew, Greek, and Egypt—all included dances among their ceremonies; but apart from the dance of the dervishes I believe there is no other modern instance known of a sacred dance.

This priestly city deserved a thorough study, even more than its famous rival Kunbun, but we could not undertake it; the young lamas were still extremely hostile towards us, being furious that we had crossed their hitherto inviolate country; and on several occasions, despite the presence of the delegate of the Living Buddha, we were very near being stoned. The greatest reserve was essential; but for that matter the negotiations already spoken of occupied the greater part of our time.

Finally, on the sixth day, we obtained from the Mongol king a letter which contained an explicit statement of his apologies and regrets, and which promised both the punishment of the guilty persons and the restitution of the articles stolen from us. This diplomatic success allowed us to leave Tibet not only with the consciousness that our scientific objects were attained, but also with the hope that we had effaced the impression produced by the murder of the valiant and unfortunate Rhins, which until then had been extremely vivid, and exceedingly dangerous to Europeans.

An unexpected and almost incredible proof has lately attested that this hope of ours was justified, and that we had really contrived to make ourselves respected: *a year later the objects stolen outside Kortsei were forwarded to the French Minister at Pekin.* The patient and persevering efforts of the Mongol king and the lamasery had resulted in the recovery of everything we had lost. I would not say that not a pin was missing, for there *was* a box of pins missing, but *nothing else!* Carbine, cameras, cartridges, watches, jewellery—everything else was safe.

This is an extraordinary proof of the fact that those peoples which are apparently the most refractory to all authority and discipline cannot live and subsist without an organisation capable, provided the proper measures are taken, of producing results that civilised societies well might envy. Do not let us despise the Barbarians!

*

* *

Rapidly descending, after a day and a half of marching we once more crossed a "Barrier of the Empire" and re-entered China.

Immediately all was different. From Alpine heights we went down into scorching valleys; from the kingdom of Buddha into one of the centres of Islam. We should be blinded no longer by the snow, but by the sun, the dust, and the sand, for we were entering the country of the *loess*, that light yellow earth which the least wind sets flying; and later on we should cross the dunes and steppes of Mongolia, which advances to within thirty miles of Pekin.

The narrow belts of fertile land which surround or cross these deserts, and which imply the mastery of the desert, have from all time been the battle-field of Tibetans, Mongols, Mahommedans, and Chinese. A new task lay before us; but these countries have been traversed by many travellers, so I reserve the results obtained for our scientific publications and will henceforth go forward at a run, merely mentioning a few characteristic episodes.

At Ho-Chu, an important Mahommedan centre, we made some particularly interesting discoveries relating to Chinese Mahommedanism, and discovered the exist-

MOUNTAINS OF LOESS.

BRIDGE AT LAN-CHU.

To face page 288.

ence of Western confraternities whose presence in China had never been suspected. We were extremely thankful that we had with us a Mussulman scholar, for without his help we should no more have suspected these secret relations with the Levant than our predecessors had done.

Crossing mountains of *loess* which the force of the winds had worn into the most fantastic forms—shapes of castles, towers, temples, sphinxes—we came to Lan-Chu, the capital of the province of Kan-Su. Surrounded by heights picturesquely crowned with pagodas, it is built on both banks of the Yellow River, which is crossed by a bridge of boats over 200 yards long, known in China as "the most beautiful bridge in the world." It has not its like in the Empire; it is the only bridge across the Yellow River, and across the Blue there is none.

This bridge unites two different worlds: China proper, and the vast solitudes of Mongolia, Tibet, and Turkestan, beyond which lies the Western world. It supports a constant stream of passengers, and the spectacle is almost comparable to that of the Bridge of the Golden Horn. All races elbow each other on this bridge; Tibetans clad in blazing colours, Turks with cloth overcoats, Mongols, Hindoos of the Punjaub, and Chinamen of every province.

Here ends the empire of the camel arriving from Mongolia, as also that of the mule and the pack-horse which come from Sze-Chuan or the mountains which stretch away to Tibet. On the great route which leads from China to the plains of Turkestan the typical means of transport is the cart with two wheels: a vehicle some five feet wide and ten feet long, covered with a cradle-shaped tilt and drawn by three, five, or seven horses; one harnessed as a leader, and the rest to a pole, in twos or threes. Carts! To those who know the dizzy trails we had been following for eighteen months the very word speaks of a new world!

Alas! the "most beautiful bridge in the world" will soon cease to be. Modern utilitarianism has reached Lan-Chu. As the whole structure has to be removed each winter, when the frost sets in, lest the thaw of the following spring-time should carry it away, it was thought prudent to employ European engineers to build an iron bridge resting on piers, and this bridge is already nearly finished. The people were greatly irritated: they were convinced that the Genius of the river, outraged and wounded by the steam pile-drivers used to sink the caissons, would take a cruel revenge. Already the rains had been scanty; the harvest was lost, and famine threatened. Nearly ten thousand agricultural peasants, entirely without resources, had arrived in the suburbs to beg for a living, and encumbered the gates, for they were not allowed to enter. They were selling their children, whom they could no longer support, and the market-price for daughters ran as follows: one tael (about 3s.) per year of age, so that a child of one year was worth 3s. and a child of ten 30s.

The reader will perhaps be indignant. What? Should the parents prefer to see their offspring die of hunger before their eyes? It is the poverty of the country that is guilty, and the inclemency of the climate. Slavery, moreover, is a paternal institution in China; so much so that the slaves are always known as "children."

Here the valiant Father Dury left us to return to Sze-Chuan. Without him, without the simple devotion with which he accepted our invitation to accompany us, our expedition would have been impossible, or must have ended in disaster; for how could I, with no other interpreter, have parted with Captain Lepage and sent him ahead for assistance? All the honour of our success must be attributed to this modest missionary, who, after enduring sharper sufferings and taking more trouble than any of us in a cause that was not his own, returned quietly to his apostolate, without even suspecting that his conduct had been heroic.

The reader may remember that while we were crossing Asia from south to north, the Pelliot Mission started six months earlier, in June, 1906, to cross it from west to east. A number of journals had not hesitated to state that we should infallibly encounter it, since our routes cut across one another. One individual, full of a touching confidence in the assertions of the newspapers, actually sent me a letter with a request that I should hand it to Dr. Vaillant, the second in command of the Pelliot Mission, on the occasion of this inevitable meeting. Since our own departure we had heard nothing of it.

On reaching Lan-Chu we had been astonished to hear that the Pelliot Mission had not yet passed ; no one knew what had become of it. Three days later a telegraphic dispatch arrived : it was from M. Pelliot, who, on reaching the first telegraph office, inquired where we were. Thus, after two years just as we emerged from the unknown, we were about to meet, as the papers had foretold ! The newspapers are always right !

In marching northward from Lan-Chu towards Leang-Chu we passed many ruins. This route, which traverses a narrow ribbon of fertile soil lying between the deserts of Tibet and Mongolia, and is the only connecting link between China and the Western world, has been one of the favourite battle-grounds of humanity. The Chinese, who required it in order to attack, in their deserts, the unseizable nomads, the plague and terror of the Empire, and to ensure the safety of their trade with the Levant—for this is the famous " silk route "—lined it with defensive fortifications. In the first place there is the Great Wall, one of whose branches runs alongside the road ; then there are innumerable forts, connected by a system of castles, towers, and blockhouses or signal-posts. Everything speaks of warfare ; a warfare which commenced with history and is not yet at an end, for on the accumulated ruins of successive defences—the last dating from the thirteenth century—rise other ramparts, more formidable than ever.

It is a singular thing, and I suppose the explanation is to be found in superstition, that nowhere have the new inhabitants occupied the dismantled defences, although they might almost anywhere have found walls that were still solid and houses that only need re-roofing ; for in this country, where it never rains, walls of sun-dried brick are almost indestructible. They have preferred to build themselves new houses ; but, instructed by centuries of experience of the fate which threatens them, they have fortified them as carefully as did their predecessors. As a result, one journeys through a profusion of towers and ramparts, some ruined and others recent, but seeming to wait for the assaults that will level them also to the ground.

With its feudal castles in the midst of the sun-scorched landscape, this country evokes a vision of Palestine at the time of the Crusades. This impression of the Levant is heightened by a thousand characteristic details, such as the well with its counterpoised arm, which may be seen elsewhere in China, but rarely ; the abundant waters flowing almost everywhere on the surface, and rendering the wells useless ; the *noria* precisely like those of India, Syria, and Algeria. On the wide, dusty roads which lay bare the yellow earth or the sand the camels are numerous, and even more so are the lively little donkeys, the brothers of those of Egypt or Judæa.

On July 6th we reached Leang-Chu, an interesting city which contains various ancient monuments. On the following day the Pelliot Mission arrived. After making excavations in various parts of Turkestan, M. Pelliot had the good fortune to make a valuable discovery in the grottoes of Tuan-Huang, although these

THE GREAT WALL (DESERT OF GOBI).

WE MEET THE PELLIOT MISSION.

To face page 292

were already known. A few years ago a bonze discovered a secret chamber which had been walled up since the eleventh century, and was full of books, which were consequently the most ancient in all China. The English explorer Stein had passed that way and had bought a portion of these books, but had left enough to enrich many libraries, and Pelliot had suffered a real *embarras du choix*. He arrived straight from the cavern, with carts laden with these precious acquisitions, which had so happily crowned the patient search he had conducted in Turkestan.

The next day we passed in company. Each expedition had religiously preserved, for more than a year, in the recesses of its baggage, a bottle of champagne reserved for some sensational event. Anticipating by a few days the occasion of the national festival, it served to celebrate the meeting of the two Missions which were occupied in serving science and their country, and whose meeting in the heart of Asia, after so many marches and adventures, testified to the scientific activity of France

Then, having brought one another a whiff of our native air, we separated: the Pelliot Mission to reach Pekin by the ordinary high-road, that of Si-Ngan-fu, while we were to pass through Mongolia.

We intended at first to follow the border of the desert of Gobi, skirting the Great Wall. This gigantic construction, so famous that it is, to the general public, one of the characteristics of China, has evoked more mockery than admiration; unkindly critics have refused to see in it anything but the foolish cowardice of a race which imagines that to defend itself it has only to cower behind a wall. It needed some boldness on my part to attack this prejudice in a former work, by maintaining that the continuity of this wall, apparently so absurd, in reality corresponds to an irreproachable military conception: it constituted a strategic route, enabling the Imperial troops to move surely and rapidly *on the platform which surmounts it*. This idea resulted from a previous study of the ancient fortifications of India.

I must, however, admit that the aspect of the wall where it skirts the desert is not of a nature to confirm this theory. Its narrowness makes it plain that it was merely an obstacle to the passage of nomadic horsemen, and nothing else.

But reflect a moment! Here, upon perfectly level ground, the defenders had no need of a paved road; but when we follow the wall into the rugged mountain-ranges we find a width of several yards, and an insignificant height, proving that it was not raised as an obstacle, so that the double function of the wall seems clearly defined: to check the enemy in naturally open country, and in impracticable regions to provide a roadway for the defending forces. This is a perfect realisation, having regard to the period and the circumstances, of the most modern principles of fortification.

Into what a deplorable condition has this great outwork fallen to-day! Although in some parts it still rears its imposing outline, in others the searcher can barely find a few remains. Its decadence is not the result of peace and civilisation, but of death and decay. The desert invades all, submerging with its sands the old cultivated plains which their inhabitants have deserted; and it is a melancholy experience to see this great war-machine stretching its carcass across the ruined solitudes, and to reflect that we cannot now guess what peoples it once protected, nor against what enemies.

However, at Chong-Wei a new loop of the capricious Yellow River has for the moment restored the fertility of the soil, and a fairly large population is supported by its waters, which are drained into a multitude of canals.

Here my party was to be once more divided, and now for the last time. My officers were exhausted by their long and severe labours ; the overwhelming heat of midsummer in the desert of Gobi, comparable only to that of the Sahara, following immediately upon the Arctic rigors of Tibet, was in danger of seriously injuring their health ; so I sent them off in the direction of Tai-Yuan-fu, the nearest point on the railway, which was distant about thirty days' march. On the way they passed through the south of the country of the Ordoss Mongols, and were able to gather a mass of valuable information and of documents, notably in the neighbourhood of Swei-To-chu, where they discovered the tomb of the celebrated General Mong-Tien, who built the Great Wall.

*
* *

Left alone, I decided to complete, by an inquiry conducted on the spot, the information collected from Mahommedans throughout our travels concerning a kind of Mahdi who was born in these regions : a very interesting character, who from 1860 to 1871 was the leader of the Mussulman insurrection, and nearly created a Mussulman state. He founded an extremely active sect, of which we had found traces as far away as the south of Yunnan.

Then I intended to visit the Mongol King of Alashan. Various travellers having visited this prince already, I will not trouble to describe my experiences here. I was preceded, at an interval of a few days, by the Russian Kozlov Mission, which had just visited all the rulers of Mongolia.

Thence I gained the Catholic community of San-Tao-Ho. Nothing could be more curious than this creation of the Belgian missionaries. In the heart of Mongolia they have succeeded, by dint of sheer labour, by planting trees, and by excavating irrigation canals, in redeeming from the sands a tract of arable soil, and there, surrounded by disciples who have come from every direction, they constitute a kind of tiny Christian republic. There are thirty villages there, divided into eleven parishes grouped around a bishopric. In these deserts, where no mandarin was ever seen, the bishop and his curés are the sole rulers of this little nation of 5,000 souls; it is they who administer justice, appoint the "burgomasters," apportion the soil, and supervise the execution of the works which save the community from extinction. It is a new Paraguay; but I do not imagine that its people, whose numbers are augmented daily by the arrival of Chinese attracted by the fame of this Eden, are ever likely to raise a revolution.

Three days from San-Tao-Ho, in the solitude of the desert, the Comte de Lesdain and Father De Boeck discovered, in 1905, the vestiges of a vanished city buried beneath the sand. Their narrative had persuaded me that it would be of interest to examine the spot, as excavation might perhaps enable one to determine the period at which a country which now presents the most perfect picture of death and desolation was able to support a numerous population, and also what people had lived there. Another missionary, Father Van Havere, who had visited these ruins since 1905, but without the means of excavation, generously offered to guide me thither.[1]

With a small army of labourers we spent a fortnight digging on the site of Poro-Khoto, the Grey City. To my great disappointment we found no written document. But a great number of objects—vases, money, arrow-heads, and utensils of various kinds—were unearthed. The wholly individual type of the tombs is of a nature to provoke the keenest interest, as is the strange mode of burial, which consisted of

[1] This excellent Father, whom I remembered with the greatest gratitude, died four months later. How many others, among the missionaries who so generously received and aided us, have since vanished, exhausted by their life of privation and overwork!

DWELLINGS IN THE LOESS, NEAR SWEI-TO-CHU.

To face page 206.

placing the corpse in a jar—a method only recorded, to the best of my belief, among the ancient Persians and the Indians of the Peruvian Andes. The photographs of their ancient funerary jars in two portions show them to be identical with those of Poro-Khoto.

In the hollows of the wild Mount of Wolves, whose jagged crests overlook the sea of sand, we visited lamaseries like those of Tibet, but even remoter from the world ; more monastic and more impressive. Their existence in the midst of these majestic but barren rocks, surrounded by the desert, is something of a prodigy. Whatever opinion one may hold of Buddhism, one cannot but be filled with admiration for a faith which transforms the most ferocious swordsmen on earth into ascetics, and these seemingly lifeless gorges into homes of prayer and sanctity. So, when at night the gigantic trumpets sound the motive of the Grail—for such one would swear it to be, so great is the resemblance—one feels no surprise ; for is not this the Mountain of Salvation?

Forsaking the camel, I profited by the long navigable reach, too little known, of the Yellow River, which traces a great loop across Mongolia, in order to take boat down-stream. Thus I came to the famous Blue City—Kuku-Khoto. The four cities which it comprises to-day—the Mongol, Manchu, Chinese, and Tibetan cities—show to what an extent Mongolia has suffered invasion wherever a little good soil is available. The Tartar shepherd is gradually driven westward, and on leaving the Blue City and marching south-east I might well have thought myself in the heart of China, although in reality I was many days' march beyond the Great Wall. Such Mongols as one encounters there—and they are numerous—are only pilgrims making for the famous monasteries of Wu-Tai-Shan, and it is they who seem the strangers in this ancient home of their fathers.

The road follows a series of wide valleys, whose gentle contours, infertile slopes, and rare inhabitants would produce the impression of a stagnant and insignificant region, did not innumerable vestiges recall the fact that we are passing through an age-long battlefield.

These characterless hills are crowned by the Great Wall ; these level valleys are traversed by its multiple ramifications : for it was triple, and even quadruple, wherever the passage of the enemy had otherwise been easy. It is in the recesses of its irregular lines, in the ancient strong places, that the modern inhabitants shelter their miserable dwellings. Here, of old, were the ceaseless conflicts between the Barbarians and the " Golden Empire " ; nowhere have men more continually killed one another, because here Nature had raised no barrier between men. A banal antithesis, yet how striking when it rises from the very ground one treads !

The evocation of those centuries of conflict, which barely ceased two hundred years ago ; the thought that the Barbarians have been repulsed only by a few days' march ; that perhaps we shall see them yet again, charging over this soil where the ruined Wall of China will no longer check them : such thoughts possess the mind of the traveller through this historic plain.

But suddenly my meditation was pierced by a feeling of utter amazement, which rooted me to the soil. From *within* the hill-side, where a rugged slope became a cliff, and receded in a bay, a giant face regarded us ; a vast, calm countenance, smiling an ironical smile. Was it a hallucination? There were other faces also, peering out of the very bowels of the hill : the gods were looking through the window to watch us pass ! There was even one, affable yet majestic, who welcomed us : the hill-side opened before him, revealing the whole colossal figure—nearly sixty feet in height—seated in an attitude of eternal peace, and seemingly the very spirit of the soil.

EMBARKING ON THE YELLOW RIVER.

EXCAVATION IN THE DESERT.

To face page 298.

Fantastic vision! All this wall of rock, for a distance of nearly two-thirds of a mile, is peopled by a race of gods, surrounded by a train of innumerable worshippers. Each one has his palace. It is entered by a door some twenty feet in height, hewn in the hill-side, and appearing anything but lofty. Once the threshold was crossed an august shadow enveloped us; only on high, and it seemed at a great height, was a plane of light, and throwing back the head we recognised the serene countenance that had contemplated our arrival. An opening pierced through the rock before it allows it to gaze out upon the world.

Little by little we distinguished in the darkness the body which supported that luminous head; a prodigious body, shaped in the living rock. Then the celestial retinue became visible; from the vault, the walls, issued an army, a cohort of spirits of all sizes and all forms. The shadow grew lighter. A whole people was there, in adoration and ecstasy: saints, self-absorbed in ineffable meditation; spirits flying to carry the divine orders; apostles, their hands raised and their mouths open, celebrating the praises of the divinity.

It was a marvellous phantasmagoria. Such an overwhelming profusion of art, which could only have been realised at the price of labours worthy of Egypt, confounds the imagination. But what completes the wonder of the beholder is that he finds these masterpieces in the womb of the earth, and almost in darkness. They were not executed to excite the admiration of man; you may find faces sculptured in absolutely dark corridors, and in the base itself of the colossi. No, the outer world has disappeared; the god and his adorers are at home here, in peace and silence, and beside them nothing exists.

These temples were not unknown: they are mentioned in Chinese works, more especially because of the restorations undertaken there by the Manchu emperors; and a number of missionaries have seen them. But nothing concerning them had ever been published in Europe, and I was congratulating myself that it was reserved for me to reveal these wonderful monuments to an admiring public. But that very night, running through a bundle of journals and newspapers given me by the Fathers of San-Tao-Ho, I found therein an account of these temples written by M. Chavannes, the eminent member of the Institute of France, who had visited these rock-temples six months earlier, and had taken numerous photographs.

Such a predecessor excused me from doing more than admiring these splendid grottoes on my own account and at perfect leisure. To my mind they equal the marvels of Abu-Simbel, Ellora, and Ajunta. Certainly the restorations of the three last centuries have diminished their archæological value; and from the artistic point of view also one could wish that they had been left as the centuries had left them. But I bear the restorers no grudge; we are so given to relegating all these gigantic works, the fruit of an intense faith served by an unlimited power and will, to so remote a past as to feel that we have nothing in common with them. When we find them fresh, sharp, and new we suddenly receive a most vivid impression that this past is not abolished; that it lives on into the present; and the survival, in the age of electricity and aerial navigation, of this colossal, refined, yet barbaric art, moves us as a revelation of unsuspected, adverse, and formidable forces.

*
* *

Now our efforts to complete the work of so many great explorers, and finally to raise the veil which hides the mysteries of Tibet from the world, were at last to be rewarded. Not far from where I was, at a distance of five days' march, in the retirement of the famous

VAULT OF A SUBTERRANEAN TEMPLE, YUN-KANG.

To face page [illegible]

THE COPPER PAGODA, WU-TAI-SHAN.

To face page 301.

mountain of Wu-Tai-Shan, there resided, at that moment, the Dalai-Lama, the Living Buddha, the inaccessible pontiff-king of Tibet, whom none of our predecessors had succeeded in approaching.

The sensation caused by his recent flight to India had attracted universal attention to this divine personage. We knew now that he was the permanent incarnation on earth of Pradjapani or Avalokiteshvara, the chief of the spirits after Buddha, who is the very perfection of God. When his corporeal envelope is about to die, his soul passes into the body of a new-born child, who, himself revealing his quality, becomes the new Dalai-Lama. He enjoys the profoundest veneration of all Tibetans and Mongols.

But to this title are added two others. He is the direct superior of the Saskya, the most powerful of the monastic orders, whose convents are scattered not only all over Tibet and Mongolia, but are even to be found in China, on Mount O-mei, on Wu-Tai-Shan, and in Pekin.

Finally, since 1722 he has been king of the central portion of Tibet, or Debadjung: at that date China deposed the king of that period, and transferred all his powers and honours to the incarnate deity, under the suzerainty of the Emperor.

We see that although in certain senses he deserves the name of the Buddhist Pope, which has so often been bestowed upon him, the resemblance to the sovereign pontiff of the Catholic religion is far from being perfect. He is at once more and less powerful than the Pope: more venerated as God, but less powerful as spiritual chief and less independent as sovereign.

In 1904 the English, during the period of the Russo-Japanese War, entered Tibet through India; the Tibetan defence was feeble, and the English entered Lhassa. The Dalai-Lama fled, taking refuge in Mongolia, at the great monastery of Ourga, near the Russian frontier. Since then the English had withdrawn their expeditionary force; but China was not willing to restore the Dalai-Lama to the throne, save upon conditions to which he would not subscribe. It was to facilitate the negotiations with China that he had installed himself upon Wu-Tai-Shan.

Wu-Tai-Shan, the "mountain with five terraces," is one of the holy places of the earth. For four long days, after leaving the plains of China, the traveller continually ascends. By valleys ever growing narrower and steeper he finally reaches, at a height of 8,100 feet, a summit surmounted by one of the outlying portions of the Great Wall; for here, in other days, the territory of the Empire ended.

This formidable witness to human power and human weakness still marks the frontier between the terrestrial and the divine. Immediately beyond the wall is a high-lying valley, with gently sloping sides, carpeted everywhere with turf. Here are no villages, no farms, no fields, but monasteries, ever more and more numerous. Around each monastery presses a grove of pines, making a rampart of shadow and mystery. These sacred woods, which form an integral part of the convent, extend its sanctity to the summit of the mountain. There is a sense of something mysterious and august in all this landscape; the mountain-tops are just so high as to raise the eyes towards the sky, without overwhelming the sense; there is something indescribably pure and ethereal in the light and the atmosphere of these lofty heights, so that even in the depth of the valleys one does not forget that one is high above the world in which men strive and drown. Great rocks of violet porphyry, which pierce the green mantle of the grassy slope, give relief to the lines and contrast to the colours of the landscape, while pine-trees, harmoniously grouped, crown the spurs and rounded summits of the lesser heights. The mountain atmosphere, the majesty of the peaks, the sombre violet of the rocks, the solemn serenity of the pines, the many widely scattered monasteries, and, above all, the peculiar beauty of the valley—all seems to have been arranged by some divine architect in order to produce the most perfect picture of the Buddhist paradise.

A narrow ravine below, the valley widens as we climb, but there is yet no sign that we are nearing the summit: the farther mountains reveal fresh peaks, always loftier and loftier. Finally an amphitheatre, spacious and bathed with light, opens at the confluence of several valleys. Temples appear on every side: on the level ground, on the slopes, and on the heights of the spurs which divide the valleys: it is the first of the five terraces, known as the southern terrace.

Here it is that the pilgrim, arriving, like ourselves, from Mongolia, enters the sacred precincts. Impatient to arrive at our destination, let us cross this first terrace; there will be time to visit it later.

Like a vast corridor uniting two temples, the valley becomes a narrow defile, its rocky walls sculptured in low relief. It opens finally on a wide circular plateau, which is crowned on the north-west by a diadem of dazzling snow. This is the central terrace. In the midst rises a hill, from base to summit covered with temples. A portico and a majestic staircase, the Propylæum of this Acropolis, leads to a first platform from which rises a white stupa, eighty feet in height, which from that point of vantage seems gigantic, and has a magnetic power of capturing the attention. Pagodas, heaped one above the other, climb to the summit of the hill, which is occupied by several temples with red walls and roofs of yellow, the colour reserved for the Emperor.

Thither, in all ages, from all points of China and Mongolia, pilgrims have flocked; their gifts sufficing to support, in the midst of this solitude, a whole race of monks, and further to enrich the pagodas, many of which are extremely beautiful. At the time of my visit the presence of the Dalai-Lama was attracting an even greater concourse than usual. Mongol kings were there, with numerous retainers. A thousand Tibetans forming the escort of the divinity, some clad only in skins of beasts, others in stuffs of brilliant hues, completed a strange and many-coloured pageant.

The Dalai-Lama had decided to accept the invitation of the Emperor, and to proceed to Pekin, where negotiations could be more easily concluded. He was to start in two days' time, so that this did not seem a favourable opportunity for attempting to approach the inaccessible divinity.[1]

However, since he was going to the capital, he would there have to deal with various matters relating to Europeans, and notably the murder of numerous French missionaries. I therefore had his chanceller informed that I, newly come from Tibet, should have been happy to salute the Dalai-Lama, but that in view of his departure I did not wish to seem importunate; yet I was sure that he would regret to learn that his subjects had attacked us and had wished to massacre us, as they had killed so many missionaries of our country.

My interpreter gazed at me with astonishment while I gave him these instructions. "Do you think that this message is going to give him any particular pleasure?" he asked me. No, I was not so ingenuous, but it was precisely upon the Dalai-Lama's displeasure that I had counted.

[1] We must remember that no European had ever seen the Dalai-Lama, nor even, with the exception of Fathers Huc and Gabet, who were disguised as lamas, succeeded in approaching his place of residence. However, since his arrival at Wu-Tai-Shan, he had grasped the fact that the support of the Occidental Powers would be of assistance to him in resisting the demands of China, and he had received Mr. Rockhill the famous explorer of Tibet, who had been appointed United States Minister, and a Russian officer, Baron de Mannerheim, who had just been exploring in Turkestan and the borders of Tibet.

THE GREAT BUDDHA OF YUN-KANG.

[To face page 304.]

And, sure enough, I received a message that very evening, stating that he would receive me on the following day. He had perfectly comprehended that it would be better that he should not, on arriving in Pekin, receive a fresh complaint from the French Minister concerning the treatment we had suffered.

The commandant of his Chinese guard of honour came for me, and conducted me to the uppermost temple, which commands the whole valley. There the Tibetan guard was drawn up; the men wore a highly original uniform, red with orange straps and facings, and a three-cornered hat; the whole exactly resembled a European uniform of bygone date, and was doubtless based upon such a model. But their weapons were Russian repeating-rifles of the latest type.

The Dalai-Lama was seated upon a throne, which stood up on a raised platform. Facing him an arm-chair had been placed for me; all about the room his councillors stood erect.[1] The god-man wore a short tunic of yellow silk, orange trousers, and boots of a bright yellow, of the form peculiar to the Tibetans; about his neck was a red scarf. His head was bare; his hair clipped short, but not shaven; he wore a moustache, and his features were absolutely European in type. One might well have taken him for some French officer, but for his complexion, which was neither brownish-black, like that of the Tibetans and Mongolians, nor yellow, like that of the Chinese, but of a true orange colour, which gave a striking and

[1] The illustration given below depicts the scene better than I could describe it. Alone of all the illustrations in this volume, it is not the direct reproduction of a photograph, but was drawn from a sketch made by me the moment I left the temple, with the help of photographs taken the following day as the long procession set forth—photographs too bad, unfortunately, to be reproduced. Anxiety to be guided by these photographs has resulted in a slight inexactitude; the costumes of the lamas are those which they wore on the following day. During my reception all were wearing capes of cloth of gold, and were bareheaded, as was the Dalai-Lama.

peculiar aspect to a face which was otherwise so similar in type to our own.[1]

I offered the Living Buddha a *khata*, in accordance with the curious ceremonial prescribed. This immense scarf, some ten feet in length, had been previously rolled up from either end towards the centre, thus forming two parallel rolls, which I held upon my hands, the latter being pressed together. At a slight movement of the fingers the two rolls fell downwards, unrolling, and suddenly displaying their brilliance. The Dalai-Lama immediately responded to this offering by that of a similar scarf.

My presents were then laid before him, and in return he offered me ten pieces of the precious red cloth of Tibet, and ten bundles of sticks of the famous Tibetan incense.

The Dalai-Lama is supposed to know all languages without having learned them ; however, as my interpreter ironically remarked, it apparently pleases him to conceal the knowledge, which does not make intercourse easy. I spoke in French ; my interpreter translated my words into Chinese ; a lama repeated them in Mongolian ; and another, bowing before the man-god, transmitted my words to him. He replied in a low voice ; then the same series of translations brought me his august reply. It was a truly miraculous thing, but the replies very nearly corresponded to the questions, and it was not absolutely certain that we did not understand one another.

He questioned me as to my travels in Tibet, and expressed his regrets at the barbarity of the nomads, who refused to obey him, and also his sorrow at learning of the murder of the missionaries. He reminded

[1] So-called photographs of the Dalai-Lama have been published as taken in Pekin. They represented various persons, who had *no* resemblance to him, either as to features, hair and beard, figure, clothing, or general appearance. In reality the lower part of the face is rather less delicate than it appears in the illustration.

COMMANDANT D'OLLONE OFFERING THE SCARF OF FELICITY TO THE DALAI-LAMA.

To face page 306.

me that he had formerly sent rich presents to the son of the king of the French—Prince Henri d'Orléans. When I rose to take my leave he offered me another scarf; then, at a sign from him, a lama brought him yet another, even larger and finer than the first, and the god-man, presenting it, begged me to bear it, as a sign of his friendship, to our emperor![1]

The interest of such a visit, as may be imagined, does not lie in the remarks exchanged, which are necessarily insignificant. What was of interest was the aspect of this divine incarnation before whom a notable fraction of the human race bows down. Was he a monk, pickled in sanctity? or a mere puppet, intentionally besotted since infancy by those who surrounded him? or a strong and remarkable personality?

The two first hypotheses must emphatically be rejected. Not only does the Dalai-Lama speak and act as a man habituated to command, but there is nothing of the monk in his manner, nor even in his clothing. He is a vigorous man, with a soldierly face and figure, and the sight of him explains his unexpectedly adventurous career. Among the lamas who surrounded him I noticed many faces of a Hindoo type, full of refinement and intelligence.

On the following day the Dalai-Lama took the road for Pekin. From daybreak thousands of camels, led by Mongols, filed down the mountain, carrying his baggage. Then followed groups, always at shorter intervals and always more and more numerous, of Tibetans, Mongols, and lamas.

At eight o'clock a gun was fired, and from the open doors of the upper pagoda issued a double file of lamas robed in red; they took up their positions all along the monumental stairway of marble which led from the summit. Finally, amid the detonation of salutes, a glittering group appeared; followed by his

[1] This confidential mission was fulfilled: I had the honour of handing this scarf to the President of the Republic.

high dignitaries, clad in capes of cloth of gold, the Dalai-Lama slowly descended the staircase, supported on either hand by two young priests. The file of lamas already in position on each step of the stairway began to advance in step; it was as though the stairs themselves were descending, bringing the divine procession from the sacred heights.

At the foot of the hill, in the midst of an innumerable crowd which had gathered from all directions, the Dalai-Lama was awaited by a tao-tai, or governor, a general, two prefects, and numerous squadrons of cavalry, sent by the Pekin Court to escort the pontiff-king. This little army began to march. The Dalai-Lama, at first carried in a chair of yellow silk, resembling that of the Emperor, soon emerged from it in order to mount on horseback, in the midst of his Tibetan guard, and the whole cortège, with trumpets sounding, set off at a rapid pace. The god-man had abandoned the somewhat bored expression which he had worn the night before, and was looking about him attentively. With his cardinal's hat of golden lacquer and his short doublet of yellow silk, vigorously trotting in the midst of his men-at-arms, he was more like Richelieu at the Pass of Susa than the inert idol which men have imagined him.

All that day I travelled with the Living Buddha, sometimes mingling with the cortège, sometimes drawing aside to enjoy and to photograph the pageant. At the entrance of every pagoda the monks were drawn up to salute the Lama; he halted to receive their homage, and this multitude of prelates, mandarins, and Chinese and Tibetan soldiers, assembled in those singularly beautiful surroundings, composed on each occasion a picture of incredible strangeness and beauty. When the march was resumed, when the pageant of all that royal pomp swept through the solitary valley, when the trumpets sounded as though to tell the rocks, the pines, and the mountains what sacred host it was that passed, I admit that I was filled with a religious emotion; and in spite of the Far-Eastern colour, and the taint of modernism introduced by the rifles, I seemed to see the People of God marching past the foot of Sinai.

On the morrow I pushed forward, leaving the Dalai-Lama, who started late. I was thus able to see with my own eyes the preparations—doubtless in all ages the same—which rendered possible the journeys of the Asiatic monarchs, whose luxury in the midst of countries bristling with obstacles and void of all resources was at first sight incredible.

Thousands of labourers, brought from the plains, were finishing a road some yards in width, which had been laid out in the course of a few days. This road they had levelled, freed of every pebble, and raked; over the rivers bridges had been thrown; structures which would doubtless be swept away by the first rains, but which to-day provided a safe and easy passage. Camps were pitched in advance, where the pontiff-king might halt or pass the night at will; in these everything was prepared: tents, aligned in perfect order, and proportioned to the rank of the personages of the suite, provisions, stores of fodder, watering-troughs, and lanterns; and a magnificent tent, fully furnished, awaited the Dalai-Lama.

After his passage the staff of workers attached to each camp would rapidly dismantle it, and, marching all the night, would re-establish it at some well-chosen point the next stage of the journey. Everywhere I saw triumphal arches of verdure, decorated with lanterns, oriflammes, and inscriptions, and the whole desert seemed to be transformed into a pleasure-garden.

As I descended towards the plains the preparations glorified the god less and the monarch more. Generals, governors, and viceroys attended his passage, and a veritable army was assembled to do him honour. The

Imperial Court had prepared a triumphal march, a thousand times more imposing than the entry into Pekin, which took place under the eyes of foreigners. These extraordinary honours, which were heaped upon him here, where the presence of no witnesses had been anticipated, were a sufficient proof of the actual power of this fugitive monk.

I could not have anticipated a termination to my Mission better calculated to give the reader a synthetic picture of the strange world in which we had lived for two long years. A primitive, violent, barbaric world; in a word, a world some fourteen centuries behind our own, yet near enough in terms of space; for at the end of this apotheosis the Living Buddha and his mountaineers were one and all to enter a railway-train, albeit they lost naught of their barbaric rudeness, nor he of his divinity.

*
* *

What, in the end, did we gain by this long exploration? Five thousand miles of itineraries, of which 1,670 were absolutely unknown; 2,000 photographs of types, costumes, monuments, and characteristic landscapes; more than 200 complete anthropological mensurations; 46 vocabularies of non-Chinese dialects; 4 dictionaries of native characters previously unknown or undeciphered; 32 Lolo manuscripts; 225 inscriptions relating to historical events, in Chinese, Sanscrit, Tibetan, Mongol, Manchu, Arabic, and Lolo; the almost unique and undiscoverable monographs of 42 cities; numerous weapons, utensils, examples of pottery, currency, paintings, &c., and finally, an abundant harvest of observations. The whole mass of our documents could not be presented in less than seven volumes. Of these the publication has already been commenced, with the kindly collaboration of certain eminent scholars.

It would be premature to hint at the conclusions which will result from this aspect of our labours. If I have sufficiently denoted the width and diversity of the problems which presented themselves the reader will not expect a solution in the immediate present, nor even in the immediate future. The non-Chinese races of China form a whole world in themselves ; long study, and ample research on the spot, will still be necessary before it issues from the obscurity into which its downfall has plunged it. We shall be only too happy if the results of our efforts succeed in attracting the attention of the general and special publics, and provoke the searching inquiry which the subject demands.

But I may be permitted to attribute all the honours of these results to those who gave me assistance ; and firstly to the missionaries, who everywhere, with the most patriotic devotion, placed their persons and those of their flock at our disposal ; and above all to my devoted companions.

The zeal of M. de Boyve in taking charge of all imaginable detail left the other members of the expedition absolute freedom for their scientific work. By his courage and devotion he saved Captain Lepage, and thereby the whole Mission. No previous expedition in western China had included a Chinese-speaking member. The presence of Captain Lepage saved us from the customary treachery and inaccuracy of interpreters, and enabled us to understand such written documents as we had to deal with. This explains why we encountered no obstacles in localities reputed to be difficult. That our harvest was so abundant, not only in unknown countries, but even when we passed through countries already known, was due to this officer's knowledge and scholarship.

The enormous amount of geographical work accomplished was almost wholly due to Captain de Fleurelle, who was my second in command, and who directed, in full liberty and with perfect success, several particularly difficult pieces of exploration.

Thanks to such help, the programme assigned to me has been fulfilled. Yet now that we have come to the end of our task we feel that everything has still to be accomplished. So vast, so varied is the world of the Barbarians that each discovery only measures the profundity of our ignorance.

Yet, having penetrated that world, we feel in our hearts a little of that sacred horror which the revelation of the mysteries evoked in the initiates of old. It seems to us that a corner of the veil has been raised, allowing us to divine, in the darkness, something of the past which yet survives and of the future which is now in preparation.

THE END.

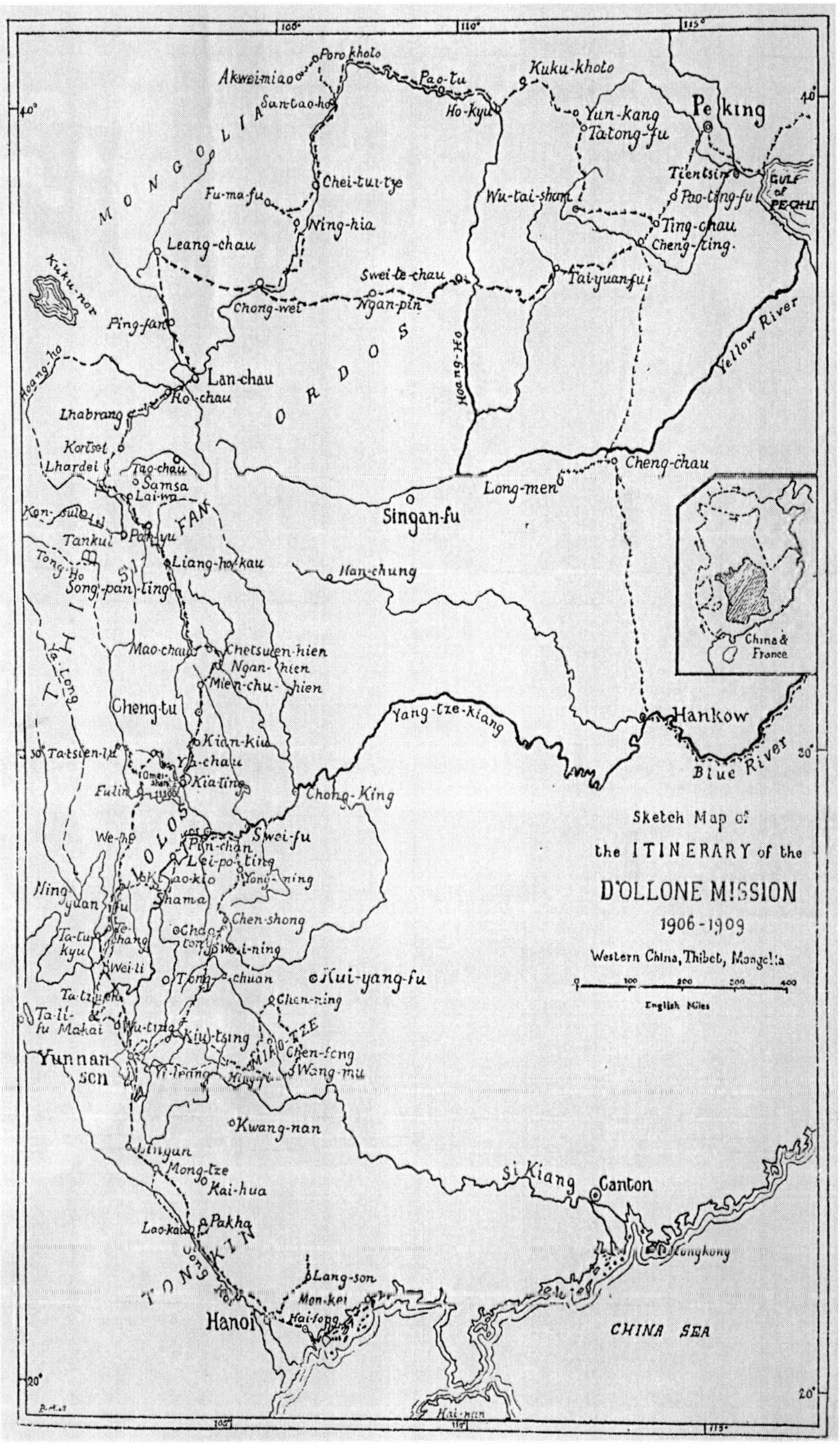
Sketch Map of
the ITINERARY of the
D'OLLONE MISSION
1906-1909
Western China, Thibet, Mongolia
English Miles
0 100 200 300 400
China & France
Pe king
Tientsin
Gulf of Pe-chi-li
Yellow River
Blue River
Yang-tze-Kiang
Hoang-Ho
Si Kiang
CHINA SEA
Hai-nan
MONGOLIA
ORDOS
THIBET
SI-FAN
LOLOS
MIAO-TZE
TONGKIN
Kuku-nor
Poro khoto
Akweimiao
San-tao-ho
Pao-tu
Ho-kyu
Kuku-khoto
Yun-kang
Ta-tong-fu
Pao-ting-fu
Ting-chau
Cheng-ting
Wu-tai-shan
Tai-yuan-fu
Chei-tui-tze
Fu-ma-fu
Ning-hia
Leang-chau
Swei-te-chau
Chong-wei
Ngan-pin
Ping-fan
Lan-chau
Ho-chau
Lhabrang
Hoang-ho
Kortset
Lhardei
Tao-chau
Samsa
Lai-wa
Kon-sum
Tankul
Pan-yu
Tong-Ho
Song-pan-ting
Liang-ho-kau
Cheng-chau
Long-men
Singan-fu
Han-chung
Mao-chau
Chetsuen-hien
Ngan-hien
Mien-chu-hien
Cheng-tu
Ta-Long
Kian-kiu
Ya-chau
Ta-tsien-lu
Omei-shan
Kia-ting
Fulin
Chong-King
Hankow
Swei-fu
Pin-chan
Lei-po-ting
Yong-ning
Ning-yuan-fu
Shama
Chen-shong
Ta-tu-kyu
Chao-tong
Wei-ning
Wei-li
Tong-chuan
Kui-yang-fu
Chen-ning
Ta-li-fu
Makai
Wu-ting
Kiu-tsing
Chen-fong
Wang-mu
Yunnan-sen
Yi-leang
Kwang-nan
Mong-tze
Kai-hua
Canton
Hongkong
Lao-kai
Pakha
Lang-son
Mon-kai
Hanoi
Hai-fong
100°
105°
110°
115°
40°
30°
20°

INDEX